World Politics on Screen

WORLD POLITICS ON SCREEN

Understanding International Relations through Popular Culture

MARK SACHLEBEN

UNIVERSITY PRESS OF KENTUCKY

Copyright © 2014 by The University Press of Kentucky

Scholarly publisher for the Commonwealth,
serving Bellarmine University, Berea College, Centre College of Kentucky,
Eastern Kentucky University, The Filson Historical Society, Georgetown College,
Kentucky Historical Society, Kentucky State University, Morehead State
University, Murray State University, Northern Kentucky University, Transylvania
University, University of Kentucky, University of Louisville, and Western
Kentucky University.
All rights reserved.

Editorial and Sales Offices: The University Press of Kentucky
663 South Limestone Street, Lexington, Kentucky 40508-4008
www.kentuckypress.com

18 17 16 15 14   5 4 3 2 1

Cataloging-in-Publication data is available from the Library of Congress.

ISBN: 978-0-8131-4311-8 (hardcover : alk. paper)
ISBN: 978-0-8131-4312-5 (epub)
ISBN: 978-0-8131-4313-2 (pdf)

This book is printed on acid-free paper meeting the requirements of the American
National Standard for Permanence in Paper for Printed Library Materials.

Manufactured in the United States of America.

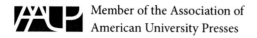 Member of the Association of
American University Presses

For my father,
Charles Sachleben

CONTENTS

Introduction

INTERNATIONAL POLITICS IN FILM AND TELEVISION

It has become a cliché to point out that we live in a world in which international events affect our lives. Yet when most people think of television and international politics, they naturally assume that the connection has something to do with the news. This book starts from the premise that television and film can actually give us a deeper understanding about world politics. It will not argue that film and television can replace reading and research—but, by understanding how important political topics are covered in popular culture, we will have a better appreciation of how societies understand issues, problems, and potential solutions. To begin with, consider some important questions: What is the relationship between popular culture and politics? Why should those of us interested in politics pay attention to popular culture? The answers can be complex and multifaceted. Popular culture is a reflection of the way society believes the world operates. As the name suggests, popular culture has broad appeal. This is not a culture that is available to only a few; it is widely available to many people. Although popular culture has existed in all societies and all times, the unprecedented power of film and television as media has meant that the dissemination of messages now transcend time and place. Films and other moving-image mediums have the ability to convey a great deal of information and emotion, often without words. Ideas and reactions can be transmitted with a glance or a smile. Film and television are powerful ways to transmit messages and ideas.

We live in a world in which the moving image is ubiquitous. The process of incorporating moving images into our popular culture began in the 1890s with the invention of motion pictures on filmstrips, and continued in the 1940s and 1950s with the mass production and acquisition of televisions by millions of people. Such images are constants in our lives today, with motion pictures being delivered to us by a plethora of electronic devices. While the method of delivering moving pictures to audiences continues to change, there is no doubt that the moving image will remain an important—and perhaps ever-increasing—facet of modern life.

If you stop and think about it, it is remarkable how much of our every-day lives are shaped by popular culture. Sometimes we build our schedule around accessing popular culture. Our adherence to our favorite television program or song is often an indication of who we are as a person. On a date, a question about popular culture is often a way to get to know another person ("What's your favorite band?" "What's your favorite TV show?"). Sometimes our pretensions might get the better of us and we might claim not to be impacted by popular culture, but even for such individuals it takes only a few seconds to realize how pervasive film and television are in our lives. Many people like to quote favorite scenes from movies in everyday language—who doesn't know someone who says, "Show me the money!" (from *Jerry Maguire*, 1996) or "I'll be back" (*The Terminator*, 1984) in an Arnold Schwarzenegger voice? The idea of "an offer he can't refuse" from *The Godfather* (1972) has become a verbal shortcut for an unpleasant task that must be done, or else severe consequences will ensue. On a deeper level the stories we tell each other describe who we are, who we want the world to think we are, and what we think the world looks like. Stories become metaphors for our lives.

In 2006 an online news organization announced that Americans know more about *The Simpsons* (the animated television family) than they do about the First Amendment. Indeed, a survey by the McCormick Tribune Freedom Museum found that more than half of Americans could name at least two members of the animated family, and 22 percent of Americans could name all five members of the family (Homer, Marge, Bart, Lisa, and Maggie). On the other hand, only one in one thousand (one-tenth of 1 percent) of Americans could name the five freedoms protected by the First Amendment to the Constitution (freedom of speech, religion, press, assembly, and petition for redress of grievances).[1] One could interpret this as how ill informed Americans are about their constitutional rights and history (which might be true). Another interpretation might be to note the overwhelming influence of popular culture. *The Simpsons* is showing on television almost daily around the world; on the other hand, it is very rare that there is an entertaining discussion of constitutional rights playing around dinnertime in the United States. Further, it is not as if there are there are no political messages contained in *The Simpsons*. That television program is replete with information that also serves the audience, at times even in education about First Amendment rights in the United States.

We could speculate that there are three possible relationships between popular culture and politics: (1) popular culture reflects politics; (2) popular culture shapes politics; and (3) there is an endogenous relationship between popular culture and politics—in effect that popular culture helps to inform and shape politics, and politics help to inform and shape popular culture— a symbiotic relationship. Popular culture, or "pop culture," can take many different forms, including art, mass media, popular novels, cooking, and clothing—all of which are enjoyed by most people in a society. This book will focus primarily on film and television, with slightly more emphasis on film. As we begin to think about the relationship between film and television programs and politics, it is helpful to remember each of the three possible relationships. As you read this book, watch films, and discuss films and television programs with others, ask yourself: Is this an example of a film trying to shape political culture? Or is this a film that reflects political culture? Or does it do both?

Popular culture and mass communication can have dramatic consequences in national and international politics. Imagine two people: Sally, who lives in Detroit, and Stephan, who lives in San Francisco. Because they live in the same country, the United States, they sense that they have something in common; a bond exists between them. This in spite of the fact that they probably will never meet, that there is over two thousand miles between them, and that they may not even like each other should they ever meet.

Consider Angela, who lives in Toronto: she lives approximately 250 miles from Sally (ten times closer than Sally to Stephan). Sally and Angela might experience similar weather, they might share the same weekend getaways (maybe a cabin on Lake Erie or the casinos in Windsor), and they speak the same language. The realities of geography might suggest that Sally and Angela are more closely tied. Yet because Angela lives in Canada and Sally lives in the United States, they do not share the same sense of commonness that Stephan and Sally share.[2]

In the modern world we draw lines, imaginary boundaries, that appear only on the map. For most of the U.S.-Canadian border, the only way one can tell where the border exists is to see the signs humans have erected to demarcate it. If those signs were not there one could not tell the difference between the two countries (the grass, trees, geography, animals—even the people—all look the same). The people who live on either side of the border of Montana and Saskatchewan speak the same language, look remarkably similar, work in similar jobs, have similar political philosophies, and often watch the same television programs. Despite all of this, and despite the imaginary nature of the border, this line between the United States and Canada is real and has a real impact on lives.

Countries have a vested interest in cultivating this sense of belonging. First and foremost, it makes governing easier. A population whose members believe they belong together and share similar characteristics is more likely to accept, or legitimize, political leadership. Before the industrial revolution, nationalism and a sense of community was limited to elites. A feeling of community among most people was limited to their immediate surroundings. As the importance of the state grew, people began to feel a sense of commonality, what Karl W. Deutsch called "shared meanings" brought on by "interlocking habits of communication."[3]

Benedict Anderson has noted that even in the smallest country an individual will never know, meet, or even hear from the vast majority of other members of the society. Yet, despite this, the members of the society believe that they are a part of the same community. Anderson argues that the idea of nationalism, a sense of belonging together politically, is a product of the industrial age. In order for people who had never met one another to sense they belonged to the same community, there had to be a way for them to share the same stories, common reference points, and concerns. For stories to be widely distributed there had to be some mechanism by which those stories could be consumed widely. For scholars like Anderson, this required industrialization and the process of mass distribution, or mass media.[4]

In his book *Imagined Communities*, Anderson explains how, through newspapers, human beings began to create a feeling of community with people they had not met. The process of disseminating stories, through which readers could begin to identify, helped to create a sense of commonality. As Anderson points out, early newspapers in the Western Hemisphere would report on the life of the area in relationship to the rest of the world: when ships were due to arrive, who was marrying whom. One might read a newspaper from a different part of the world, but it probably did not have much to say about the reader's experience.[5] Somewhat unconsciously and apolitically, the newspaper was creating a sense of community among readers.[6]

As technology has developed, other forms of information and entertainment have emerged to help create a sense of community. Instead of literary journals, magazines, and newspapers, today most people are entertained by stories through other media outlets: television, radio, movies, or the Internet. And, as technology has continued to evolve, the ways in which people are acclimated to their surroundings, taught the norms of their community, and generally socialized into their society have changed as well. Today, popular culture is the repository of many of the seminal elements that define a society—its important figures, cherished values, and shared experiences—which in turn shape individuals' relationships with, and views of, the rest of society. In this book, we will concentrate on the medium of film; however, other forms of popular culture are worthy of consideration as well.

In the modern era, popular culture helps to reinforce a sense of community. This book works from the premise that popular culture can provide clues as to what is important to a political society. Each of the chapters in this text discusses an important concept in world politics today. This, by no means, suggests that the films discussed here are definitive, nor is it argued that the impact of popular culture is consistent. For example, one could argue that the messages contained in popular culture are a reflection of the values of society. Others may argue that those constructing the message (through film, art, music, or commentary) are attempting to create a message that will have some resonance within the society. Such messengers may use their craft to reexamine the past, redefine the status quo, or perhaps imagine the future. Other examples of popular culture could be alternative voices expressing what the society *should* value or protesting the existing values.[7] Regardless of whether popular culture is shaping, is shaped by, or has some endogenous relationship with politics, understanding film gives us insight into understanding politics and ourselves. In this sense, narrative films need not display the "truth" because they help us to understand how others understand a topic.

Films: What to Look For

One problem in writing a book such as this is the availability of so many films, especially documentaries. Many documentary films have been avoided in this book due to a lack of accessibility, though I do include several documentary films that are immediately available to the public because they help to further ideas and points that are being made. But for the most part, in this book I am more interested in a narrative that is constructed by filmmakers about topics in international politics. The films that are examined here are not necessarily based on true stories. Thus in a narrative film (one in which a story is told rather than a documentary), actors play parts, the filmmakers establish scenes, and the film creates a narration of a story.

It can be quite intimidating to "read" films. As an undergraduate, I had no patience for people who sat in the back of the room, often smoking cigarettes, lecturing others on the *true* meaning of a film. This book works from the assumption that films have different meanings for different people. I illuminate some of the meanings people have ascribed to a film or the stated meaning according to filmmakers. Yet one of the most satisfying exercises is to discuss what films mean to us with others. In a time in which DVD and Blu-ray mean that many films are viewed in solitude, we often forget that films are usually made to be seen in a darkened theater with many other people. Theaters were built to provide grandeur to the viewing experience, signifying its importance. People would sit in a darkened auditorium so as to minimize distractions. Much of that experience has been lost today, yet it is important to remember that most films were made for a communal experience—one in which people would react and discuss the film as they left the theater.

Because this is a book about international politics, I have made a conscious effort to include a number of international and foreign-language films. Many people, especially novices, will say they do not like foreign films because of the distraction of reading subtitles. But I see foreign films as an opportunity for individuals to escape the "Anglosphere" (the English-speaking world). English-language films dominate the film industry;[8] however, only half a billion of the world's six and a half billion people (about 7.5 percent) speak English, including those who speak it as a second language.[9] If you are going to consider different perspectives from around the world, limiting yourself to English-language films will severely limit the perspectives you will consider.

Foreign-language films allow us as viewers to travel without leaving our seats. We are transported to seeing into a different culture, to hearing foreign languages (while simultaneously understanding through the subtitles), and to peering into a different perspective for a couple of hours. Foreign-language films provide an insight into how much of the rest of the world understands our world, and how other parts of the world construct their identity. I have every confidence that if you are reading this book, once you get accustomed to reading subtitles, it will become very easy and natural to do so. No doubt, in time, some people will not remember if a film was even subtitled.

This is not a book about film criticism or editing; however, we should say a word about films and their construction.[10] Many of the films made today (sequels, fast-paced action dramas, and those with familiar characters) are designed solely to make money. Opening weekend box office receipts often determine the "value" of a film. For the most part, these are not the types of films we will be considering. To be sure, all filmmakers want to make money. But what we want to consider is the message, or the story, that filmmakers want to tell. That is not to say that we will not be exploring some very popular films, but the criteria used to select the films is how well they demonstrated the ideas under consideration, whether they offered a perspective that you might not have considered before. At the same time, I want to demonstrate that familiar films have many subtle messages as well.

It is difficult to pinpoint exactly where a film's message originates. Other than small documentaries, the process of creating a film is a collaborative project. Films are sometimes adapted from written works; therefore, the writer plays an important role. The director is the head of the production and often puts his or her personal stamp on a project. Actors are often the people whom the public associates with a film, because they are the most visible part of a finished project, and thus have an important role in interpreting their parts. Producers organize the making of a film, including financing, hiring of key individuals, and distribution deals; thus they have a role in determining what is made. Many would argue that without financial backing a film would never be made; therefore, the person with the money can often control the message. We could spend thousands of pages describing how a film project is a collaborative project (witness the hundreds of people who are credited at the end of any feature film today). Many times this book will refer to "filmmakers" as a phrase to encapsulate this collaborative process.

The role of editing in film and television production is a very important process. If it is done right, most of us do not realize that editing has occurred. Creating a film is more than pointing a camera and just shooting film. Many of the most famous films in history achieved their status because of editing. Moving pictures aim and shoot; film is constructing a series of shots to mean something. Students of filmmaking spend a great deal of time studying specific scenes from films, such as the Odessa Steps sequence from *Battleship Potemkin* (1925) or the shower scene from *Psycho* (1960), to understand editing techniques. Editing is the process of selecting, organizing, and arranging scenes. In some cases it also includes emphasizing points, deleting scenes and, perhaps, even distortion.[11]

Even in documentary films or reality television, editing is very important. What is left out of a film, a television program, or even a reality show is just as important as what is left in. Take, for example, a popular reality program in which people are continuously arguing. What is not being shown is all the time those people are not quarrelling. If there is no conflict, then it is rather boring; without conflict, there is no drama. Therefore, all the footage in a reality series where things are going along just fine is left out of the program. While this makes sense, we should not dismiss the implications: such programs can lead to a sense that people are naturally quarrelsome or prone to conflict, when in actuality we might be missing a great deal of evidence. It leads us to question what is "reality." Is reality people arguing all the time? Or is life rather dull most of the time, punctuated with a few minutes of drama? Regardless of the answer, remember that almost any visual image produced for mass consumption contains a heavy dose of editing.

For those who make documentary films, the question of editing is very important. Most documentary filmmakers, as the name suggests, are trying to document what has actually happened. Editing can be very tricky; it can be a way to manipulate what has been shot. In 1945, when the concentration camps of Europe were being liberated, Allied Forces wanted to document and detail the atrocities of German concentration and death camps. The British Army shot footage of concentration camps, including Dachau, Buchenwald, and Belsen, to demonstrate the gross human rights violations of the Germans. The film was partially assembled and stored in the Imperial War Museum; it became known as *Memory of the Camps* when it was restored and aired on PBS in 1985.[12] Because the actions and results were so horrific and unbelievable, the British Army called on filmmakers, including Alfred Hitchcock, to help construct the film. One of Hitchcock's chief concerns was to make sure that the film could not be accused of being a fake or a fraud. The film used editing techniques, such as long shots of mass graves and close-ups of survivors, to undermine the claims of skeptics.[13]

A similar situation arose during the Bosnian War in 1992 when a short video and photographs were made at the Omarska Camp, where the plight of a group of emaciated Bosnian Muslims was reminiscent of Nazi concentration camps. The images were made and distributed worldwide by the British Independent Television Network (ITN) and helped to galvanize world support for action in the Balkan wars.[14] The footage was convincing and evocative;

however, some Serbs claimed that the original footage would have proved the men were being treated humanely had it not been edited out of the final story. This led to a legal battle between a pro-Serb magazine, *Living Marxism,* which disputed the claims, and ITN. ITN was eventually vindicated in the courts and *Living Marxism* was forced to shut down after losing, but the controversy demonstrates the importance of the process of editing and film construction.[15]

For people just beginning the study of films, one of the most difficult things to get accustomed to is the pacing of some films. Most people today enjoy a diet of rapid-fire films with numerous explosions and witty banter for dialogue. It is not to suggest there is anything wrong with these films, but most are designed to stimulate the senses rather than to make people think. Many of the films we will be considering in this book take more time to establish the story—they tend to be complex stories. Most of the time, real life does not happen at a rapid-fire pace, and if these films are seeking to explain something about real life, their pacing attempts to mimic the real world. Thus pacing is an important aspect of the films we will consider. Some films deliberately slow down the action in order to give the audience an opportunity to think about what is being said. There also is a cultural difference. This, for some, will take time to get used to as well. European cinema often spends more time on nuance, whereas American cinema offers bold and definitive answers to the situations protagonists face.

It is sometimes difficult to know how to begin to discuss and analyze films. Our first temptation is to say whether we like the film, which is a perfectly reasonable place to start. Yet if you begin to ask other questions it might be helpful in dissecting why someone might, or might not, enjoy a film. Here are a few suggestions to ask when watching films:

- What is the message(s) that the filmmakers are trying to convey?
- Is the message(s) a reflection of society? Or is the message trying to change society?
- Who are the powers behind the message?
- Who is the target audience for the message?
- How effective is the message in attempting to convince the target?
- Do people or places represent something?

The beauty of film is that it can be interpreted by different people in different ways. A discussion of film can provide a discussion of various understandings of a film.

I encourage you, whether in class, as a group, or online, to discuss films with others. Undoubtedly, you will take different points and be struck by ideas different from your own. Discussing a film gives you a fuller insight into how film impacts others, just not you. It is also a demonstration of how films and popular culture impact individuals; the process of finding shared meaning in a piece of work is a collective process. If a piece of art has cultural significance, then it must be seen and discussed by several people; but not necessarily everyone. Being seen and understood by elites is good enough in many cases. It is the elites in a society that help to shape public perceptions of the meaning of a particular work. Who are elites? Elites are those who tend to dominate the political process and thereby shape opinion and understanding within society.[16] Because humans tend to work from the basis of heuristics, we use stories and past experiences as a guide to understanding current situations. By constructing a story in a certain way, elites can point to a particular piece of work and identify it as noteworthy. Thus politicians, journalists, educators, and pundits can identify a film as relevant and cite its importance to understanding a particular issue.

Interaction among Film, TV, and Politics

There is a good deal of evidence to suggest that popular culture, film, and television have helped to shape politics across the globe. For example, the novel *Uncle Tom's Cabin; or, Life among the Lowly* (1852) by Harriett Beecher Stowe helped to bolster the cause of the abolitionists in the minds of the American public prior to the beginning of the American Civil War (1861–1865).[17] The novel's central themes are the immorality of slavery, the rightness of abolition, and the need for Christian teachings in American political life, especially when it comes to slavery. In the novel, Uncle Tom is a deeply religious and loyal slave whose qualities do not protect him from the harsh realities of slavery. Although Tom is a "good slave," he is eventually separated from his family and beaten to death. Many scholars have argued that the novel helped to galvanize the cause of abolitionism, bringing it into the mainstream. Subsequent films—of course all made at least a half century after the American Civil War—serve as a reinforcement as to why the war was important and a condemnation of the institution of slavery. The term *Uncle Tom* would eventually become an epithet for African Americans considered to be too accommodating to whites in power.

Film is a particularly effective medium because it can connect distant people and events for the viewer. The documentary *How the Beatles Rocked the Kremlin* (2009) argues that the famous rock band from Liverpool was instrumental to the demise of Communism in the Soviet Union. While the premise may seem farfetched, Leslie Woodhead, the director and narrator of the film, points out that in the 1950s worldwide Communism was on the rise and many people, including intellectuals and artists, saw Communism as the future of world ideology. Communism was understood to be international, even cool. Yet when the Beatles emerged as the most popular musical group in the West, even in the world—more than a band, a phenomenon that transcended national boundaries—the reaction of the Soviet leadership was to ban the group's music. As counterrevolutionary, the music of the Beatles was rarely confrontational; it was engaging and decidedly upbeat. Suddenly, the Soviet Union went from appearing to be a forward-looking society to seeming like a reactionary one in its attempt to suppress a popular, influential, and nonconfrontational band that heralded the future of music. Many Russians went to extraordinary lengths to procure the Beatles' music despite the government ban. The documentary argues that the Soviet leadership's refusal to allow young Russians to get music that their counterparts in the West had ready access to was an example of tactics that ultimately helped to undermine the legitimacy of the regime—and that lack of legitimacy eventually led to the dissolution of Communism in the Soviet Union. *Searching for Sugar Man* (2012), a documentary of an obscure Detroit rock artist's impact on the antiapartheid movement in South Africa, is yet another example of the intersection of music, politics, and film.

Films and television series also have the ability to provoke national conversations. The television miniseries *Holocaust* (1978) followed the story of the Weisses, a Jewish-German family, over the course of Nazi rule in Germany. As the anti-Semitic policies of the Nazi regime evolve into genocide, the family finds itself in increasing peril; many family members eventually die. The Weiss family's story is contrasted with that of a distant family member (through marriage) who is transformed by Nazi ideology from a mild-mannered lawyer into a leading advocate for the "Final Solution." Despite what many critics referred to as its soap-opera style and some minor historical inaccuracies, the miniseries had sensational ratings in the United States and was a critical success for the NBC television network. The broadcast had an important impact within the United States in discussions of racial and religious freedoms, support for Israel, and the role of the United States in refusing Jewish refugees prior to and during the Second World War.

The airing of the miniseries prompted many discussions and the funding of several foundations.[18] One could even argue that it led to the eventual creation of the Holocaust Museum in Washington, DC.

While *Holocaust* helped to transform the way in which Americans understood and memorialized what happened in Europe during the 1930s and 1940s, perhaps the miniseries had a more significant impact when it was screened in West Germany in 1979. In that country viewers reacted very strongly and the miniseries led to a discussion about German complicity during the Second World War.[19] Prior to the miniseries, many Germans had simply blamed "the Nazis" for the Holocaust, but now German society began to recognize wider culpability. This period of reflection culminated in 1985, when Richard von Weizsächer, president of Germany, noted that it was not merely "Nazis" who were to blame, for Nazis consisted of German citizens—ultimately, the German people as a whole were guilty of genocide.[20]

The impact of films on society is not necessarily always as dramatic. Vice President Al Gore's *An Inconvenient Truth* (2006) sparked a national dialogue inside the United States on climate change and environmental pressures. The documentary presented Gore's lecture on climate change, which was meant to educate and to serve as a warning about the consequences of inaction. The documentary sparked interest and discussion about the impact of climate change caused by humans and was engaged with not only by those who supported the vice president's claim, but by those who doubted that humans caused climate change as well. Gore would win both an Academy Award and a Nobel Peace Prize; however, most of the suggestions made by the film have gone unheeded. The point is not that a piece of popular culture necessarily changes the body politic in a particular way, such as the way the filmmakers desired, just that it changes politics in some way.

In recent years many television programs have resonated within political discussions, especially in the United States. The television program *24* (2001–2010) sparked a great deal of controversy in the U.S. debate about the efficacy of the use of torture as a method to fight terrorism. *24,* which starred Kiefer Sutherland, followed the exploits of CIA agent Jack Bauer as he tried to prevent terrorist plots against the United States. The series, though some of its plotlines are farfetched, is well written, and it was extremely popular at the beginning of its run. One of the novelties of the series is that it plays out in real time, meaning that each episode simulates an actual twenty-four hour period in the life of Jack Bauer. The series seemingly advocated the use of torture as a way to prevent terrorist attacks and protect civilians. Traditionally, the use of torture has been strictly prohibited under domestic and international law; however, the use of "enhanced interrogation" methods after the September 11, 2001, attacks on New York and Washington, DC, was seen by some as an acceptable means to deter and prevent terrorism. Opponents of enhanced interrogation saw the methods as torture. Some critics have argued that the series had a specific political agenda, seeking to create fear of external enemies in the public's mind, so that domestic dissent would lessen and military spending increase.[21]

Regardless of the controversies surrounding the series, it became a touchstone in the debate about enhanced interrogation.[22] Speaking in Ottawa, Ontario, in 2007, U.S. Supreme Court Justice Antonin Scalia argued that Jack Bauer saved hundreds of lives in Los Angeles, asking rhetorically, "Are you going to convict Jack Bauer?"[23] Critics point out that *24* is a fictional program; Jack Bauer, a fictional character, has not saved anyone (in Los Angeles or elsewhere). But supporters claim that *24* represents potential threats that people and governments must consider. This raises an interesting question: Are examples of popular culture viable evidence in making policy decisions? It is difficult to assert that a work of fiction, where the writer can take dramatic license to craft a situation to meet the needs of the story instead of reality, can be used as evidence. Yet this is done occasionally.[24] And certainly, it demonstrates the importance of film and television to political discourse.

Such controversies are not limited to the United States. In 2008 the Russian government began considering a ban on the animated series *The Simpsons* (1989–) and *South Park* (1997–) from Russian television. Members of the Duma (the Russian parliament) argued that the foreign programs, which contain foul language and satirical depictions of religion, should be replaced with patriotic children's programs. The television channel that broadcast *South Park* even faced a criminal investigation.[25] Each of these series prompted societies to discuss their core values and the role of popular cultures created in other countries in those discussions.

Science fiction films and television have often been an important topic of debate and discussion within the wider public. The *Star Trek* franchise is an excellent example of provoking discussions of issues as diverse as racism, war, and environmentalism. More recently, *Battlestar Galactica* (2004–2009) also sparked debate and conversation in the political discourse. The original series, *Battlestar Galactica* (1977–1978), was seen as an allegory of the cold war, with the robotic Cylons representing the followers of Communism. It has been conjectured that the 2004 series, much darker and intense, relates to the September 11, 2001, terrorist attacks and the subsequent American invasion of Iraq. Despite the controversial nature of the allegory, the latter series of *Battlestar Galactica* did not rely on standard clichés of the War on Terror. It explored ideas of human rights, terrorism, religion, and civilian-military relations. The series was a critical success, although it struggled in the ratings. It was so well thought of that in March 2009 members of the cast and executive producers Ronald D. Moore and David Eick were invited to participate in a panel discussion on the ethics of war at the United Nations to celebrate the series finale.

Not all films that have a significant intersection with political discussions are necessarily controversial because of their message; many generate interest because of film techniques. *La battaglia di Algeri* (The Battle of Algiers, 1966) is an Italian-French film that explores the anticolonial movement in Algeria from the standpoint of both the French and Algerian communities. The project's filmmaking technique suggested a documentary feel; it was so persuasive that the director thought it necessary to open with a title card explaining that no documentary footage was used in the making of the film. The film is based on actual events, showing the Algerian Front de Libération Nationale resorting to violence to achieve independence from France, as the counterinsurgency efforts of the French become increasingly repressive. The conflict among the French electorate surrounding the methods depicted in the film actually led to a constitutional crisis in France, resulting in the dissolution of the Fourth Republic and the establishment of the Fifth. The French forces were successful in quelling the insurgency initially, but Algeria eventually achieved its independence in 1962. The film would be brought to the forefront again some forty years later when it was revealed that the American Pentagon was regularly screening the film in the hopes of learning lessons that could be applied in its battle with the insurgency in Iraq.[26]

As demonstrated above, film and television programs offer a forum for learning about problems, debating their influence and effects, and posing solutions for them. This is why there can be a significant debate about film and television programs (as well as music and books). Famously, in 1992, then U.S. vice president Dan Quayle criticized the television series *Murphy Brown* (1988–1998) for depicting a single professional woman having a child out of wedlock. He accused the program of "mocking the importance of fathers."[27] The controversy generated a debate about single parenthood, working mothers, the availability of contraceptives, and abortion rights.

These debates already existed, of course; what popular culture did in the instance of *Murphy Brown* was to focus attention on the interrelatedness of several debates and give people a common reference point.

Film and television have a significant impact on our understanding of the political world, although most of the time it is less dramatic than *Uncle Tom's Cabin* or *Holocaust*. Many times film and television simply reinforce a belief that is already held in society. Not all films considered in this book are political films; that is, not all the films are about politics.[28] In fact, some of the works we will consider are films whose underlying message we are still trying to discern.

There are a number of films and television programs that are deliberately attempting to impact the political dialogue of a society. *The Daily Show with Jon Stewart* (1996–) has had a massive impact on American political dialogue. Jon Stewart has even been cited as the most trusted man in America, even though he anchors a broadcast that is self-described as a "fake news show." Other late-night television hosts have similar impacts (David Letterman, Conan O'Brien, Jay Leno, to name a few).[29] Films such as the ones produced by Michael Moore (*Roger & Me*, 1989; *Bowling for Columbine*, 2002; and *Fahrenheit 9/11*, 2004), by Robert Greenwald (*Outfoxed*, 2004; and *Wal-Mart: The High Cost of Low Prices*, 2005), and those made to counter their views attempt to affect the political discourse in favor of their preferred political outcomes. With such films, there is no mistaking the intended messages. In the end, these films usually are viewed only by people who are already predisposed to the messages they offer. As important as these films and television programs are, they are not the focus of this book. A more important skill is to discern more subtle messages contained in films and television programs and to understand how broader political culture is reflected in popular culture.

Some Final Thoughts

This book is designed to give an overview of some of the more pressing issues in world politics today. It is not meant to be definitive—but it is hoped that you will think more critically about how moving images today, brought to us on theater screens, through the television, or via the Internet, have shaped or have been shaped by politics. If we are to understand the politics of the world, then we must understand how political messages are shaped and how different people understand problems differently.

The book is divided into three sections. The first provides some background information about film and politics as a jumping-off point. It includes a brief chapter on international relations theory to help elucidate key terms and theoretical motivations. The second section is a consideration of the perennial issue of conflict and cooperation in world politics. The third section will examine some important vexing issues that are current in world politics.

Understanding how stories are constructed, the messages and symbols they use, and the point of view of different protagonists is an important undertaking that helps us to understand politics better. The remainder of this book examines how issues affecting world politics are captured on film and television. It is hoped that you will see film and television in the future not simply from an entertainment perspective, but with awareness of the implications that latent and blatant messages have in framing our understanding of the political world.

Part 1

WORLD POLITICS, FILMS, AND EXPLANATIONS

1

THE MODERN WORLD AND THOSE WHO TRY TO EXPLAIN IT

Sometimes a movie about zombies is not really about zombies, and aliens from outer space are not aliens from outer space. For instance, a recent zombie film from Cuba is a commentary about life under the Communist regime.[1] Sometimes there is no overt political message, but there are hidden, sometimes unintentional, messages. Films and television *can* be about escapism and fantasy. But even those films with no overt political agenda or message contain the essential fundamentals of a culture and are a product of that culture. Contained in the film are subtle messages and cues about how the world *should* work. People act in a particular way with one another, and there are norms and values that the audience and filmmaker share about the nature of society, which is shaped by culture. This is why when a film or a television program steps outside the norm of expected behavior there is a cultural conversation, usually condemning the program.[2] The study of popular culture, specifically in films and television, is so important to the study of politics, and this book is designed to bring to the table a wide variety of films to help illustrate issues and trends in world politics.

By viewing, analyzing, and studying films, we are observing the attitudes, values, and cultural conversation of a community.[3] As an example, consider the case of Ellen DeGeneres and the depiction of homosexuality on American television. In her relatively successful sitcom, *Ellen* (1994–1998), the actress portrayed a woman who in the fourth season of the series reveals that she is gay. As such, DeGeneres became the first openly gay lead character in American television. The program caused some controversy and a cultural conversation about the meaning and significance of the episode and the series.[4] When DeGeneres debuted with a daytime television talk show a few years later, *The Ellen DeGeneres Show* (2003–), there was rarely discussion of her sexuality in the media, and her program has become very successful and popular. In the interim between the two programs, several gay characters began to appear on American television screens. Examining these programs (and others) gives us an insight into the politics and cultural dialogue regarding the inclusion of homosexuals into American popular culture and politics.[5]

We live in a world that contains a vast amount of moving images. This is a fact that began long ago and continues to grow today. Not only movie and television screens, but computer, Internet, and handheld devices employ moving images as well. This chapter is designed to provide a background to the politics of film and politics on film and introduce some key ideas to help explain why films and television are so important to politics.

It's a Big World After All

In an age of globalization and global threats, such as environmental disaster and nuclear weapons, it is tempting to remind ourselves of the song "It's a Small World," the plea for international harmony that has become a familiar tune in Disney theme parks around the world. While there is no doubt that there are global threats, it is important to remind ourselves that our experience is not necessarily the experience of the 7 billion–plus other people on the planet. It is dubious, and perhaps a little egotistical, to assume that our stories, lives, and problems are similar to those of other people around the world.[6] This means that there remain, despite dramatic changes in recent decades, differences in ideas and cultures around the world.

By the 1920s, because of the First World War and other economic forces, Hollywood had become the largest film production center in the world, a dominant position it retains down to the present day.[7] Although it is true to say that American films tend to dominate the global market, that dominance is restricted to films of a particular genre: the action-adventure film. Typically, these films employ the latest special-effects technology and can count on attracting a mass audience across cultural barriers to create a blockbuster megahit. Yet American comedies, which rely on cultural cues and references, typically do not do as well in foreign markets.[8] Other film production centers do well, as evidenced by the popularity and appeal of British dramas, even in the American market. British films, or at least Anglo-American coproductions like *The English Patient* (1996), *Shakespeare in Love* (1998), and *The King's Speech* (2010), tend to be fairly popular at the box office and have garnered many awards, including the coveted Academy Award for Best Picture. Even British television programs such as *Upstairs, Downstairs* (1971, 2010), *I, Claudius* (1976), and *Downton Abbey* (2010–) have proved to be very successful, celebrated as cultural events in the United States.[9]

While it is tempting to think that everyone sees the same movies, watches the same television programs, or listens to the same music, it is simply not true. Our choice in entertainment is often a reflection of our cultural preferences and practices. The values and references depicted in films and television are extremely important. Thus watching films from around the globe can give us a peek into the cultural conversations of other societies as well as explaining some of our own practices. As pointed out in the introduction, popular culture relies on the shared experience of audiences. Those who enjoy particular films and other forms of popular culture develop catchphrases and shortcut references for them. This shared experience helps to build community and relationships between people. Part of the importance of literature, music, and film is the sharing of events; humans tell stories and share their experiences so that others will understand them.[10]

While the dominance of American popular culture is by no means complete, it is almost axiomatic that there is a prevalence of American culture on movie and television screens around the world. The television series *The Simpsons* (1989–) is dubbed in several languages and subtitled in many others for international audiences. The popular American sitcom *Friends* (1994–2004), which chronicled the lives of twenty-somethings in New York City, was reported to be a major underground hit in Iran.[11] Films from the United States, too, are typically at the top of foreign box offices.[12]

World Politics and Film

Films have long been recognized as a way in which messages, themes, and ideology can be disseminated to many people. In an era of mass media and globalization, telling a story to many people is vital to establishing a frame of reference. Consider any issue in politics: getting to the story first is extremely important because the subsequent recounting of events or ideas must reference the first cut. Whoever can tell a compelling story first gets to set the agenda.

It has been argued that the real instructors of young people today are not schoolteachers or university professors but motion pictures and television.[13]

The actor Richard Dreyfuss has said that he was far more influenced by film than he was by textbooks or lectures while he was at university.[14] There is no doubt that filmmakers have understood this for a long time. Darryl Zanuck, legendary producer and head of 20th Century Fox studios, saw his role as an opinion leader. He thought a good producer was one who could determine what the public would want even before the public knew it.[15]

Realizing the influential nature of film, some countries have taken measures to protect and develop their domestic film industry. For example, in France and Quebec, the initiatives to protect the French language from the dominance of other languages, particularly English, has prompted governments to fund the production of domestic-language films. Further, under French law, 60 percent of television programs and films shown must be European made.[16]

As film historian Steven Boss has pointed out, it is conventional wisdom that Hollywood is a bastion for leftist (or liberal) ideology; however, Boss argues that while there have been high-profile liberals in Hollywood, such as Charlie Chaplin, Humphrey Bogart, Katharine Hepburn, and Warren Beatty, individuals on the right (or conservatives) in Hollywood have had far more impact on the politics of the United States. Hollywood figures who have held elective office and thus direct political sway on the American political system are all conservatives: Ronald Reagan, Charlton Heston, and Arnold Schwarzenegger.[17] An analysis of American films demonstrates that both sides of the political spectrum are present in film and television. It is important to note, however, that there are deeper tendencies than simply partisan ideology at work within films and television. At the core of many films is a basic belief in how politics work; these messages are frequently unstated. The messages are not designed to change the audience's beliefs or outlook but, instead, to reinforce them. Think about the animated television series *The Simpsons* or *South Park:* while both frequently make political and social commentaries, some background messages are taken for granted. Characters participate in politics, which denotes a core belief in participatory forms of government (that is, democracy); there is a general observance of tolerance, as demonstrated by the religious diversity of the characters; and the importance of education as foundational to democratic participation is highlighted by the frequency with which school and education issues are showcased. These trends extend to nonpolitical programs and films as well. Television series such as *CSI* and *Law and Order* highlight the work of society's civil and public servants. These are ideas and concepts that are rarely questioned. These subtle messages can be observed in many films from different cultures, and they give us important clues and information about how different societies operate.

Even the ways in which a story is approached are indicative of the culture that produces the film. In almost every American film that deals with political, economic, and/or social issues, problems and situations almost invariably respond to individual solutions rather than community problem solving.[18] Thus in a film such as *Casablanca* (1942), overcoming the Nazis and Germany aggression relies on the action of one man, Rick Blaine (Humphrey Bogart) rather than the collective action of the entire community of expatriates. This approach reflects the American political culture trait of individualism. On the other hand, the classic Japanese film *Shichinin no samurai* (Seven Samurai, 1954) takes a different approach to the similar problem of thievery and banditry. A Japanese village of farmers hires a diverse group of samurai to protect them from extortionist thievery. It takes the entire group working as a cooperative unit to defeat the bandits.[19] In fact, in one scene the samurai training the farmers explain the necessity of collective defense to those who resist military training.[20] The French-Spanish coproduction *L'auberge espagnole* (The Spanish Apartment, 2002), a metaphor for the European Union, is about a group of university students from across Europe sharing an apartment while studying in Barcelona. The film argues that cooperation and dialogue are necessary to avoid or manage conflicts, a process that mirrors what occurs in the political institutions of Europe. In each of these films, we see how cultural and political norms help to shape the story. Yet in none of these cases are the stories *about* political culture—rather, the stories are shaped by it.

Films are expensive to make. Even the lowest-budget documentary can cost tens of thousands of dollars to produce. If a filmmaker wants a film to be seen by a wide audience, then considerably more money must be spent. It is unlikely that filmmakers would take a stance too far outside the mainstream of existing political and cultural beliefs because the likelihood of recouping the investment would be negligible. Thus films, more so than other art forms, tend to conform to prevailing political views and social norms.[21]

Nevertheless, it has become commonplace to label films one disagrees with as "propaganda." In today's world, propaganda carries a negative connotation, but this has not always been the case. Supporters of the same film might view it as a documentary. In recent times, the distinction between the terms *propaganda* and *documentary* has become increasingly blurred.

Regardless of the correct application of terms, viewing these films can help us to understand and explain politics. Propaganda can be defined as a deliberate attempt to manipulate symbols and concepts in order to change people's behavior, attitudes, and thoughts so as to achieve desired outcomes. This attempt will cause controversy among the people who are targeted by the manipulation.[22]

Many film scholars cite the cinema of Nazi Germany as among the best at practicing propaganda. For Adolf Hitler the use of the new media of motion pictures and radio was important in creating new adherents and converts to National Socialist ideology. The method of propaganda favored by Hitler was a direct approach, one that condensed complicated ideas into a few simple ideas or slogans. He thought that the state could create effective propaganda by intense repetition and exaggerated symbols. Hitler's minister of propaganda, Joseph Goebbels, favored a more indirect approach to propaganda; he believed that *how* the information was presented was far more important than the actual message.[23] An acknowledged masterpiece of the technique is *Triumph des Willens* (Triumph of the Will, 1935), in which, as the film begins, Hitler descends from the clouds in an airplane. The film's director, the controversial Leni Riefenstahl, said the intent was to make it seem as if he were coming down from heaven as a god.[24]

Distinguishing between documentaries and propaganda films can be very difficult, and the charge of propaganda can be damning. It is a psychological truism that when we like or agree with the message of a film, we tend to consider it a documentary; when we do not, then it is propaganda. Typically, a documentary film is one in which the viewer learns something—there are truths or information uncovered. On the other hand, a polemic typically reinforces already believed ideas and aspirations. Film critic David Denby has argued that a documentary filmmaker should not be "a collagist who assembles miscellaneous footage in order to support what he already believes."[25] Instead, a true documentary film is one in which the filmmaker undertakes an investigation to learn something, and the audience witnesses the investigation and learning process.

In the aftermath of the American invasion of Iraq in 2003, Michael Moore's *Fahrenheit 9/11* (2004), which questioned the Bush administration's use of the terrorist attacks of September 11, 2001, to justify the American invasion of Iraq, became a lightning rod in the debate between documentary and propaganda. On one side, Moore won the Palme d'Or, the highest award, at the prestigious Cannes Film Festival in France; however, supporters of the

Bush administration claimed that the film was nothing more than left-wing propaganda masked as a documentary film. Because France had opposed the American invasion of Iraq, critics claimed, French approbation for the film was nothing more than anti-Americanism.

The debate over Michael Moore's films and several filmed responses to them led to renewed interest in documentary films in the first decade of the twenty-first century. The question we should ask is: At the end of the day, how effective are these films in persuading the public? Is this a case of preaching to the choir? For instance, imagine a documentary filmmaker making a film about polar bears and their plight in the Arctic, where they are facing a warming environment and declining fish stocks. The documentarian can set out to make a reasonable, well-researched, and rational case about the polar bear, but a person who is unsympathetic to polar bears or the effects of climate change is not likely to spend time or money to see such a film. Who will go to see such a film? Typically, those people who are already inclined to accept such a message. While the goal of a film might be to introduce an audience to a topic, the audience must be receptive to the message.[26] Thus a film such as *An Inconvenient Truth* (2006), in which former vice president Al Gore made the case for action on androgenic climate change, or the similar *The Eleventh Hour* (2008) by director John Lyde, is not likely to be seen by those who are skeptical of climate change, while it is likely to be embraced by those who see climate change as a real problem. There is an old philosophic thought experiment that asks, "If a tree falls in a forest, and no one is around to hear it, does it make a sound?" We can ask a similar question about documentary films: Does a documentary film whose purpose is to persuade people to change their mind about an issue have any impact? One contention is that it does by coalescing those who are already similarly inclined; however, the impact among the general population might be to harden positions against the film's message. Regardless, observing this debate and reviewing these films can be instructive. They can help us understand and dissect the political debate that might be occurring within a society.

Who Has Power?

Historically, power in world politics has been measured in terms of resources. One political scientist, in an effort to quantify power, argued that the power of a state consists of three basic resources: population, economy, and military prowess.[27] Critics of this approach note that simple measurement of resources doesn't account for the intangible assets or skills a state might possess, such as persuasiveness or ideology. Despite the frequent use of the term, the definition of power is somewhat contentious and political science's ability to measure power has been elusive.[28]

Whether power is the ability to make someone do something he or she otherwise would not, or is simply the ability to influence, the concept is important and an essential part of world politics. Political scientist Joseph S. Nye Jr. argues that simply defining power as a set of tangible resources misses a big piece of what makes powerful countries powerful.[29] In fact, the resources of power depend on the context of a situation.[30] Nuclear weapons, for example, are not likely to be useful in trade negotiations. Instead, so-called soft power consists of attractive ideas or qualities that entice others to change or modify their behavior and can be the ability to persuade others through the framing or establishment of an agenda, rather than a reliance on force.[31]

 The concept of soft power is particularly important to this book because film and cinema represent a manifestation of soft power. A couple of years ago a student from Paris spent the summer studying at my university in rural Pennsylvania. Given that she was from a glamorous and sophisticated city and was living in a small town in Pennsylvania, I wondered if she felt isolated and lonely. She said she did not; in fact, the attractiveness and allure of the United States was just as she had expected. Intrigued, I was curious as to how she developed her favorable impression of the United States. The young woman told me that she imagined the "real" United States to be a place of tree-lined streets and white-picket fences where families work and play together—in short, an idyllic and bucolic place. Where did she get this impression? From her favorite television program, *7th Heaven* (1996–2007).

Whether *7th Heaven*, *Gilmore Girls* (2000–2007), *Friends*, or *How I Met Your Mother* (2005–), popular television programs paint an enticing picture of the United States, making it attractive to many viewers around the world. This attractiveness means that the culture can set the standard of success and establish the agenda of how to measure that success.[32] This attribute is not unique to the United States. Other countries produce films and television programs that have the ability to establish paradigms of success and consumer demands as well; an example is the influence of French media on countries in Africa.[33] In fact, many scholars have pointed to the burgeoning of soft power through the development of film and popular culture.[34]

Some Final Thoughts

Watching films is not a shortcut to understanding world politics; instead, it adds a layer of nuance and complexity. The reason that this book examines a number of older films is that we can trace the development of ideas and conceptions over time. The beginning of the cinema corresponds roughly with the beginning of the twentieth century. This means that sitting in archives around the world are images of leaders and events that are invaluable to historical research. The first "movies" as we know them today were made in the 1890s; however, the development of a cinematic language, the unique way in which film can move around time and space, did not begin until the early twentieth century. Many film historians consider the American Civil War drama *The Birth of a Nation* (1915), directed by D. W. Griffith, as the film that perfected the techniques of cinematic storytelling. Other directors, such as the Russian director Sergei Eisenstein, most famous for his film about the abortive 1905 Russian Revolution, *Battleship Potemkin* (1925), were innovators who helped to cement film as an art form.

One interesting phenomenon, somewhat counterintuitive, should be noted. Most films made before 1930, depending on the region of the world, were known as silent films. These films were never really silent; films prior to the introduction of spoken dialogue were projected with musical accompaniment in the movie theater, designed to help facilitate the story. Technical innovations in the 1920s put sound directly on the strip of film that was run through the projector. This introduced spoken dialogue to films, but in an odd way had another effect. Films made during the silent period were remarkably international, because title cards (written words either describing the narrative or substituting for dialogue) were relatively rare. It was easy to provide translations of film in many different languages. Thus a German film could have the title cards translated into English and placed in the film, rendering the nationality of the actors unimportant. With the advent of sound films, the entire dialogue of a film had to be translated for a film, either by dubbing the voices of the actors or providing subtitles throughout the films.[35] Thus films became less international, at least initially, because of linguistic barriers. Later, improved techniques of dubbing films and providing subtitles would be developed.

There are at least three important events of the early twentieth century that still have an impact on world politics, making the consideration of silent films of continuing importance. First, the silent film period coincides with the First World War (1914–1918), a war that notably remade borders in Europe, but also a war in which the full impact of the industrial revolution came into play, resulting in killing on a scale never before witnessed. Because the war was so horrific in terms of deaths and destruction, after it worldwide peace and antiwar movements began to emerge. A second reason why silent films should be considered is that the birth of the cinema roughly coincided with a massive wave of immigration to North America in the 1920s. As we will see in chapter 11, films have played an important role in educating both immigrants and the public at large. Finally, another event that had a lasting impact on world politics is the rise of Communism in world politics, and the decline of ideological homogeneity.[36]

In addition to a few silent films discussed, this book has included as many non-English-language films as possible. One of the primary goals of the book is to introduce world politics through the examination of many filmic interpretations of concepts and events. The films are not always equally engaging, but the different responses and interpretations go a long way to explain why there are so many perspectives on world politics.

2

A PRIMER ON IR (INTERNATIONAL RELATIONS) PERSPECTIVES

Scholars and students of world politics look for tools and devices to help make sense of the world. Political science, like most social sciences, is premised on the idea that there are discernible patterns in the world that we can categorize, explain and, in some cases, predict.[1] Thus, if we know and understand the patterns, it will help us comprehend world politics. International relations (IR) perspectives are meant to do just that: identify patterns to explain and sometimes predict the course of world politics.

Despite the variation in understandings of world politics among different perspectives, there are some general points upon which most scholars agree. Political scientists concur that the primary unit of world politics is the state. A state, which is a legal term, has the basic characteristics of defined territorial borders, human population, government organization, and demonstrated sovereignty.[2]

Perhaps the most important characteristic of the modern international system is that there is no world government. International politics is said to exist in a state of anarchy (without a ruler or government), because all states are sovereign. Sovereignty means that each state has exclusive jurisdiction over its territory, free from outside interference. Since sovereignty exists, and world politics occurs in a condition of anarchy, states must be concerned with their own security because no one else will.[3]

The study of the interactions between states is referred to as international relations, and the major schools of thought are referred to as perspectives. Perspectives are a tool to give us a shortcut in our understanding of world politics. Many people describe them as a lens, or glasses, that will help us filter out less important, or extraneous, information. A perspective allows us to focus on the main details of information. It is difficult, and perhaps a bit disingenuous, to summarize broad, complex schools of thought in a few sentences. Scholars have conducted vast amounts of research, writing, and interactions with other scholars that are not reflected in this brief essay, yet for the purpose of this book it will be helpful to review the major premises of the perspectives in order to demonstrate, in subsequent chapters, how films reflect contemporary understandings of world politics and international relations theory.

Realism

The oldest and most established of the schools is political realism (realpolitik), which finds its origins in focusing on the resources and capability of a state. As the school has developed, there has been more emphasis on the power a state possesses. Specifically, realism assumes that those states that have more power are dominant and shape the politics of the system. The anarchical nature of the international system requires states to be concerned, even obsessed, with power because it is the only way to ensure security or even survival. Thus, for most realists today, the study of international relations should concentrate on how power is distributed among states.

Realists argue that the struggle for power and security is timeless and often cite Thucydides, the Greek historian who wrote in 380 BCE, "The strong do what they can, and the weak suffer what they must."[4] Since, according to the realists, the issue of security cannot be resolved, states are trapped in a series of competitions over power, resulting in continual military conflicts. The emphasis on power leads realists to assume that very little weight should be given to other motivations, such as ideology, religion, or even characteristics of leadership.[5]

Liberalism

The primary alternative to the realist school is known as the liberal perspective. Rather than focusing on the power of the state, liberals tend to focus on the decision of individuals (sometimes these scholars are referred to as *idealists* or *pluralists*). Based on the work of philosophers such as Jean-Jacques Rousseau and Immanuel Kant, liberals argue that there are always opportunities for people to cooperate; however, this does not mean that they will always do so. In fact, there might be significant barriers that might preclude or inhibit cooperation, including ideological, cultural, racial, or economic differences. While liberals will maintain that the security dilemma is a major problem, most contend that these barriers can be overcome through cooperation.

Liberals also acknowledge that power is a key issue in world politics, but they point out that there might be other interests that drive state behavior, such as economics, ideology, or religion. Thus the liberals argue that to reduce politics to simply one motivation, the quest for power, is an oversimplification of world politics. Many liberal scholars point to the substantial forms of cooperation that exist in world politics, such as international trade, diplomacy, and space exploration. Therefore, many liberals contend that cooperation among democratic countries produces peace, and the more states cooperate, the less the chance they will go to war.[6]

Social Constructivism

Although the realists and the liberals have been the dominant perspectives in research and writing on international politics, other perspectives offer alternative interpretations. A central theme in the constructivist perspective is that new knowledge changes interests, values, and dynamics in the international system. The perspective argues that actors construct a reality based on their perception of a situation. Thus, constructivists claim that just as individuals emphasize different roles within their own lives, states may value different things depending on the current situation and the role they are taking within it. Although states have interests, these interests are changeable, depending on what the states (or the leadership within states) think is most important at any given time.

For the constructivists rules are created depending on the situation, so that what is considered appropriate can change over time. The perspective points to the evolving norm patterns in world politics for many issues, of which slavery is a notable example. For many centuries slavery was accepted as completely normal in the international system; however, the acquisition of knowledge and the generation of new thinking prompted a change in the international system. Likewise, prior to the twentieth century, the issue of human rights was not a matter for discussion in world politics. Thus Alexander Wendt's dictum "Anarchy is what states make of it" refers to the idea that the rules of the international system are not set in stone and can be changed over time.[7]

Structuralism

Another broad school of thought is collectively known as the structuralist perspective, which argues that politics can be explained by understanding who has power and who makes decisions. Within this perspective there is a tendency to highlight the historical development of world politics to demonstrate its evolution and trends. Structuralists argue that by analyzing these trends, one can observe patterns of domination.

The perspective accounts for the uneven distribution in wealth and power around the world and among groups. For example, feminists will argue that because men make political decisions, they shape politics to reflect the interests of men and privilege those interests over others. Other scholars in this perspective will focus more prominently on the role of wealth and economic classes, noting that decisions are made by those who have financial wealth. While Marxists will focus on the relationship between economic classes worldwide, world-system theorists claim that the development of historical trends leads to a situation of dependency between the industrialized north and the lesser-developed (poorer) countries of the south.[8]

Some Final Thoughts

By no means does this short primer provide details or give the complete nuance of some very sophisticated debates. Please consult the citations for more information. It is unwise to focus solely on one perspective or to ignore one that does not initially sound appealing. These perspectives are helpful because they make the amount of information about world politics manageable by asking you to focus on what the different schools see as essential. None of these perspectives seeks to explain all things, but all are designed to demonstrate trends in world politics.[9]

Part 2

CONFLICT AND COOPERATION IN WORLD POLITICS

3

WAR IS SOMETIMES UNAVOIDABLE

War has driven the development of the field of international relations more than any other concept. Originally the study of international relations was the study of why countries go to war; even today the basic premise of the field of international relations is to understand why states do what they do, including why they go to war. There is a plethora of works speculating about and analyzing why wars occur. One of the great theoretical divides among international relations scholars is whether wars are ultimately avoidable.

Under the current configuration of international politics, known as the Westphalian System, because states are sovereign, they must depend on themselves for their own security and survival. Unlike the case for citizens who live in countries where there are working governments, there is no police, no judicial mechanism to rescue states. Political scientists often refer to this as a system of anarchy because there is no overarching world government. Given this, those from the realist (realpolitik) theoretical perspective argue that conflict is unavoidable. The rival theoretical perspective, liberalism, is less sure about the consequences of the Westphalian System. Liberals know that war will not necessarily be avoided, but they believe that it could be avoided.

This chapter and the next will explore how war has been depicted in films: this will explain the theme that wars are unavoidable, and the next will analyze films that are decidedly antiwar. Subsequent chapters will explore variations, including nuclear war and the opportunity of international cooperation. The goal of these chapters is to examine why wars occur, different perceptions of the results of war, and the consequences of war in today's world.

The Study of War

Few rational people are pro-war. Wars cause destruction, misery, and degradation. John Mearsheimer opened his famous 1990 article on the future of international politics at the end of the cold war by stating that peace was wonderful and he had no desire to be overly gloomy in the face of a seemingly wonderful event. Yet for all the optimism that marked the collapse of Communism in Europe and the end of the cold war, Mearsheimer wrote, one had to be realistic: his analysis predicted an increase in military conflict in the coming decades.[1] Other scholars who examine the prospects and probability of war in the twenty-first century argue that one must not let optimism and hope cloud the analysis. Certainly after the terrorist attacks on the United States on September 11, 2001, and subsequent attacks in Bali, London, and Mumbai, many have been skeptical about the possibility of peace in the twenty-first century.

At first glance, historical evidence appears to suggest that war is a natural occurrence in international politics. Quotes such as von Clausewitz's maxim that war is an extension of politics through other means[2] and the Vegetius's dictum "Si vis pacem, para bellum" (If you wish peace, prepare for war) seem to indicate that war is inevitable and a natural human condition. Indeed, much of our history revolves around war and conflict. We measure time and mark phases based on war. Consider our use of terms such as "postwar period." It seems that war is a constant and punctures our history.

In Kenneth Waltz's seminal work *Man, the State and War,* the author attempted to decipher the causes of war.[3] To better understand what led to war, Waltz divided causes into three categories (or images): the individual level, the state level, and the system level.[4] Each of the levels was designed to organize one's thinking about where the primary factors (or causes) of war are located. For example, John G. Stoessinger uses the individual level to argue that the decisions, perceptions, biases, and opinions of individual leaders are the primary explanatory factors in understanding war. On the other hand, several authors, including Bruce Russett and Michael Doyle, argue that the characteristics of a given state, including whether it is democratic and the level of economic development it has attained, help to explain how likely it is to go to war.[5] Waltz, however, concluded that the main reason states go to war is because of the nature of the international system (the system level). He argued that because the international system is in anarchy (it lacks government), states have to rely on increasing their own power to obtain security. The competition to increase power inevitably leads to conflict.[6]

Many political scientists and historians agree with Waltz when he argues that war is a natural outcome of an anarchic world.[7] Because countries are insecure, and the measures they take to make themselves feel more secure inevitably make their neighbors feel less secure, conflict and war become inevitable. In political science this is known as the phenomenon of the security dilemma. States that are insecure will constantly try to increase their power in order to satisfy their security needs, which often leads to the security dilemma. This is because, inevitably as states increase their power when feeling insecure, their neighbors will respond in kind, increasing their power to meet their insecurity. Both states find themselves caught in a game in which they are suspicious of each other and find that they have to respond because anarchy means no one else will do it for them.[8] Film can both illustrate this concept and help contribute to it. *Dr. Strangelove* (1964) and *The Russians Are Coming! The Russians Are Coming!* (1966) critiqued and poked fun at the suspicions (or paranoia) existing between the United States and the Soviet Union during the cold war. *High Noon* (1952), arguably one of the greatest westerns ever made, is often read as a parable of the dangers of paranoia and a disengaged citizenry. Commenting on the cold war period, the townspeople represent an American public unwilling (or unable) to stand up for basic principles. Alfred Hitchcock's *Rear Window* (1954) is ostensibly about a man with a broken leg who is looking out his window and sees a murder, but it can be read as the paranoia of the United States as it looks out on the world and sees all its petty disagreements. Hitchcock's films often focused on the suspicion of others and what deeds they might be engaging in (or not), helping to capture the paranoia of the cold war in the United States. On the other hand, films that cast suspicion on the other side, for example, *Big Jim McLain* (1952), *Red Dawn* (1984), and documentaries such as *The Hoaxters* (1957), help to raise and sustain suspicion about the Soviet Union. The same is true of Soviet films at that time about the United States. The very amusing *Neobychainye priklyucheniya mistera Vesta v strane bolshevikov* (The Extraordinary Adventures of Mr. West in the Land of the Bolsheviks, 1924) uses American certitude coupled with lack of actual knowledge to cast aspersions on the society. Other films, such as the ones contained in the DVD collection *Animated Soviet Propaganda,* attempt to build the case that the capitalist system of the West inevitably leads to imperialism. In both cases, the films cast suspicions on the other side.

This does not mean that people want war to occur—quite the contrary; however, the implication is that wars are difficult to avoid. The anarchy of the international system is seen as a major obstacle to peace in the film *The Day the Earth Stood Still* (1951). This is actually an antiwar film, but because it sheds light on the reasons why wars occur, it will be considered here. The film opens with a large flying saucer landing on the Mall in Washington, DC. The spaceship is immediately surrounded by military personnel and equipment. When the door of the spaceship begins to open, the military brings more machine guns to surround the ship. When the alien (Klaatu) emerges and tries to proffer a gift, he is wounded by a nervous soldier looking on. There is no mistaking that the filmmakers are highlighting the essential insecurities of humans and countries.

Klaatu takes on the form of Mr. Carpenter and makes his way to a boardinghouse where he surreptitiously tries to learn more about humans.[9] He is befriended by Bobby, a young boy who lives there. One day Bobby takes Mr. Carpenter on a tour of Washington, DC. They visit Arlington National Cemetery, where Bobby's father is buried. The broad shots of the cemetery allow the viewer to consider how very many people are buried there. Klaatu is amazed that everyone buried within the cemetery had died in war.

The film constantly reinforces the notion that war is a result of our insecurities. In a scene at the boardinghouse, the residents sit at the table discussing the landing of the spaceship. Several are convinced that the landing is a prelude to invasion; Mrs. Barley (played by Frances Bavier, who played Aunt Bee on the *Andy Griffith Show*) opines that Klaatu is not really from outer space, but right here on Earth. She raises her eyebrows suggestively, saying, " . . . and you know where I mean" (a reference to the Soviet Union). This is a hint to the viewer that the story is not about outer space, but about current politics.

After the narrative of the film plays out, Klaatu delivers the message for which he has come. He tells the people of Earth that other worlds have observed the wars of humans and the development of their crude atomic weapons. In the future, he says, Earth will not be allowed to export its violence into outer space. Klaatu explains that the other worlds had overcome their insecurities with each other by turning over ultimate control of power and security to a group of robots. He warns Earth residents that if they do not join the security of the robots, the Earth will be reduced to smoldering embers.[10] Klaatu is calling for an end to anarchy and the creation of a government (albeit one led by robots) to manage the insecurities of people.

Many scholars, particularly political realists, will agree that without a world government, wars are a inevitable part of human existence.

Particularly for the Allied countries (especially the United States, Canada, and the United Kingdom), the Second World War is often viewed as a war, above all others, that was legitimate and just. Several films about the Second World War reflect the notion that sometimes wars *must* be fought, however reluctantly. To explain the implications of these films, this section is organized into three justifications for war: (1) self defense; (2) the preservation of some ideas and values that are transcendently important; and (3) resistance. These are not discrete categories; films will overlap in categories quite frequently, but these categories give us a way to think about different types of war films and the messages they contain.

War as Self-Defense

For many who believe that war is sometimes inevitable, they point no further than the concept of self-defense. If a country is attacked militarily, then it has no choice but to respond militarily. A country can be very committed to peace, but unless other countries also are committed to peace, then war is always a possibility. It seems only logical in a system where there is no judge and no police that if you are attacked, you must respond, for no one else will be there to help you. Several propaganda films from many countries make this point,[11] probably none as familiar as the Why We Fight series under the direction of Frank Capra, director of several famous Hollywood films, including *Mr. Smith Goes to Washington*.[12] In *Why We Fight: The Nazis Strike* (1943), the second in the series, the film recounts the understanding of the United States as to why war is necessary against Nazi Germany—even the title suggests the aggression and militarism of Hitler's regime. Between the Japanese surprise attack on Pearl Harbor and the threat posed by German militarism, the film argues, the United States has no choice but to fight a war of self-defense.

Military preparedness often is seen as a method of preserving a state's security, and thus ultimately peace. Several narrative films have made this argument implicitly and explicitly. From this perspective, there are enemies out in the world, known and unknown, for which a country must prepare. A handful of films prior to the First World War argue this point, sometimes to absurdity. For example, *The Battle Cry of Peace* (1915) and *The Fall of a Nation* (1916) used fictional invasions of the United States as a warning against those who advocated peace at any cost. At this time World War I had already broken out in Europe and there was a debate about what role, if any, the United States should play. In *Battle Cry of Peace,* the United States is secretly and efficiently invaded by an unnamed European army, whose soldiers wear mustaches remarkably similar to that of the German Kaiser. The occupied United States is rescued by a group of women who are seemingly complicit with the invaders but are actually loyal Americans who use their feminine charms to lure the occupation force from its post to allow American soldiers to regain the upper hand. In *The Fall of a Nation,* a sequel to the much more famous *The Birth of a Nation* (1915), the film's writer and director, Thomas Dixon, argued that Americans who advocated peace were supporting foreign powers. The reviewer for the *New York Times* thought the premise was absurd, but nonetheless it was an entertaining film. One might speculate that this was of little concern to Dixon. As the reviewer pointed out, the film was designed to cast suspicions upon anyone who opposed an increase in military appropriations.[13] The argument Dixon employs, that opposing military spending is tantamount to supporting the enemy, is not unique and has been frequently employed by many people in different countries.

Films in the 1950s sometimes reflected this concern of known and unknown enemies as well. Because of the dominance of the United States in the immediate postwar period, some American films took on a different look. Films such as *Strategic Air Command* (1955) and *Battleground* (1949) reminded the audience of the hard work and sacrifices of individuals who were engaged in the defense of the country. One could argue that the introduction of nuclear weapons meant that military preparedness took on a new dimension (see chapter 6). In films such as *It Came from Outer Space* (1953), *The War of the Worlds* (1953), and *The Thing from Another World* (1951), the invaders were ostensibly extraterrestrials; however, there is a subtle message about the value of scientific research and the need to maintain spending on technology to maintain a predominant position in the modern world. Improbably, scientists are portrayed as sexy intellectuals, risking life and limb in an effort to understand the threats we face. The message of these films was that a threat clearly existed, and in our own world—outer space was just a metaphor for other countries so that the filmmakers did not have to identify and potentially offend a particular country. That choice also makes the enemy interchangeable, meaning that a filmmaker does not need to correctly identify a potential enemy—just to suggest one exists. Thus, in *The*

Day the Earth Stood Still, Mrs. Barley casts a wary eye on other countries rather than focusing on the message being delivered by Klaatu.

During the late cold war period in American cinema, a handful of films, like *Red Dawn* (1984) and *Invasion U.S.A.* (1985), again reflected the possibility that the United States could be invaded. These films were made at a time when there was a debate about increased military spending. While the premise of these films might seem preposterous, the overall message is clear: the United States needed to make sure it engaged in military preparedness. The premise of *Red Dawn* is that the United States is invaded by Warsaw Pact countries, led by the Soviet Union. Most of the action takes place in Colorado, where a group of high school students create a resistance force against Cubans, who constitute part of the multinational Communist occupying force. The film offered early starring roles for a number of young actors, including Patrick Swayze, Charlie Sheen, and Lea Thompson. By explicitly identifying the Soviet Union as the invader, the film came to be seen as anachronistic with the end of the cold war.[14] Other films use an unidentified enemy so that the film lives on, even if the potential enemy becomes a friend. *Invasion U.S.A.* stars Chuck Norris as a former CIA agent fighting off Communist terrorists who have invaded Miami. There are a number of not-so-subtle references in the film, including having the terrorists invade on Christmas Day and destroy churches. Because most Communist countries were officially atheist, the filmmakers surmised it would be only natural for these terrorists to attack these institutions. Such a scenario is unlikely. Most invaders would know that such a tactic would only antagonize the local population rather than make it more quiescent. Yet psychological accuracy is not the point of these films. The motivation of any film that urges military preparedness is to tell not a believable story but an entertaining one that reinforces the need for military vigilance. Note that, despite the fact that there are seventy years between *Battle Cry of Peace* and the films *Invasion U.S.A.* and *Red Dawn,* all have the same premise—that there are countries out there willing to attack the United States and that invasion is imminent. Despite their far-fetched plotlines, all the films call for American military preparedness.

Such films are not unique to the United States. Many countries draw on their historical past to remind citizens that military preparedness might be necessary. One of the most famous examples is the Russian-language film *Aleksandr Nevskiy* (Alexander Nevsky, 1938). The film was directed by Sergei Eisenstein, the most famous and influential film director of the

Soviet Union. The film tells the story of the thirteenth-century Russian hero, Nevsky (Nikolai Cherkassov), probably the most famous Russian of the medieval period. The opening titles of the film explain that outsiders are drawn to Russia because of its wide-open spaces and its great resources. As the film opens, Mongols, who have just launched a major attack against Russia, are seen patrolling the Russian hinterlands. Nevsky is recognized as a good leader, and the Mongols ask him to join them because they are always looking for good leaders. Nevsky declines, citing patriotic reasons. One of Nevsky's men asks if they should fight the Mongols. Nevsky answers that they should deal with the Mongols later because the Germans (Teutonic knights) are more of a threat and should be dealt with first. When the film was released in 1938, there was significant concern in the Soviet Union about the threat Nazi Germany posed. Examining the costumes that Eisenstein uses for the Teutonic knights leaves no doubt as to whom they are supposed to represent: The knights wear interesting helmets that evoke the image of Nazi Stormtroopers.

As the Germans approach the city of Novgorod, their capture and occupation of the city of Pskov is brutal. The priest traveling with the Teutonic knights declares that anyone not submitting to Rome should be destroyed. The Russians, who are Orthodox Christians, refuse. German soldiers level their lances and systematically kill the Russian prisoners. The knights then turn on the women and children, ripping male children from the arms of their mothers and throwing the babies and toddlers into a raging fire. The German treatment of Pskov rallies the people of Novgorod to action, and they call on Alexander to lead them in defense of all Russian lands.

The film uses Russian history to demonstrate that Russians had repelled attacks from the West before and could do it again. The climactic battle in the film takes place at Lake Peipus, which historically occurred on 5 April 1242 and is remembered as a great military victory. After the battle, Nevsky says, "Go home and tell all in foreign lands that Russia lives. Let them come to us as guest and they will be welcome. But if any one comes to us with sword he shall perish by the sword." This film, made by the Soviet Communist regime of the time, evokes nationalism and the defense of the homeland as a central theme.

These arguments can be made for contemporary audiences while using information from the past. The Finnish film *Talvisota* (The Winter War, 1989) documents the Russian invasion of Finland in 1939 from the point of view of two brothers. The film is a commemoration of the sacrifice of the Finnish people on the fiftieth anniversary of the war. Yet it also serves as a reminder that fifty years later Finland is still located next to Russia and the need for vigilance remains. There are many more films that display this theme; unfortunately, when the background to a conflict is not widely known outside their country of origin, these films tend not to travel well. Because the films are created for domestic audiences they do not usually resonate in other countries. Nevertheless, films such as *Britain Can Take It!* (1940), *Battle of Britain* (1969), *Tora! Tora! Tora!* (1970), and *Pearl Harbor* (2001) provide stories that serve to entertain audiences while pointing out the importance of military defense.[15]

These types of film might work in reverse as well. In the atmosphere of confrontation between the West and Iran over Iran's suspected nuclear program, Warner Brothers released the special-effect-laden film *300* (2006). The film recounts the battle of Thermopylae in 480 BCE, in which a small Greek force led by King Leonidas and three hundred Spartan soldiers held off the much larger Persian forces, led by King Xerxes, at a mountain pass. Many commentators noted the allegories of the story to current political tensions: the West (Greeks) versus Iran (Persians). The timing of the release of the film drew criticism from the Iranian government (modern Persia) that Hollywood was making anti-Iranian films and insulting Iranian history.[16] The intent of the film thus backfired, serving not so much as a call to the West against Iran as a call to Iran against the West.

Wars over Ideas Worth Fighting For

Perhaps more realistic and persuasive is the idea that sometimes one has to fight for important ideas. In American and British films there is an emphasis on protecting individual liberties and a democratic way of life. Self-sacrifice and giving for the common good are often hallmarks of this type of film. Sometimes the fight must be taken up even if one is reluctant to do so; sometimes one must actively resist an overbearing force or ideas that are repulsive. Regardless, there are those ideas—ideological, religious, or for the good of the community—that require a good fight.

The rise of fascism in Europe corresponded with a number of films that used the logic that there are ideas worth fighting for. Even before the outbreak of the Second World War, the Spanish Civil War led liberals and socialists worldwide to argue that the heavy-handed tactics of fascists in Spain (and the rest of Europe), including intimidation, violence, and assassination, meant that the fascists had to be opposed militarily. Thus, *Blockade* (1938) and *For Whom the Bell Tolls* (1943) both urged military resistance to the growth of fascism. People from around the world poured into Spain during the civil war (1936–1939) as volunteers to fight the fascist forces led by Francisco Franco in an engagement many historians consider a prelude to World War II. Those who served, including Americans from the Abraham Lincoln Brigade, were later lionized in documentaries like *The Good Fight* (1984).[17]

Very often films in this genre are subtle and tell a great story, but behind the story are ideas about the importance of the protection of certain values.[18] At first glance, *Casablanca* (1942) is a great love story; however, further study reveals important political messages in the story as well. The film helped define Humphrey Bogart as an important Hollywood star. Before this he played tough-boiled detectives and gangsters. Initially, this is how his character, Rick, appears on the surface; yet as the movie develops it becomes clear he has a conscience, he is a patriot, and he loves Ilsa deeply. Rick Blaine, as portrayed by Humphrey Bogart, becomes an idealized hero.[19] The film employs a type of hero very appealing to the moviegoing audience. Men identify with the strong silent type who is motivated by noble passions (patriotism and love); his flaws are the result of a deep wounding. Women often see the man who is quiet, hard, and difficult (the "bad-boy" image) as one who can be transformed by a woman's love. As an archetype, the film is a great draw for film aficionados. *Casablanca* is consistently on lists of the ten greatest films ever made.

The prevailing view is that *Casablanca* was arguing in favor of U.S. engagement against fascism and on the side of the Allies.[20] It is difficult to argue against that analysis. From this interpretation, the city of Casablanca is a microcosm for the world in 1941. There are three primary instances in which the film represents world politics at the beginning of the Second World War: first, early in the film Rick repeats the mantra "I stick my head out for no one," which was seen as the U.S. attitude toward the rest of the world; second, when the entire bar stands up and sings "La Marseillaise" to shout down the Germans singing war songs, it is meant to signify the need for internationalism and cooperation to defeat Germany; and third, at the end of the film, when Captain Renault drops Vichy water into the trash, it means that the United States and the rest of the world should drop that regime in favor of liberating France.[21] The overwhelming sense is that war must be engaged; the stakes are too high and a way of life has to be protected.[22]

Today, *Casablanca* continues to be a favorite film for many. Its story seems timeless, reminding people that there are causes worth fighting for. The way in which the film builds empathy for refugees of the Nazi regime certainly helped the American public empathize with the plight of occupied Europe. The remarkable thing about the film was that it was almost entirely fictional. By the screenwriters' own admission, the story was cobbled together. There was no such thing as a letter of transit, and any Germans who might have been in Casablanca were certainly not in uniform.[23]

A similar American film of the same period is *Sergeant York* (1941), which also references the idea that there might be causes worth fighting for. The film is a biographical account of Alvin C. York from his time as a young man in Tennessee until his return to the United States after World War I. Alvin York, played by Gary Cooper, is a young man who seems to have little purpose but to spend his time drinking and gambling, much to the consternation of his family. Gradually his interest in a local girl (Joan Leslie) and the guidance of the local pastor lead him to become a very religious man. When York is drafted he tries to obtain an exemption based upon his religious belief that it is wrong to kill. His petition is turned down. York is forced to report for training and while there his skills as a hunter serve him well and he demonstrates that he is an expert marksman.

When York is offered a promotion to help train soldiers, he is willing to help other soldiers learn how to shoot, but he declines the promotion. As a conscientious objector, York faces some hardship and endures negative comments from his fellow soldiers. When military officers press him about his religious beliefs, York details why he believes that the teachings of the Bible prevent him from killing another human being. Major Buxton argues that York's freedom to practice his own religion is dependent on freedom guaranteed by the United States and that sometimes it is necessary to defend those freedoms through war. Thus, as distasteful as it is to fight and kill, there are ideas that must be fought for to be protected. In his study of both American history and the Bible, York stumbles across this passage from Matthew: "Render unto Caesar that which is Caesar's." He takes this as a sign that he must do his duty for the country.

York fights with distinction and eventually is forced to take command of his unit because of battlefield deaths. With only a handful of men, York is able to neutralize several machine gun nests and capture 132 German soldiers. He is awarded the Medal of Honor and returns to the United States a hero, the most decorated American soldier in the First World War. After receiving the key to the city of New York, he is offered a number of employment opportunities, including breakfast-cereal endorsements and the chance to appear in motion pictures. However, he refuses all accolades, explaining he is not proud of what he did in France; he did it because he considered it his duty. In the end, knowing that whether he fought or not, thousands would die, it was his duty to fight and kill in order to save lives in the long run.

The timing of *Sergeant York*'s release, July 1941, is important. This was after the Second World War had begun in Europe but before the entry of the United States in December of 1941. At the premiere of the film, Alvin York expressed his hope that the film would create a sense of "national unity in this hour of danger."[24] The film was clearly designed to persuade a wary American public that war is sometimes necessary to save the lives of people and protect freedom, even if one is opposed to the ideas of war and killing. Using the true experience of a real person (who was still living at the time of the film's release) who had opposed war on religious and moral grounds but in the end became a significant war hero also bolstered the idea that Americans had a duty to perform in Europe that it would be morally unconscionable to shirk.

There are a number of films that portray other ideas that their filmmakers thought worth fighting for. Yet some of the ideas are no longer considered virtuous. Kipling once wrote that Europeans had a "white man's burden" of civilizing the rest of the world.[25] To those who advocated an imperial policy, the idea was very appealing. Kipling's poem evokes both responsibility and costs in that it was not only appropriate but justified that Europeans fought and died in an attempt to bring Western values to the world. Films such as *Charge of the Light Brigade* (1936), *Gunga Din* (1939), and *Beau Geste* (1926, 1939) are stories in which colonizers attempt to quell dissent over European rule. Never do these films question why the soldiers are there, or if they should be; the assumption is that their motives are noble and their opponents' are not. Many times these films are a cover for the racist belief that whites are superior. Similarly, films of the Old West, particularly those that pit whites against Indians—those of European descent against Native Americans—make generalities as well. As a contrary approach, the Ivorian Coast film *Noirs et blancs en couleur* (Black and White in Color, 1976) portrays the actions of white colonists in Africa during the First World War. The absurdity that a group of ill-prepared French colonists would fight a group of undermanned German colonists using local Africans as proxies, while not knowing why the larger war is being fought, calls into question who is really civilized in the story.

Similarly, it is rare that films of the golden age of Hollywood question the alternative view that European conquest might not be such a good and noble idea. Yet more recent films, such as *Dances with Wolves* (1990), provide a more favorable image of Native Americans. From this point of view one might argue that those suffering from the effects of colonial conquest are fighting wars of defense or resistance.

Wars of Resistance

Another popular theme in films about war is the idea that wars need to be fought to resist an occupying or overbearing force. For example, U.S. films such as *Johnny Tremain* (1957), *Revolution* (1985), and *The Patriot* (2000) all celebrate the American colonists' resistance of British domination and rule. Resistance is a common theme regardless of nationality; American films do not have a corner on this market. Even wars that are remembered differently, such as World War I, have propaganda films that make the argument that fighting the war is necessary because it is resisting tyranny or domination.[26] Several foreign films follow this same pattern, sometimes overtly, sometimes less so.

The difficulty of this genre is that receptiveness to this type of film is very dependent upon the sympathies of the viewers. American viewers of films about the American Revolution might be very sympathetic to a film that depicts British troops as brutal, manipulative, and not very nice; British viewers might not appreciate such a depiction. Likewise, a Vietnamese film about what is locally referred to as the American War (such as *The Sound of My Violin in My Lai*, 1999) would be substantially different from an American film about the Vietnam War. A Vietnamese film would likely focus on the resistance offered by the Vietnamese people to Japanese, French, and then American domination and occupation.[27]

Wars of resistance are events that can create a national identity and stories that help identify and shape a nation. They also create epic tales in which protagonists have pure motivations of defending family, faith, country, and ideals. Thus, films like *Alexander Nevsky* paint the Russians in favorable terms and Germans, the invaders, in decidedly negative terms. Even when the subject of the film is mythical, the story can create very strong emotions and allegiance. The original trilogy of the Star Wars films, *Star Wars* (1977), *The Empire Strikes Back* (1980), and *Return of the Jedi* (1983), is about a war of resistance against the Empire. Luke Skywalker, Princess Leia, and Han

Fantastic Planet uses an animated film format, which at first seems bizarre, to demonstrate how an overly oppressive and strong regime can be brought down through ingenuity and cooperation. (Still from the author's collection)

Solo, those who are considered heroes in the films, are resisting the brutal and dictatorial tactics of the Empire and are depicted in terms of good, while those siding with the Empire, particularly Darth Vader and the Emperor, are cast in dark and negative terms. The film is constructed in a way that makes it very easy for the audience to root for the rebels.

Many films and resistance causes are familiar to Western audiences. For instance, the 2008 film *Defiance* recounts the efforts of the Bielski partisans, who resisted the German occupation of Belorussia during the Second World War while simultaneously protecting hundreds of Jewish refugees in remote forest locations. Along the same lines, the Czechoslovak film *Ostre sledované vlaky* (Closely Watched Trains, 1966) highlights the sacrifice of individuals in the face of German occupation. It is interesting that while the film sets up the dichotomy of "good" Czech resistors versus "bad" German occupiers, in the case of *Closely Watched Trains*, the motivation of the protagonist, a young man, is more about a sexual liaison with a local partisan than it is about the ideals of resistance. Another Czech film, *Musime si pomahat* (Divided We Fall, 2000) allows that not all resistance is necessarily military resistance.[28] In the film, a childless Czech couple thinks it their duty to protect a local Jewish man from the Nazi occupiers and their allies. The story depicts the idea that there are sacrifices to be made in the cause of resistance, both small and large. *La planète sauvage* (Fantastic Planet, 1973), an animated French-Czech coproduction, uses an allegorical story to make a similar point.

Perhaps one of the most famous and influential films about colonial occupation is *La battaglia di Algeri* (The Battle of Algiers, 1966). The film tells the story of the attempts by a rebel group in Algeria, the National Liberation Front, or Front de Libération Nationale (FLN), to secure the independence of Algeria from French colonization in the early 1950s. It is a film that could be discussed in a number of different chapters in this book and that will be referenced briefly elsewhere. The style of the film is an attempt to give the audience a sense of what the situation actually looks like—*cinéma vérité*. The film does not romanticize either side. It is an attempt to portray the French occupation and the Algerian resistance to French colonialism (led by the FLN) as accurately as possible. The film opens with a note that no documentary footage was used in the making of the film. It is a testament to the realistic detail that the director, Gillo Pontecorvo, placed in the film. Both the French and the Algerians use methods that many would question, including torture and the bombing of innocents. At the same time the film also highlights the rightness of each cause.

The Battle of Algiers creates in the viewer's mind the trap that both sides of the conflict find themselves in. In the film, there are no easy answers and certainly no unsoiled heroes. Those fighting against the occupation are not Luke Skywalker or Han Solo; they are real warriors ready to kill and they can be indiscriminate in their violence. By the same token, the French military that tries to strike back against the FLN uses tactics that most would consider torture and a violation of human rights. At one point, when the French colonel in charge of the anti-insurgency operations is asked about the methods being used against the Algerian rebels, he replies that if the French people want to stay in Algeria then they must accept all the consequences. So powerful and realistic is *The Battle of Algiers* that in 2003 screenings of the film were held in the Pentagon. Pentagon officials were using the film to help identify tactics and motivation that might be helpful in combating the strong insurgency movement in Iraq.[29]

Some Final Thoughts

In the end, it may not matter what starts a conflict, just that once it begins, the cycle of violence seems nearly impossible to escape. At times the Israeli-Palestinian conflict appears to be intractable. The Israeli film *Ha-Buah* (The Bubble, 2006) bears this out. The film concerns a group of young Israeli roommates living in Tel Aviv, a city some consider an impregnable bubble away from the reality of Israel. Lulu, Noam, and Yelli, the latter two gay, all seek meaningful relationships with men, enjoy partying, and steer clear of most politics. That begins to change after Noam returns from his national guard duties and his lost identification papers are returned to him by a young Palestinian, Ashraf. Noam and Ashraf fall in love, but it is illegal for Ashraf, as a Palestinian, to stay in Tel Aviv. The couple's efforts to stay together become increasingly difficult. The roommates are part of an ad hoc group to promote peace, and even attempt to throw a "rave for peace," but prejudices (both between Israelis and Palestinians and toward gays) lead to deadly complications. At the end of the story, the viewer is left with the notion that the situation might be hopeless. The film was about young urban people who were not ideologues but simply wanted to live their lives; they were looking for love, they felt compassion for others, and they were generally unconcerned about politics; however, by the end of the film their bubble is burst and they are left with the realities of war and politics. In such a world it seems difficult to conclude anything but that war is, at times, unavoidable.

There is a common theme that runs through many of the films discussed in this chapter. World War II is what author Studs Terkel called the "good war."[30] Films that are ostensibly about the virtuous necessity of war are often set during the Second World War. There was and is very little dissent on the part of citizens in Allied countries regarding the necessity of that war. Even in countries where the leadership was not considered legitimate the war against Germany, Japan, and Italy was seen as patriotic. This is in contrast to World War I, which is often seen as a tragic, horrific, and senseless war (see the following chapter).

Whatever the cause of or justification for war, the films considered in this chapter all give a sense that war is a natural, if unpleasant, part of human existence. What is interesting is that the messages contained in a number of the films were not considered appropriate for those who were actually doing the fighting of the war. Scholars and analysts have suggested that the people who actually fight wars are not as motivated by the themes covered in this chapter. For instance, *Casablanca* was never screened for the troops during World War II. The messages of overt, unquestioned patriotism were often rejected by those who had seen war up close. War is a nasty, brutish, and dirty business. Many soldiers experience things that would horrify most of us, including the deaths of friends and comrades. The notion that a film such as *Casablanca* could motivate soldiers on the ground is questionable. In fact the newspaper of American troops, the *Stars and Stripes,* denounced the film in an editorial in 1943, describing the flag-waving in the film as "sickening."[31]

4

THE CASE AGAINST WAR

Anthony Swofford, a corporal in the U.S. Marines during the Persian Gulf War in 1990–1991, famously wrote that there is no such thing as an antiwar film. He argued, "Filmic images of death and carnage are pornography for the military man."[1] Despite this admonishment, several filmmakers have attempted films that paint war as devastating, dehumanizing, wasteful, and absurd. This chapter is not limited to antiwar films alone; it examines the horrendous effects of war as well. In doing so, the chapter seeks to explain the reasons behind antiwar films and films that illustrate the effects of war.

There are several reasons and methods to avoid war; however, this does not mean that any or all of these efforts will be successful. In fact, war holds a certain fascination for many; war permeates our popular culture and inspires research, discussion, and even reenactment. This poses an interesting and vexing question: If war is, indeed, so terrible, why does it happen? While the realist perspective of international relations theory predicts war as an inescapable result of human greed, selfishness and, ultimately, insecurity, the pluralist (or liberal) perspective is slightly more hopeful—but only slightly more. Instead of believing that war will be overcome, the pluralist perspective contends that people have an *opportunity* to cooperate. When people (and states) cooperate, benefits accrue. Thus pluralism argues that cooperation can greatly reduce the chance of war. There is a caveat; there are many barriers to cooperation. In world politics different ideologies, turbulent histories, poor communications, different approaches to economics, and differences in race, ethnicity, and religion, among other factors, can inhibit cooperation among actors. For pluralists, in order to prevent conflict and war, one must understand and overcome these barriers to cooperation.

Despite some arguments to the contrary, many would argue that the effects of war are so devastating that if people understood the impact of war they would avoid it at all costs. War has multiple impacts, mental and physical, on those who are combatants, those caught in the fighting, and society at large. Film provides an opportunity for those who have not experienced combat to get a sense of what it is like. By using a narrative structure not bound by space or time, film allows the viewer to see multiple impacts of the effect of combat on individuals over time. While the individual who experiences the effects of war might be able to relay the experiences and emotions of war, few have the ability to contextualize those experiences and emotions. Films, both narratives and documentaries, try to encapsulate more than just individual stories and provide a meaningful context to war. Those who make and endorse the idea that wars should be opposed try to present an accurate depiction of the effects of war to generate sentiment.

It was mentioned in the previous chapter that in the Anglo-American world the Second World War (1939–1945) was seen as evidence that sometimes a war has to be fought; alternatively, the First World War (1914–1918) is usually depicted in film as the epitome of the senselessness of war. Millions of young men from across Europe (and around the world) were killed and maimed because of outdated military tactics in the face of new, efficiently lethal combat technology. The exact reason(s) for the war seemed lost on those who were fighting it. After the war was over, most people thought it was completely preventable in retrospect.[2] What appeared to many as senseless slaughter resulted in an antiwar sentiment in European and American popular culture. Similarly, the American involvement in Vietnam (1963–1975) prompted many antiwar messages, including the film and television series *M*A*S*H* (1970, 1972–1983), which helped to introduce antiwar messages into the mainstream of American culture during the 1970s.[3]

Of course, some of the oldest pieces of literature are concerned with the dramatics of war, although not many of them are antiwar but instead usually narratives that emphasize the heroics of war. One of the few surviving plays penned by the famous classic Greek playwright Aristophanes, *Lysistrata,* is a classic of the antiwar genre. The lead character, a woman named Lysistrata, organizes the women of Greece to withhold sex from their husbands until the men of Greece end the Peloponnesian Wars. Lysistrata argues that war is a concern of women because it affects their lives in many ways (including denying the women their husbands and sons and making it harder to find mates). The story is often bawdy and very funny. *Lysistrata* has since become a symbolic piece of art representing antiwar, feminist sentiments and reminding the viewer that it is not just the combatants who are affected by war. The play has been filmed several times; some of the versions concentrate more on the licentious aspects of the play than on the message. Other films remain faithful to the play, including a Greek version, *Lysistrata* (1972), and an Austrian version, *Triumph der Liebe* (Triumph of Love, 1947; English-language title, *Lysistrata*).[4] There are also films that use the message and tactics employed in *Lysistrata* in other settings, including *The Second Greatest Sex* (1955), set in late nineteenth-century Kansas, and *Absurdistan* (2008), a Russian film shot in Azerbaijan, in which women use a sex strike in order to get the men in their village to repair a water system. The original play also resonates with pacifist movements; readings of the play in fifty-nine countries (and all fifty states in the United States) in 2003 were staged to protest the American invasion of Iraq.[5] The documentary *Pray the Devil Back to Hell* (2008), which is about the civil war in Liberia and will be discussed in a subsequent chapter, describes how women in Liberia used a sex strike to force their husbands to work toward peace.

There have been many studies of war and why wars occur. It is an important issue to political scientists and the study of international relations. There has been quite a bit of academic attention paid to war; however, only more recently have the consequences of war been addressed. This chapter is organized to consider these impacts, highlighting the consequences on individuals (largely combatants first, then others) and the effects on societies that are engaged in war (including those who do not engage in combat). The chapter will consider how war changes societies and, finally, how films have been utilized to prevent wars. A subsequent chapter (chapter 6) will address the prospect of nuclear wars, which assuredly have prompted a number of antiwar themes as well.

The Effects of War on Individuals

The first and very important impact of war is that people die. Men and women lose their lives in war; not just those who fight battles, but those who are in proximity to combat as well. Civilians—especially women and children—are often casualties of war. While figures vary, it is clear that a large proportion of the people who die in modern wars are civilians.[6] Beyond that, deprivation is experienced by many—and critics would point out that those who suffer this are not those who decide whether to engage in war.

When wars occur, people lose loved ones; this has been true throughout history. Motion pictures help people visualize death. Prior to the invention of photography in the mid-nineteenth century, people might have been notified of the death of a husband, brother, or son during war, but the specifics of what happened were often left to the imagination, based on literary or news accounts. Although people might have seen more death in general at the time, they did not always understand the horrendous conditions of combat.[7] It is not that literature had not adequately described death and battle before, but the medium of film makes those descriptions more immediate to the senses and available to a wider audience in a shared communal setting. Filmed battle scenes show death on a wide scale. Early films such as *The Birth of a Nation* (1915), which depicted events surrounding the American Civil War, typically glorified battlefield death. As technology and special effects improved, combat scenes became more precise and graphic. By the end of the twentieth century, special effects could simulate both battlefield experiences—for example, *Saving Private Ryan* (1998) and *Un long dimanche de fiançailles* (A Very Long Engagement, 2004)—and the consequences of battle—for example, the digitally removed legs of Gary Sinise in *Forrest Gump* (1994).

As the medium of film was reaching maturity simultaneously with the devastation of World War I, the silent cinema of the 1920s often reflected an understanding that war was brutal and horrible. During the war a number of essentially propagandistic films were produced that did not engage in such sentiments;[8] however, as the decade of the 1920s progressed and a period of reflection occurred, films, particularly Hollywood films, began to focus more on the horrors of war. Many historians of film would point to this era as one in which there was a decided emphasis on antiwar messages. Often actors, directors, and writers had firsthand knowledge of combat. Two major productions, *The Big Parade* (1925) and *Wings* (1927), demonstrate the general anxiety about war in a way that makes the war very emotional and accessible. Both films use a love story to help push the narrative. While the primary protagonist in each of the films (John Gilbert and Buddy Rogers, respectively) suffer injuries and lose friends, the films have a happy ending as the soldiers find love. While this might have been popular filmmaking, it was not grounded in the reality that most soldiers faced.

Perhaps one of the most effective films of the post–First World War period, in terms of describing the war to a mass audience, is *All Quiet on the Western Front* (1930), an adaptation of the Erich Maria Remarque novel of the same name. As a foreword to the film, the opening title card explains to the viewer that the film is not intended to be accusatory but is designed to tell the story of a generation of men who were destroyed by war, even if they had escaped death. Nevertheless, while claiming that it does not lay blame for the war, the film is a clear indictment of at least World War I, if not war in general. The four years between 1914 and 1918 were so devastating and horrific that everyone in Europe knew someone who had died or was seriously injured on the battlefield.

All Quiet on the Western Front, set in Germany, opens with soldiers triumphantly marching in the streets of a small town. The primary protagonist is Paul, a cheerful student. Students are urged by their teachers not to sit on the sidelines but to be a part of history—to do their patriotic duty. The students are motivated to enlist by slogans claiming that their country and family need their protection. The film illustrates how the state, through its resources in schools, recruits students to be soldiers. The students are a captive audience and their lack of knowledge and experience make them perfect targets for manipulation. The use of metaphors, such as sitting on the sidelines, creates peer pressure and motivates students to join up.

After Paul is wounded he returns home to see his family, but he no longer thinks he belongs with civilians—he has seen and experienced too much. When he goes to the local pub with his father, the men tell him that the food is better at the front because all the best things have been sent for the soldiers. Of course, Paul knows better; the soldiers often have to scrounge, forage, and steal food. (While this point is not explicit in *All Quiet on the Western Front,* other films, like *Paths of Glory* [1957], illustrate that, while common soldiers survive on meager rations, officers, often from the aristocracy, fare much better in their food and lodging.) The civilians insist that the soldiers must fight on and march to Paris. It is clear that Paul is dubious—to him, being at the front is about survival; there is very little thought about why he is fighting. Before returning to the front Paul visits his school, where he hears the young students still being conditioned to fight in the war. Compelled to speak, Paul tells students that dying for one's country is painful and dirty. There are millions of people dying for their country and no one seems to know why.[9]

All Quiet on the Western Front is a testament to the psychological pressures of constant bombardment, hunger, fatigue, and a never-ending battle with rats. The former students see horrors that they could not have imagined; the film allows the viewer to witness conditions and observe the psychology of the trench. Some men (or, perhaps more accurately, boys) do not survive this pressure: soldiers go mad and rush into an incoming hail of bullets to be released from the pressure; others wander off only to be captured as deserters and executed. War is depicted not as a glorious event, but solely as something to survive.[10] The confusion of attack and counterattack and hand-to-hand combat does not encompass great ideas; there is no meaning beyond a mere will to survive in an utterly chaotic situation. The theme of just surviving is consistent in many films. In *Paths of Glory*, soldiers are given the task of securing a particular hill without adequate resources. The generals assume that the men can achieve the objective simply because the officers say they can. When they fail, the soldiers are held responsible for the failure rather than those directing the tactics. This is also the premise of the Australian film *Breaker Morant* (1980), set during the Boer War.

All Quiet on the Western Front takes a break from the action to consider *why* the soldiers are in the trenches in such horrible conditions. After their first decent meal in weeks, soldiers have a chance to sit down and discuss what everything means. They wonder why they are there; why is there war? One soldier suggests that one country has offended another. But how can a German mountain offend a French field? another asks. The soldiers speculate that every emperor needs a war to make him famous—a far cry from the classroom call to arms for great and noble causes. This very powerful scene concludes with an older soldier, Cap, saying that next time the powers that be feel like having a war, they should rope off the area, put all the kings and generals inside, and let them fight it out with clubs. This scene rarely fails to provoke reactions among the audience.

This theme, the seeming uselessness of World War I, is common in many depictions of the war. The British television series *Blackadder Goes Forth* (1989), the fourth in the series, is an excellent example. The *Blackadder* series, starring Rowan Atkinson, was generally a comedy detailing the vain attempts of the members of the Blackadder family to secure wealth and power; however, the fourth entry was much darker, and focused on Blackadder trying to escape from the front, where certain death awaits the combatants. Similarly, the Australian film *Gallipoli* (1981), which stars a young Mel Gibson, questions the slaughter of Australian and New Zealand troops in Turkey for seemingly no military value.

Another film made roughly at the same time captures much of the same sentiments as *All Quiet on the Western Front*. The German film *Westfront 1918* (1930) was adapted from the novel *Vier con der Infanterie* (Four from the Infantry) by Ernst Johannsen. At first glance, it is stunning how much *All Quiet on the Western Front* and *Westfront 1918* are similar to one another.

The films were made in two different countries that were on opposite sides in the war, but they mirror one another in eerily similar ways and convey to the viewer a lot about the horrendous conditions of World War I, if not the conditions of war in general. Both films were early efforts following the advent of sound in motion pictures; *Westfront 1918* was the first sound film produced by the famous German director G. W. Pabst and is considered a technical achievement of the early sound period.[11]

Just as *All Quiet on the Western Front* does, the film follows a group of four German soldiers through the horrors of the First World War. Unlike *All Quiet,* however, *Westfront 1918* takes less of an emotional approach to the war and more of a detached observance. Thus one should not be surprised by the racist and sexist language in the film. The soldiers see this as completely appropriate.[12] The use of stereotypes during war situations allows for prejudices to be established, and the film demonstrates this as a pattern of dehumanizing others. It has been postulated that people have a cognitive barrier to killing other human beings. If others can be perceived as less than human, then the moral weight of killing them is not as burdensome.

Although initial reviews of the film were positive, Pabst would later face criticism from across the political spectrum in Germany. The film does not examine what causes war (such as lack of democracy or extreme nationalism), which made liberals in Germany unhappy; on the Right, critics said the film depicts a demoralized German people and takes a defeatist attitude.[13] Because the film did not use emotional messages and symbols, which were, and are, common in Hollywood films, some critics thought the film was not effective to a neutral observer who might have ambivalent feelings about war. It was considered by some critics an effective antiwar film but not very good entertainment.[14] The film does not contain a romantic subplot or any of the trappings of a so-called Hollywood movie. Nevertheless, today many critics consider *Westfront 1918* the more effective antiwar film of the period. It is also worth mentioning that at the premiere at the Capitol Theatre in Berlin in May 1930, at least twenty people who attended *Westfront 1918* fainted during the screening. A few years later, in 1933, the film was banned by the Nazis after Hitler came to power.[15]

Many films were produced in the aftermath of World War I that expressed the general repulsiveness and horror of the war. Some were more effective than others; many have been forgotten today. For film historians, Abel Gance's *J'accuse* (1919) is one such forgotten masterpiece.[16] The title (I Accuse) was indicative of the anger Gance and others felt about the war.[17]

Many authors would argue that most humans have a natural reluctance to kill.[18] Thus countries use various methods, including military discipline, regimentation, and the use of popular culture (including film) to persuade soldiers to overcome this reluctance.[19] Soldiers must distance themselves from the humanity of their targets; in reference to *J'accuse*, Abel Gance said, "What one shoots at in war is not men, but uniforms."[20] Gance was not a pacifist; he intended to demonstrate that if war does not serve a specific purpose, it is horrific, terrible, and ultimately inhumane.[21] At the climax of the film, the dead of the war rise, and the sight of them so horrifies people that they reconsider the usefulness of war. In the 1938 version, which is significantly different from the original, Gance used members of the Les gueules cassées, an organization for soldiers with "broken faces," to demonstrate the impact of war on individuals. Poignantly, during the filming of the original version Gance persuaded the French government to allow him to use soldiers on leave from the First World War to spell out "J'accuse" for the film. The soldiers who appeared in the film returned to the front a few days later—and almost all of them would perish in action.

As devastating as combat can be on individuals physically, the psychological aftermath can be just as horrific; many combat veterans witness events so terrible they find it difficult to cope. Others have described the adrenal rush of combat as addictive; the former war correspondent Chris Hedges commented that he knew reporters who would seek out duties covering wars just to make themselves feel alive.[22] Antiwar films that focused the story on injured veterans were attempting to dissuade the public from recklessly endorsing war. Such films are designed to let the viewer contemplate the implications of war. Some films are more effective than others. Since the end of the First World War, films became less sentimental and more nuanced in their treatment of the subject. For example, although at the end of the film, Jim, the hero in *The Big Parade,* is wounded and he loses his leg, he finds the girl he fell in love with in France (Melisande) to resume what the audience believes will be a well-fulfilled life. The film ends as the two lovers are reunited; while the film charts the physical damage done to Jim, it does not contemplate, or invite the audience to think about, the life that is to come for Jim as an amputee. Films such as the psychedelic cult film *Johnny Got His Gun* (1971), which takes the effects of wars on those who fight them to an extreme, and *Born on the Fourth of July* (1989) examine the effects of war in terms not only of physical damage but of the emotional and psychological effects of injuries suffered during war.

Perhaps the preeminent film that captures the postwar experience is set not during the First World War but the Second. *The Best Years of Our Lives* (1946), which won the Academy Award for Best Picture, focuses exclusively on the aftermath of the war for three returning American veterans, examining their very real problems of readjusting to civilian life. One of the three veterans, Homer (Harold Russell), has lost both arms and has been fitted with metal prosthetics that allow him to do most things (for example, eat, smoke cigarettes, and drive a car).[23] He worries about how his family and fiancée will accept him. Of course, his family is overwhelmed with joy to see him home and alive, although at the sight of his metal arms his mother breaks down. His fiancée welcomes him unreservedly. As his buddies Al (Frederic March) and Fred (Dana Andrews) watch Homer and his fiancée embrace, their faith in Homer's girlfriend is confirmed. Fred observes that Homer can do almost anything with his prosthetics and he will get along fine. Al replies, "They couldn't train him to put his arms around his girl and stroke her hair."

The other two veterans are not physically damaged, but the war has taken a toll. Al has missed four years of his children's lives, which he finds distressing; it also disturbs him that his family survived and thrived without him. Al also misses the action and excitement of combat; the prospect of returning to a life of sitting quietly and reading the newspaper in the evening no longer appeals to him. Ultimately, he finds comfort in alcohol. Fred, who married a woman before the war whom he did not know too well, craves companionship but finds that his prewar bride has moved on emotionally. *The Best Years of Our Lives* is not an antiwar film per se; it is, however, a film that chronicles the very real impact of war on the individual soldier and his family.

With the onset of the Vietnam War, American films, for the most part, once again returned to an antiwar stance. Along with *Apocalypse Now* (1979) and *Platoon* (1986), *The Deer Hunter* (1978) is considered one of the best films about the Vietnam War. The psychological toll of the war is brought home to three young men of rural Pennsylvania: some of them face physical injuries, but undeniably all of the men suffer psychological hardships. The Iraqi film *L'aube du monde* (Dawn of the World, 2008) also addresses the suffering caused by war, which can go beyond physical damage. The continuing and unrelenting psychological pressures of war eventually take their toll on combatants and civilians alike.

The Effects of War on Women and Children

One of the more obscure topics in relation to war is the role of women. While historically it is men who engage in combat, it is not the case that war does not affect women—quite the contrary. All too often wars are fought on the grounds that they are necessary to protect the women of a society. Yet in the end it is the women who suffer greatly as a result of war. On the home front, women lose husbands, sons, and lovers. Author Virginia Nicholson points out that after World War I there were 2 million more women than men in Britain. A substantial number of young women lived their lives without hope of ever marrying—a grim prospect in the rigid formality of 1920s Britain.[24] Sometimes women would pine for their men at the front, hoping against hope that their loved one would return. Like the character Mathilde (Audrey Tautou) from *A Very Long Engagement*, they would seek to understand the war that took their men away.

The Russian film *The Cuckoo* (2002) depicts two stranded soldiers, one Finnish and one Russian, fighting for the attention of a single woman, Anni, in rural Lapland during the Russo-Finnish War and subsequent Second World War. The film is a metaphor for the plight of women during a war. The men, who are not really that different from one another, find themselves in a competition for a prize (the woman), not dissimilar to the Helen of Troy scenario. The woman must navigate the relations between herself and the men, and negotiate the relations between the two men as well. How films depict this subject varies significantly. In *The Big Parade*, Jim (John Gilbert) establishes a relationship with a young local French woman, Melisande (Renée Adorée); the film depicts their relationship as chaste and innocent.

Unfortunately, reality was far different most of the time. In the midst of battle, women are often the victims of violence and death. Although women (and children) may not be the main protagonists in war, they are often the most frequent victims. Many men, distraught by separation from friends and family and their experiences on the battlefield, would seek fleeting distraction in the arms of prostitutes. Many women who lived in close proximity to battlefields experienced the strong possibility of rape. While there were many wartime romances and even marriages during the Second World War, especially among the British and the Americans, this was often away from the battlefield and between Allied countries. Across the battle lines, females from enemy countries are seen as the embodiment of the nation. Thus, in the minds of some soldiers, defiling a woman is tantamount to defiling the enemy nation. Because women bear the responsibility of reproducing the population of a country, they are often the targets of violence during war.[25]

The young French woman Yvette from *Westfront 1918* is not like Melisande from *The Big Parade*. At the beginning of the film, Yvette is clearly a plaything of the soldiers; she is metaphorically passed from one soldier to another. Eventually, a young student falls in love with her. Nevertheless, she is a sex object for the other soldiers, who willingly toy with her and offer suggestive comments (perhaps in large part because she does not understand them). Later in the film the soldiers meet young French women who are so hungry that they are willing to trade sex for a little bit of food. In the scene, the soldiers are expecting a romantic and frivolous night; however, the women demand to eat first.

Anonyma—Eine Frau in Berlin (A Woman in Berlin, 2008) is the filmed version of an anonymous memoir written in the closing days of the Second World War in which a German woman expresses her concern about rape during war. As Russian troops advanced on Berlin, German women were subjected to their sexual advances. The writer argues that the question of rape in Berlin was not if, but how often. Sensing the inevitability of the situation, the protagonist preemptively selects Russian officers to have sex with rather than waiting for an inevitable rape. In return for sexual favors, the woman receives protection and food, which she often shares with her neighbors. There are differences between the film and the original memoirs, published in 1954.[26] In the film the protagonist is a supporter of the Nazi Party; in the memoirs, the protagonist is much more ambivalent about Hitler and the Nazis, although she admits that she did not actively oppose the regime. Nevertheless, her actions in securing relative security and food are seen as traitorous and promiscuous by her neighbors. The author is able to fend off worse consequences, albeit for a price.

War has an impact even on those women who are left behind. There have been numerous films concerning the impact of war on women; of course, not all are necessarily antiwar films. The American film *Tender Comrade* (1943), for example, is a story of five women who share a house in order to reduce expenses and to provide emotional support for one another. Other films take a much more direct approach to establish a case for the nefarious aspects of war on women. The French-Italian coproduction *Destinées* (Daughters of Destiny, 1954) is a trilogy of stories (one of which recounts the Lysistrata story) detailing the effects of war on women, but even this is a sanitized version.[27]

Of course, children do not escape the effects of war either. On the home front, children can lose parents to battle (increasingly, in the twenty-first century, including mothers). More dramatically, in terms of combat, children are often caught in situations they do not understand and have no control over. In the Japanese animated feature *Grave of the Fireflies* (1988), two orphaned children try to survive in the closing days of World War II. By using animation the film can be somewhat less graphic while having a devastating emotional impact. In one harrowing scene, Setsuko sees his mortally wounded mother in a makeshift hospital after a firebombing raid on the city. She is completely covered in bandages and suffers tremendously from her burns. It is clear that the hospital is in no way capable of adequately caring for her. The children are the victims of more than the physical aspects of war—they are forced to see and experience things that are devastating and incomprehensible. The orphaned brother and sister in *Grave of the Fireflies* eventually face starvation as the war comes to an end. Other films, such as the epic *Empire of the Sun* (1987), in which a small boy is forced to survive the Japanese occupation of Shanghai, and *Hope and Glory* (1987), which chronicles the life of a young boy from London during the Blitz, also effectively demonstrate how children suffer during wartime.[28]

The Effects of War on Societies

Beyond the individual level, the impacts of war can be demonstrated on societies as well. Along with lives lost, war destroys culture and society. If we think of culture as concern for the arts, letters, and scholarly pursuits, then war puts an end to these things. Generally, if we define society as a group of people who organize themselves around principles of economics, beliefs, and culture, then war weakens the bonds between individuals in a society. Some authors have pointed to how wartime conditions make for a more sexually permissive society. For instance, when British cities during the Blitz were on the frontlines, men and women sought comfort from loneliness and despair in the arms of one another.[29] There is good evidence that during World War II, American girls and young women, faced with the prospect of their boyfriends going off to war, might have engaged in premarital sexual activity, which prior to the war they would not have considered.[30] Some women thought it their patriotic duty to send soldiers off with a sexual gift. These situations are the source of *The Miracle of Morgan's Creek* (1944), where in the aftermath of a sendoff party for recruits leaving for the Second World War, a young woman (Betty Hutton) wakes up married and pregnant with no memory of what happened. It is arguable whether World War II itself caused a change in sexual morality in Britain or the United States, but scholars do agree that such morals were changing in the era, and the war contributed to the phenomenon being more widely discussed and brought into the public awareness.[31]

The literary tradition of antiwar novels is particularly strong, and several of these novels have been made into films. Perhaps one of the most famous antiwar novels in Central Europe is *The Good Soldier Schweik* (alternatively, *Švejk*) by Jaroslav Hašek.[32] The novel follows the exploits of Schweik during the First World War but was left unfinished when the author died of tuberculosis in 1923. Two Czech films, *Dobrý voják Švejk* (The Good Solider Schweik, 1957) and *Polušně hlásím* (The Good Soldier Schweik 2: Beg to Report, Sir, 1958), both directed by Karel Steklý, capture the mood and sentiment of the novel. Throughout both films and the novel, it is unclear whether Schweik is an imbecile or is cleverly outsmarting those in charge.

The character of Švejk (Schweik) is very popular in Czech society. This café in Prague is named after the fictional character from Hašek's novel. (Photograph by the author)

In the films, Schweik manages to get under the skin of higher-ups and to charm and entertain his equals and civilians. He rattles off nonsensical diatribes that manage to entrance all, including viewers. Throughout the first film, Schweik chortles about how much people have to give up to allow the government to go to war. At the end of the second film, Schweik finally makes it to the front and begins to see action. When a fellow soldier asks how long he thinks the war will last, Schweik replies fifteen years, because there has already been a Thirty Years' War and people are smarter these days. In the last scene of the film, bombs are going off around the town, troops scatter, and the camera focuses on Schweik: he looks straight into the camera and yells, "Are you crazy? There are people here!" The films point out that society is going to suffer in war. In addition to people dying, cities will be destroyed, cultures will regress, and simple pleasures (such as smoking a pipe and having a beer) will be put on hold. Schweik's actions are absurd, but from the point of view of the film, so are wars. In the end the film asks: Who is crazier, the simpleton who tries to avoid combat or the people who start the war? Comedies have long been effective antiwar stories because of their willingness to laugh at authority. Films like *M*A*S*H* and *The Good Soldier Schweik* provide evidence to viewers of the absurdity of war.

There is a fair argument to be made that no work on politics and film would be complete without at least referencing *Duck Soup* (1933). At first glance, it may seem odd to include *Duck Soup* as an antiwar film. The film is a series of running gags, anarchical and nonsensical comedy, and the occasional musical number. How could a film that is so comedic, chaotic, and anarchical have a serious message? The answer lies in the chaos. As the film opens, the mythical country of Freedonia is in dire financial crisis. The country's creditor, the widow Mrs. Teasdale (Margaret Dumont) tells Freedonian ministers that she has already spent half of her husband's fortune on propping up the state and will give more financial help only if they install Rufus T. Firefly (Groucho Marx), her romantic interest, as prime minister. Everything that happens in *Duck Soup,* including romantic and financial interests, is over the top and absurd—just as war is. The final message of such comedic satires is that the reasons for war are so absurd they are laughable (not that war itself is laughable), and that it is absurd that any justification can be used to validate so much death and destruction.

On the other hand, dramatic films can have a lasting impact on the viewer by depicting stories and images that leave no doubt as to the destructive force of war. The Lebanese-French *Sous les bombes* (Under the Bombs,

2007) captures the devastation and anguish of war perhaps better and more realistically than most films. The film is set in the immediate aftermath of the Israeli-Hezbollah War during the summer of 2006. The events of the summer of July and August 2006 are confusing to many people outside the region. Technically, this was not a war between Israel and Lebanon; it was a war between Israel and the paramilitary group known as Hezbollah, which has been classified as a terrorist group by many governments, including the United States, Canada, and Israel. Hezbollah, a significant political force in Lebanese politics, used its paramilitary force to launch attacks against Israel, and during the summer of 2006 Israel responded with an all-out invasion. The conflict lasted only thirty-four days but was devastating to the infrastructure and civilian population of Lebanon.[33]

In the film a mother, Zeina (Nada Abou Farhat), comes in search of her six-year-old son as the war is winding down. She enlists the services of Tony (Georges Kabbaz), a taxi driver, to take her to southern Lebanon to search for her son and family. Zeina and Tony's relationship is complicated because she is a Shi'a Muslim and he a Christian. The search for Zeina's son is more difficult because past conflicts have complicated the relationships among people. The point of the story is that in modern war the conflict is not limited to armies or those who do the fighting; most casualties of the fighting are civilians, including a disproportionate number of women and children. The war has destroyed cities and villages and left thousands homeless. Tony and Zeina find a shared humanity and understanding during their search.

The gritty and grim realism of *Under the Bombs* is highlighted because the film was shot in the immediate aftermath of the war. Director Philippe Aractingi shot footage of the destruction of southern Lebanon as a background to the film. Late in the film, when there is a controlled detonation of cluster bombs, it is the real thing, not a special effect. There are only two professional actors in the film, Farhat and Kabbaz: all others (taxi drivers, soldiers, and villagers) play themselves. Toward the end of the film Zeina tells Tony that she does not care about politics, all she wants is to live with her family in peace. This is the sentiment that is the thesis of the film.

Often it is difficult to distinguish between individuals and societies. *Joyeaux Noël* (2008) retells the events known as the Christmas Truce during the first year of the First World War when an informal truce among British, French, and German soldiers led to enemy soldiers emerging from

Zeina navigates multiple armed forces and confusion in Lebanon searching for her son in the aftermath of the 2006 Israeli-Hezbollah War. (Courtesy Film Movement)

their trenches to share drinks and cigarettes in honor of the holiday. Some sources report that informal soccer games broke out. Observers would contend that here was evidence that humans were not prone to fight and that governments created situations in which men had to fight.[34] A film such as *Dawn of the World* demonstrates the effects of war on individuals but also examines the chaos created by the myriad of belligerents, unexploded weapons, and unburied bodies. Similarly, *Csillagosok, katonák* (The Red and the White, 1967), set during the Russian Civil War, uses a frenetic pace in the film, which is meant to mirror the chaotic nature of warfare. Combatants attack and counterattack; the viewer gets confused because it is unclear who is winning and even which side individual combatants are on. The war is nothing more than a series of seemingly disconnected events, and individuals are "subject to pursuit, capture, humiliation, and execution."[35] In both *Dawn of the World* and *The Red and the White*, noncombatants and civilians do their best to stay out of harm's way; however, the realities of war are such that societies are turned upside down and there is no escaping the death and destruction of combat.

The Moral Implications of War

Just as there can be psychological effects on individuals, the effects of war on society are not always physical. War can make it easier for societies to compromise their core values. By using a state of emergency or citing the need for extraordinary powers in time of crisis, countries can move away from internal agreements on rights and duties. For example, in the wake of September 11 attacks on the United States, some American commentators feared the reaction to a new threat would result in undermining political and civil rights inside the country. The television series *Battlestar Galactica* (2004–2009) was a remake of the 1970s science fiction series of the same name that tried to capitalize on the popularity of *Star Wars* (1977). Both versions of the program started with the premise that human civilization had been destroyed on twelve home worlds by human-created robots known as Cylons. After the destruction of the human-populated planets, the surviving humans set off to find the mythical thirteenth colony of Earth. From there the two series take radically different paths. The 1970s series was aimed at family entertainment with plots revolving around children and only mild, comic-book-type violence.[36] The version that was produced between 2004 and 2009 reflected the darkness and anxieties of a post–September 11 world and is heavily laced with religious references. In this series, the Cylons are virtually indistinguishable from humans and are motivated by the idea that humans are essentially corrupt and not worthy of being a part of God's creation. The humans, facing an enemy bent on their complete destruction, are beset with a number of ethical questions: What does it mean to be human? How should one treat a Cylon who sympathizes with humans? What role should the military play in civilian government? Where is the line between deciding what is essentially a military matter and a civilian matter in a time of war?

The series was not without controversies and is definitely not for the faint of heart. How Cylon prisoners were treated by humans was a central theme of the series. In one plotline, a Cylon was tortured and beaten badly, but the purpose of the torture was unclear. In fact, the incident served as evidence of how degraded the humans had become. Another plotline had a character who was not aware she was a Cylon exposed and arrested. After she is imprisoned, her husband disavows her and she is subsequently tortured and raped by the prison guards. Within the surviving civilian administration, the actions lead to questions of whether humanity is worth saving if it acts like this.

The post–September 11 series mirrored a number of issues that faced many Western countries, especially the United States: freedom versus security, how to manage dissent and decision making between civil and military leadership, and how government should treat its enemies, even if their worldview does not correspond to Western ideas of how the world works. The prospect of a so-called sleeper cell, individuals who blend into society and might be ready to carry out a terrorist attack at any time, was an idea the Cylons represented well. Governments in Europe and North America have struggled to find a balance between the needs of security and the demands of individual rights. The series won praise because it did not resort to platitudes or easy answers. Instead it laid out the difficulty of very complex issues involving rights and security. While most of the time the series was an allegory about the divide between the Western world and Middle Eastern societies, it does not rely on a formulaic representation (that is, humans in the series do not necessarily represent the Western world). In an interesting twist, the surviving humans on the occupied planet of Caprica resorted to terrorism and suicide bombings to fight the Cylon occupation. The audience, which ostensibly sides with the humans, is therefore brought to sympathize with the necessity and logic of suicide bombers. Overall, the series depicted humans as frail, vulnerable, and imperfect; it is not definitively clear that humans were the "heroes." While the series is not an antiwar piece, it does serve as a warning about how wars and military threats can cause societies to compromise core values and highlights the struggle to balance the need for securing society while maintaining the rights of the individual.

While *Battlestar Galactica* is full of allegories and subtle commentaries, other films take a more direct approach. Stanley Kubrick's *Paths of Glory* is set within the French Army during the First World War. The officers live in opulent surroundings (one general is complimented on his taste in rugs and paintings adorning his headquarters). Meanwhile, the lower-ranking soldiers are forced to endure filth and danger on the frontline of trench warfare. As the film progresses, the audience learns that when officers make mistakes it is to be covered up so that the public does not lose faith in the army; however, when enlisted soldiers make mistakes they must pay with their lives—either in battle or in front of the firing squad.[37]

Using Film to Oppose War

Film has been an important medium for the dissemination of antiwar messages. Historian J. M. Winter once asked a group of French veterans of war what film should be shown in a museum about the First World War. Some veterans thought that Jean Renoir's *La grande illusion* (The Grand Illusion, 1937) should be that film.[38] It is an interesting choice because much like *Casablanca,* discussed in the previous chapter, there are no scenes of combat in the film. Instead, it is set in a series of prison camps. Three French pilots who have been captured by Germans represent different socioeconomic classes within European society. The commandant of the prison, a Prussian aristocrat (Erich von Stroheim), forms a close relationship with the French aristocratic pilot. The honor that binds the two aristocrats leads to their ultimate destruction, a metaphor for the fate of European aristocracy. They had invested so much time and energy in the preparation for war, it leads to their destruction through war (the grand illusion). The future, according to the film, seems to be with the middle and working classes. When the two other pilots, a Jew and a laborer, finally escape, their relationship is tenuous, but necessary. The film suggests that the way to avoid the "grand illusion" of war is through democratization and the cooperation of different facets of society. *The Grand Illusion* is, thus, a plea to the public to embrace differences and democratic principles so as to avoid future wars. Since the film was made on the eve of the Second World War, this theme was clearly on the minds of many.[39]

These types of films can take many different forms. Some would argue that humans have a moral and/or religious duty to oppose war and have used film to remind people of such obligations. This is a tradition that runs deep in many American films, particularly in the early to mid-twentieth century.[40] The early silent feature film *Civilization* (1916) not so subtly creates a fictional story that mirrors the contemporary war of its time, World War I. At the climax of the film, Jesus Christ appears on Earth to persuade belligerents to forswear war and adhere to the Christian teachings of peace. *In the Name of the Prince of Peace* (1914) used much the same arguments, with the moral of the film being that innocents die just as frequently as those who perpetuate the war.[41] Because so many innocents die, wars cannot be just. An MGM animated cartoon made at the beginning of the Second World War but prior to American entry, *Peace on Earth* (1939), uses a Christmas setting to develop a moral basis to its antiwar message. The film opens like many cartoons of the classic war period, with rabbits singing Christmas carols and waiting for Santa Claus; however, the absence of humans in the cartoon is explained by an elderly rabbit telling his grandchildren about how humans destroyed themselves in a final cataclysmic war.[42]

Antiwar messages on the basis of religious and moral grounds are not limited to Western films or sensibilities. For instance, the Japanese films *The Burmese Harp* (1956) and *Fires on the Plain* (1959), both of which are set in the closing days and aftermath of the Second World War, examine the hardship faced by soldiers and civilians as a result of war and conclude that it is immoral to continue such a practice.[43] The Israeli film *Waltz with Bashir* (2008) is an animated film that documents the psychological toll of the 1982 Lebanese War on soldiers. *Gandhi* (1982) recounts the life of Mahatma Gandhi, his commitment to nonviolence, and his abhorrence of war. Just as with patriotic war films, societies that experienced wars, particularly fought on their own territory, often produced antiwar films. These are but a few attempts to use narrative films to convince the filmgoing public that war should be avoided at all cost. This genre would reach a zenith during the cold war, when several films were made to oppose nuclear warfare, which will be explored in subsequent chapters.

There have been a number of documentary films that have outlined the deleterious effects of war; however, most do not achieve a wide audience. *Pray the Devil Back to Hell* (2008) is an engrossing documentary that examines how the Women's Peace Initiative in Liberia helped to secure the end of a particularly nasty civil war there.[44] One of the activists, Leymah Gbowee, explains toward the beginning of the film why she was motivated to begin a women's movement for peace by describing the effect of Liberia's civil war on her children. She calculated that her children had been hungry and scared all of their lives. The effects of the war were death, destruction, rape, and hunger. *God Grew Tired of Us* (2006) chronicles the so-called lost boys of Sudan, who were forced to flee their home country as a result of civil war. The young men have difficulty adjusting to their new lives in the United States and desperately miss their homelands. Both of these films are a call to action for the audience to "do something" about war. The medium of film is used to convey messages to the audience about the result of warfare, and, without offering specific proposals, to remind the viewers of their moral duty to oppose war.

Some Final Thoughts

Political scientist John J. Mearsheimer once remarked that no one likes war; however, avoiding war, especially in a world of sovereign states, is impossible.[45] This chapter has highlighted the negative effects of war, precisely because the filmmakers, in most instances, are hoping to avoid war. Many of the stories rely on a notion that the more people are confronted with the realities of war, the less likely they will be to engage in or support war. This is a strategy that will be used in films about nuclear weapons and warfare discussed in the next chapter. A consistent theme throughout many of the films is that those who make the decisions about war often do not suffer the consequences of those decisions. Instead, it is the people who are forced to endure the hardships of warfare, whether they are frontline soldiers, women and children caught in combat, societies forced to endure hardships, or families on the home front forced to deal with the loss of loved ones.

Despite a chronicling of the horrendous effects of war, the initial evidence seems to suggest that war continues unabated. Yet there might be some reason for hope: wars between countries have declined precipitously in recent decades; in fact, the vast majority of wars that occur today are civil wars rather than conflicts between countries. Nevertheless, it would be extremely optimistic to suggest that war is likely to disappear any time soon.

From a cinematic point of view, Corporal Swofford's point that all war films are essentially pro-war is not to be taken lightly. If all drama is about conflict, then wars provide the ultimate conflict. Again and again, filmmakers return to the theme of war (and international conflict) because it is compelling. Most people live without combat going on around them; war is an anomaly, not commonplace. An interesting question to consider is, given the public's fascination with popular culture and films, does the reliance of filmmakers on war as a theme influence our ability to notice that peace is normal?

5

A PRIMER ON NUCLEAR WEAPONS

When the nuclear era began on 16 July 1945 with the denotation of the world's first nuclear device in Alamogordo, New Mexico, it opened a door to new possibilities in terms of war and peace in world politics. The Second World War saw many countries desperate to acquire a "super" weapon to ensure their victory. A nuclear weapon was thought to guarantee substantial success in the war for whichever country developed it. And indeed, the United States used its new atomic weapon to help hasten the end of the Second World War in the Pacific—and to win it. The weapon would go on to help define the politics of the cold war and beyond. Because of the substantially enhanced destructive capabilities of the weapon, many countries considered the development of nuclear arms vital to their long-term security.[1]

Countries That Have Nuclear Weapons

Typically, we define those countries that have demonstrated or tested a nuclear device as belonging to the nuclear club. In addition, Israel, which has not formally tested a nuclear device, is assumed to possess several such weapons.[2]

Four states have had a nuclear capability in the past but have voluntarily dismantled their projects or given up weapons. South Africa, under the apartheid regime, acquired a nuclear arsenal in December 1982. After the leader of the African National Congress, Nelson Mandela, was released from prison and went on to lead a multiracial government, South Africa began to dismantle its arsenal.[3] When the Soviet Union collapsed and broke into fifteen separate republics, Belarus, Kazakhstan, and Ukraine each had Soviet nuclear weapons in its territory. Unprepared to adequately defend such weapons, the three states agreed, under the Lisbon Accords (1991), to transfer the weapons to Russia (the legal successor to the Soviet Union) in

Table 5.1. Members of the nuclear club	
Country	**First weapon test**
United States	16 July 1945
Soviet Union (Russia)	29 August 1949
United Kingdom	3 October 1952
France	13 February 1960
China	16 October 1964
India	18 May 1974
Pakistan	28 May 1998
PDRK (North Korea)	9 October 2006

exchange for compensation from the international community, including the United States.

Difference between Atomic Weapons and Nuclear Weapons

Basically all atomic weapons are nuclear weapons, but not all nuclear weapons are atomic weapons. A nuclear explosion is created one of two ways. Atomic weapons produce a detonation, or explosion, by splitting either a uranium or plutonium atom. This process is known as fission and produces a great deal of energy. A hydrogen, or thermonuclear, bomb fuses hydrogen atoms together, much like the sun does. This fusion process then uses an atomic detonation to create a much more efficient and bigger explosion. A hydrogen bomb creates much more energy than does a regular atomic bomb. For example, the atomic bomb used at Hiroshima in 1945 killed about 130,000 people. Yet this is small in comparison to the destructive power of a large hydrogen bomb, which is one thousand times greater. A single large hydrogen bomb has more explosive power than all the bombs dropped during World War II.[4]

Effects on Humans of a Nuclear Detonation

There are four primary effects on humans from a nuclear detonation: blast, heat, prompt radiation, and fallout radiation. The precise effects depend on the size and location of the bomb detonation. The flash produced by the detonation is so bright that people facing the direction of the detonation can have their optical nerves burned. We tend to focus on the blast because

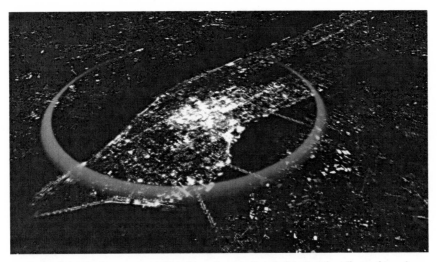

An image from the documentary film *Countdown to Zero* indicating the effects of a nuclear detonation on the island of Manhattan. (Courtesy Dogwoof Films)

the iconic image of nuclear weapons is that blast and the subsequent mushroom cloud, but other effects are probably equal to its effects or even more devastating in many ways.

The heat of a nuclear detonation is momentarily hotter than the surface of the sun. It is so intense that humans and other living organisms, as in Hiroshima and Nagasaki, can be instantly vaporized. Those further from the center of the blast can be overcome with heat exhaustion. The heat also can produce multiple spontaneous fires. These fires can create what is known as firestorms which, in their intensity, can create high winds and deplete the oxygen supply in a given area.

As a result of both the fission and fusion processes, one of the byproducts of a nuclear detonation is a high level of radiation. In hydrogen weapons, radiation is substantially higher than in atomic weapons. While the blast and heat will kill more people initially, the effects of ionizing radiation will create horrific injuries and death, but will vary depending on many factors. Some people will immediately die from massive amounts of radiation, some will succumb to radiation burns and poisoning within a few days, and others will lead a normal life until they develop delayed radiation effects (sometimes within a few years).[5]

Wind and weather can carry radiation beyond the initial detonation area.

This means that radioactive materials (such as strontium-90 and cesium-137) will enter the biosphere and food supply. Exposure to significant amounts of radiation can cause burns and death; long-term exposure to these materials can lead to increased levels of cancer.[6]

Significant International Agreements That Address Nuclear Weapons

Partial Test Ban Treaty (1963). Officially known as the Treaty Banning Nuclear Weapon Tests, in the Atmosphere, in Outer Space, and under Water, the treaty permits the testing of nuclear weapons only underground. At the time of its signature and ratification, this was seen as an important arms-control treaty. Its lasting effect has been a reduction in the amount of strontium-90 in the atmosphere and food supply worldwide since the treaty came into force.

Nuclear Non-proliferation Treaty (1968). This treaty, in which 189 countries participate, is designed to keep the number of states that possess nuclear weapons to a minimum. The treaty obligates states that possess nuclear weapons not to transfer to or encourage the development of weapons in nonnuclear states. Likewise, nonnuclear states pledge not to develop nuclear weapons capabilities. Nuclear weapon states pledge to pursue nuclear disarmament "at an early date" as well. Finally, the treaty allows and encourages the transfer of technologies that are considered conducive to peaceful uses (for example, energy and medicine). Many consider the treaty a success in keeping the number of nuclear weapon states to a minimum. There are only a handful of states that are not a party to the treaty, most notably, the Democratic People's Republic of Korea (North Korea), India, Israel, and Pakistan.

Strategic Arms Limitation Treaties (1972, 1979). These are a series of negotiations and treaties that were designed to check the arms race between the United States and Soviet Union. The treaties (SALT II was unratified but observed by the United States for several years) placed a cap on the number of missiles each side could deploy.

Strategic Arms Reduction Treaties (1991, 1993, 2010). These are a series of negotiations and treaties between the United States and the Soviet Union (later Russia) that substantially reduced the nuclear arsenals of both countries. Most observers credit the treaties with cementing the improved relationship between the two countries in the post–cold war period.

6

THE WAR TO END HUMANITY?

Nuclear War and Film

The prospect of nuclear war has led to some of the most famous political movies of all time. Several authors have analyzed films such as *Dr. Strangelove, Fail Safe,* and *The Missiles of October* and offered interpretations of their meaning.[1] These films are probably the most frequently screened in political science courses. We will consider these films, in addition to several others from this genre, in this chapter. Another focus of this chapter is to trace the perceived "usefulness" of nuclear weapons over time as well. Thus the chapter will begin with an overview of nuclear weapons and why they hold fascination among the public and are considered useful among politicians. As we will see, most films that are concerned with nuclear weapons and war were released during the cold war. The reasoning is fairly simple: the cold war began shortly after the development of atomic weapons, and these types of weapons were often the way in which people judged who was "winning" the competition between the Soviet Union and the United States. Once the tensions between the two countries dissipated, so too did the emphasis on nuclear weapons and war. Since the end of the cold war, while some attention has been paid to nuclear weapons in politics, it is rare that the issue is depicted on the screen.[2]

One of the slogans used to galvanize public support for the First World War was that it was "a war to end all wars." As we have seen previously, wars could be viewed as justified and inevitable from time to time, or they could be seen as a tremendous waste and preventable. But the question of the *utility* of wars was never seriously considered in the early part of the twentieth century; states maintained their inherent right to wage war. Yet by the mid-twentieth century, nuclear weapons meant that humans could effectively end their own existence and most life on the planet with a war. In this chapter, we will consider the politics of nuclear war as depicted through film and television. Given the amount of destructive capability, we will ask what the utility of nuclear weapons might be. Next, we will concentrate on how nuclear war has been avoided and what the obstacles to avoiding a nuclear exchange might be in the modern world. Finally, we will consider, through cinematic means, the aftermath of a nuclear war. Throughout this chapter it will be evident that the possession of nuclear weapons, their potential use, and the subsequent end of human existence on the planet represents a dramatic narrative that filmmakers have taken full advantage of.

By no means is this a complete history or study of nuclear war films. In addition, it is a little difficult to determine what actually constitutes a nuclear war film. In the years since the end of the Second World War, several films have referenced atomic or nuclear weapons or materials during the course of a story, often as a way to move the plot along. These films are not considered in this chapter. Moreover, some of the films that we will consider use the prospect of the end of the world through nuclear holocaust in order to explore other themes. For example, *Panic in the Year Zero* (1962), *The World, the Flesh and the Devil* (1959), and *Five* (1951) are stories about the aftermath of a nuclear attack that explore human nature, race relations, and prejudices in the contemporary world. Often a film about life after a nuclear war is designed to explore the nature of human beings: Are humans essentially good or bad? In truth, these films are exploring ideas about the state of nature, a condition of life that Thomas Hobbes famously called "nasty, brutish, and short." In his view, to avoid that fate, humans created the state, a leviathan, to manage people—meaning that in essence people traded freedom for security. Jean-Jacques Rousseau, on the other hand, thought that humans, as rational beings, could figure out how to cooperate with one another in the state of nature. These films reflect these different philosophies. Therefore, many films we might label as works about nuclear war do not take that as their subject per se; rather, they explore deeper themes about the nature of human beings through depictions of what a post–nuclear war world might look like—depictions that might be quite inaccurate.

The development of nuclear weapons poses significantly different problems than conventional weapons. While many people focus on the immediate destructive power of nuclear weapons, which is substantial, one of the key issues about the use of these weapons is their environmental and generational effects. The radiation associated with nuclear weapons means that not only will people die in the immediate aftermath of a detonation, others will continue to suffer from effects years after their exposure to the radiation, and their offspring will potentially suffer from birth defects.[3] Additionally, exposure to radiation means that agricultural and water resources are likely to be contaminated and carry long-term risks for inhabitants in areas that experience nuclear detonation. Aware of both the immediate and long-term consequences of the weapon, many people began to worry about the future existence of humans on the planet during the cold war.

In a speech before the United Nations General Assembly in 1961, President Kennedy argued that the world faced a situation in which nuclear weapons could destroy human civilization by accident, miscalculation, or madness.[4] He noted that the increase in the number of countries that had nuclear weapons would increase the possibility that a nuclear war would occur. Although the cold war is over and tensions have eased between the two countries that have the most nuclear weapons, Russia and the United States, nuclear proliferation remains an important and difficult problem in world politics today.[5]

The Utility of the Nuclear Weapons: A Political Tool

Given the overwhelming destructive power of the weapon and its ability to kill millions instantly, and many more later, one might ask, "Why would countries want to procure such a weapon?" Indeed, nuclear weapons are very expensive, they are difficult to maintain, and they do not appear to be very practical in settling small disputes between countries. Because the weapon destroys practically everything, it would not prove effective in securing territory, for example. In the game of diplomacy nuclear weapons might be considered a blunt instrument, along the lines of using a sledge-hammer to swat a fly. Why, then, do states think nuclear weapons might be or are useful?

Some films do help to explain the utility of such weapons; others posit interesting scenarios but are less useful in explaining the attraction of nuclear weapons in the real world. To give an example of the latter, consider the 1955 low-budget film *King Dinosaur.* The premise of the film is fairly preposterous: a new planet, Planet Nova, has been discovered and four scientists (conveniently, two male and two female) are sent to explore it. The film is marked by bad acting, poor writing, and low-budget special effects, but for our purposes, the interesting aspect of the film is when the group explores an island on the planet and finds it inhabited by dinosaurs, including a Tyrannosaurus rex. As the crew escapes from the island, one scientist turns to the other and says, "I've brought the atomic bomb; I think we should use it." The line is unintentionally funny and helps to secure this film's cult status. The audience is left to wonder why one would bring an atomic bomb when exploring a new planet or why (having escaped) one would need to annihilate prehistoric (or extraterrestrial) creatures that had never been seen by humans before. The answer is that the filmmakers could use stock footage of an atomic blast rather than the cheap special effects the rest of the film relied upon. Many science fiction films of the 1950s used images and footage of nuclear detonation to boost their otherwise meager special effects. But the film does reflect a hope that many had about the introduction of atomic energy and weapons: they would solve a myriad of problems.

In the real world of politics and war, the usefulness of atomic weaponry was, and is, far more subtle. States perceive nuclear weapons to have deterrent value. To put it simply, a country with nuclear weapons believes no opponent would dare to attack it in the first place. Generally, a strategy of deterrence requires at least three prerequisites: communication, capability, and credibility.[6] If you want to deter someone from doing something, you must be able to communicate what it is you don't want your target audience to do. You must also make it clear what penalties or sanctions the target would suffer in case of a violation. Second, you must have the ability to carry out the penalty or sanction. A threat does no good if there is no way to make the penalty happen. Finally, your opponent must believe that your threat is credible, that you are willing to carry through with your threat.

In the realm of nuclear weapons, the explosive power of the weapons is so devastating that nuclear states use them as an "ultimate" deterrent. A nuclear state will communicate to its opponent, "If you attack us, we have the capability of surviving the attack at least long enough to launch a retaliatory attack (by nuclear weapons) that will devastate your country. Make no mistake, we will retaliate. Your country will be so devastated that it is not worth the terrible price you will pay. Your best move is not to attack us." During the cold war, the United States and Soviet Union engaged in a deterrent strategy, known as MAD (mutually assured destruction), that would have meant both sides would have destroyed each other in the event of war. Each side was essentially saying, "If you attack us, we are both going down." In effect, war was to mean mutual suicide.[7] Herman Kahn advocated taking the concept further. He suggested the development of a "Doomsday weapon system" whose only function would be to destroy all human life, which would be an effective deterrent to an attack on the United States. Such a machine could be, among other things, "cheap" and "foolproof," according to Kahn.[8] The goal is to make the consequences of attack so devastating that such an attack is highly unlikely in the first place. This concept is satirized in *The Mouse That Roared* (1959), in which a tiny mythical country, the Duchy of Grand Fenwick, acquires a weapon that can destroy the Earth; of course, it is satirized in many other films as well.

But what if the two adversaries are not evenly matched? Proponents of deterrence argue that the same principles and rules apply. Imagine a scenario in which a superpower and a small state with fewer nuclear weapons face off. If the smaller power has only five nuclear weapons, it would seem to be no match for the superpower, which has, say, more than a thousand nuclear weapons. Yet, the smaller power could say, "We know you could attack us, and we will be destroyed. But before we are destroyed we will launch our weapons at your five biggest cities. You may *win,* but it will be a very costly victory." Thus, deterrence advocates argue, you do not need a lot of nuclear weapons to have an effective deterrent.[9]

Avoiding a Nuclear Exchange

Since 1945 there have been at least two times when the use of nuclear weapons has seriously been considered: the Cuban missile crisis in October 1962 and the Kargil conflict between India and Pakistan in 1999.[10] The more famous incident of the two, according to most people, is the Cuban missile crisis. This event has been analyzed by more political scientists than any other event in American foreign-policy history. The Cuban missile crisis was precipitated when the Soviet Union surreptitiously placed nuclear missiles in Cuba, which the United States perceived as a provocative and hostile action. As a result, President Kennedy demanded that the missiles be removed and instituted a "quarantine," or blockade, around the island of Cuba. Tensions mounted and, in the minds of most historians and political scientists, it was the closest that the Soviet Union and the United States ever came to war—which would no doubt have been a nuclear conflict. There have been two very prominent and successful films about the event: *The Missiles of October* (1974) and *Thirteen Days* (2000). Both films attempt to give a realistic version of the Cuban missile crisis and, in particular, the decisions faced by the Kennedy White House. While both films have been successful and are recommended, they do have limitations and drawbacks. *The Missiles of October,* a made-for-TV movie, does not have the production values one might expect of modern films; however, the tension and drama are very interesting and captivating.[11] Unfortunately, the film contains several inaccuracies. *Thirteen Days* is perhaps the more accurate film, at least from the American perspective, but it takes dramatic license with the role of the protagonist during the crisis and probably places too much emphasis on the conflicts between the civilian and military personnel in the White House.[12]

It is no accident that two very prominent films about nuclear war, *Dr. Strangelove* and *Fail Safe,* were made in the years just after the Cuban missile crisis. Filmmakers were trying to capitalize on the concern and fear generated by the situation. Without a doubt the most famous and discussed nuclear war film is *Dr. Strangelove; or, How I Learned to Stop Worrying and Love the Bomb* (1964). The film stars the imaginative Peter Sellers, who plays multiple roles, just as he did in *The Mouse That Roared. Dr. Strangelove* was released at a time when the shock and seriousness of the Cuban missile crisis was beginning to wane. Thus, the public seemed ripe for a critical interpretation of the potentially devastating effects.[13] In *Dr. Strangelove,* a paranoid American general, General Ripper (Sterling Hayden), worried that the United States is under threat of a "Communist conspiracy to sap and impurify all of our precious bodily fluids," seizes an air force base to launch an attack against the Soviet Union. The general convinces the airmen at the base that the United States is under attack and orders a bomber squadron to launch a nuclear attack. This satirical farce has become an icon of cinematic history. Toward the end of the film, one of Peter Sellers's three characters in the film, Dr. Strangelove, a former Nazi scientist, advocates the use of a doomsday weapon in a critique of Herman Kahn's concept of ultimate deterrence.[14] In the documentary *Countdown to Zero,* Bruce Blair, a former soldier working in a nuclear silo, comments on *Dr. Strangelove,* saying that it was inaccurate because prior to 1970 one did not have to be a general to start a nuclear war; two low-level silo officers working together could have launched a weapon toward the Soviet Union without any authorization from a general, much less from the president of the United States.

Perhaps somewhat overshadowed by *Dr. Strangelove's* comedic and absurdist take on madness leading to a nuclear exchange, *Fail Safe* (1964) offers a stark account of the potential of a mistaken nuclear exchange because of computer malfunctions and human errors.[15] These errors lead to a squadron of airplanes initiating a bombing run on the Soviet capital, Moscow.

The sign on a silo door, made to look like an advertisement for a pizza chain, from the film *Countdown to Zero*. (Courtesy Dogwoof Films)

Unable to recall the bombers, the American president (Henry Fonda) is forced to call the Soviet premier to warn him and explain the situation. It is clear that one of the messages of the film is that the mutual mistrust between Americans and Russians is a contributing factor to the situation. Note that in his advice to military officers and the president, political science professor Groeteschele (Walter Matthau) urges them to leverage the mistake to their advantage and use it as an opportunity to deliver a devastating first strike to what is considered to be a mortal enemy. Confronted with what such a course of action would mean in terms of human lives and destruction, the professor argues that it might save lives and protect democracy in the long run. Yet in the final sequences at the end of the film, still photography overlaid with the sounds of everyday life demonstrates to the audience what would be lost should these weapons be used. Released ten months after *Dr. Strangelove*, *Fail Safe* was not a box office success. It delivered roughly the same message as *Strangelove*, but by a much more sober and somber method. Yet one could argue that the film might have more relevance in today's world than its rival. While technology has evolved to diminish the potential of a single individual launching an attack, misinterpretation and miscalculations remain very real possibilities.

There have been occasions of so-called nuclear close calls, when accidents or misinterpreted information has led to a heightening of tensions. For instance, in November 1979, display screens at NORAD (North American Aerospace Defense Command) headquarters indicated that a large number of Soviet missiles were en route to North America in what appeared to be a devastating nuclear attack. After a few tense minutes it was determined that what technicians were monitoring was, in fact, a training tape instead of an actual attack; however, by that time American jets had been scrambled and the United States had begun moving to respond. Likewise, in January 1995, after the cold war, a Norwegian rocket was launched on a scientific mission. Although the government of Norway had notified several countries, including Russia, nine days before the test, the information never reached the Russian Defense Ministry or those operating the early-warning system. As a result, the Russian government believed it was under attack for several minutes before realizing that the rocket posed no danger. These close calls had some critics worried about the overreliance on technology, fearing that a malfunction or misinformation could lead to nuclear exchange.[16]

Using the 1979 incident at NORAD as a premise, *WarGames* (1983) is a commentary on the overreliance on technology to guarantee security. Improbably, a high school student (Matthew Broderick) hacks into NORAD's computer system to play computer games. Unintentionally, he begins a sequence that the military believes is a countdown to nuclear war. Soon government officials and the military are preparing for a full nuclear exchange between the United States and the Soviet Union. Because the computer is set up to treat the exercise as a game, hence the name of the film, it cannot distinguish between the game the student is playing and the real thing. Part of the concern of the filmmakers is that if the exercise is considered a game, rather than the deadly serious occurrence that it is, then the temptation to use the weapons becomes greater. If people consider nuclear war nothing more than a game, fought on video screens around the world, then they might not consider the millions or billions of people who will die. By putting these decisions in the hands of a dispassionate computer, rather than human beings, there was a concern that war became more likely. The film ends with what chess players refer to as a *zugzwang*, a situation in which any move you can make is damaging to your own circumstances. The pithy, and effective, conclusion to the film is this: when it comes to nuclear war, the best move is not to play.

Not dissimilar from *WarGames* is the 1970 thriller *Colossus: The Forbin*

Project (1970). In the film, the American government develops a supercomputer designed to take over the defense of the United States and provide an ultimate and dispassionate deterrence to any potential attack. The drama emerges when the computer discovers that the Soviet Union has developed a similar computer. The two computers blackmail the governments in order to carry out their mission of bringing peace to the United States and the Soviet Union; however, this is accomplished on dictatorial lines. Both *WarGames* and *The Forbin Project* appear somewhat dated today, especially in terms of how computers work. Yet both films are critical of policymaking that puts too much faith in technology. Instead, the movies argue, it is for humans to figure out how to live together. Both films question the benefit of deterrent strategy because it could lead to disastrous consequences, but they also question an assumption that we often fail to consider: the belief that more technology will ultimately lead to greater security.

Many other films of the cold war period were informed by the shadow of the bomb; there seemed to be a preoccupation with the existence and potential use of nuclear weapons. For example, in *The Planet of the Apes* (1968) humans have become subjugated to apes as the result of a nuclear war. The angst about nuclear weapons and power in films was not limited to the American cinema. British science fiction films of the period, such as *X: The Unknown* (1956) and *These Are the Damned* (1963), played upon the anxieties surrounding nuclear weapons and radiation. *These Are the Damned* even provided a way for the human race to continue in the event of an all-out nuclear war.

The trauma caused by the prospect of a nuclear exchange is evident in the Swedish film *Winter Light* (1963), directed by Ingmar Bergman. When news of the acquisition of nuclear weapons by China is announced, it causes a father to commit suicide. Similarly, *The Sacrifice* (1983) explores the angst of modern life, including the knowledge that humans could destroy themselves without rationally considering the implications. Akira Kurosawa, perhaps the Japanese director best known in the West, made *Ikimono no kiroku* (I Live in Fear, 1955) in which an industrialist goes to extraordinary measures to protect himself and his family from nuclear war, including selling all of his property and moving to Brazil.[17]

With the end of the cold war, the danger of an all-out nuclear confrontation between Russia and the United States seems to have subsided (although new fears about terrorist attacks using nuclear weapons have begun to emerge, and these fears are sometimes expressed in film and television). Many films, particularly from the late 1950s until the end of the cold war in the late 1980s, struggled with the idea of living under the shadow of the bomb. Another subgenre examined the "what ifs" should nuclear war actually occur.

Life after a Nuclear War

Since there have been only two atomic weapons deployed during war at the time of this writing, most of the films about the aftereffects of a nuclear war are speculative. Yet some films, both documentaries and narrative films, have explored the actual consequences of the bombing of Hiroshima and Nagasaki. The short documentary *Hiroshima Nagasaki August 1945* (1970) is a devastating film whose footage was shot in the immediate aftermath of the atomic bombs dropped on the two cities. The film, in a dispassionate and even tone, details the effects of the bombing on people with emphasis on the medical implications, including a woman who had the pattern of her kimono tattooed on her skin as a result of the blast. A few weeks after the attacks, the effects of radiation poisoning began to be felt. A warning: the film contains graphic images of civilians being treated for various injuries in a hospital. Because the film does not resort to hyperbole and the film-makers try to allow the horrifying images to speak for themselves, the film is perhaps more effective than many others. Although the footage was shot in the days immediately following the attack, because it was marked "secret" by the U.S. Department of Defense, the film was not assembled and released until 1970.[18]

Because Japan is the one country that has experienced an atomic attack, the nation's cinema has explored the effects of the atomic bomb many times. A common theme among many such films is the focus on innocent victims. A nuclear weapon does not distinguish between people. Thus there is an emphasis on the civilians, particularly children, who died and suffered. Based on the children's book of the same name, *Hiroshima no pika* (2005) uses the paintings artist Toshi Maruki created for her book to tell the story of Mii, a young girl who survives the bombing of Hiroshima. To heighten the plight of innocents, Mii sees birds and other animals that have been injured or killed. In the Japanese film *Genbaku no ko* (Children of Hiroshima, 1952),[19] a young schoolteacher returns to the city of her birth after the war to find the city in ruins, many of her friends and loved ones dead, and a prevailing sense of illness and despondency.[20]

While the immediate physical impact of the bombs in Japan was devastating, one of the more dramatic impacts involved the effects over time.
Kiroi Ame (Black Rain, 1988) follows the story of a young woman and her
aunt and uncle five years after the Hiroshima bombing. Although they are
residents of the city, they were spared the most horrific effects of the bomb
because they were in the countryside during the detonation, but they were
witnesses to the immediate aftermath. The physical destruction the bomb
causes, told in flashback, helps to establish the psychological impact of the
bomb.[21] Five years later, the family is living in a district where former residents of Hiroshima have been relocated. As a result of radiation sickness
many members of the community are afflicted with chronic fatigue and
debilitating diseases. Everyone in the community lives with the knowledge
that anyone could develop cancerous tumors, leukemia, or delayed radiation
sickness at any point. Psychological pressures manifest themselves not only
in those who experienced the bombing but among those who did not; some
view the Hiroshima survivors as lazy or overindulged. Even those who are
seemingly unaffected by the bomb, such as the main protagonist, Yasuku
(Yoshiko Tanaka), discover they are not unscathed. Yasuko cannot find anyone willing to marry her because they fear she will eventually become ill.

Likewise, other films focus on the psychological aftereffects of the bomb.
As mentioned above, Akira Kurosawa's *I Live in Fear* examines a man, Kichi
Nakajima (Toshirô Mifune), so frightened of another nuclear attack he is
willing to give up his substantial fortune to protect his family. The film
concludes with a psychiatrist speculating about who is actually insane: Mr.
Nakajima for becoming paralyzed by his fear of nuclear weapons, or all the
people who choose to ignore the significant threat the weapons pose to our
lives.[22]

Most films about a post–nuclear war world are speculations about what
might happen in the future. In the immediate aftermath of the attacks on
Hiroshima and Nagasaki, films that depicted a post–atomic war world often
sought to reassure the public that life would eventually return to normal. In
many of these films, the science of what was likely to happen to survivors
was either not understood or ignored. For example, cult figure Arch Oboler's
Five (1951), based on his radio play *The Word,*[23] is about five people who
survive a nuclear war. Their stories of survival are based on dubious science;
however, it is not the probable facts of post-nuclear life that the filmmaker
is interested in. Instead, it is the interesting dynamics of the survival of only
four men and one woman, mixed with ideological and racial politics, that

drive the story. *The World, the Flesh and the Devil* (1959) has a very similar plot: three people survive, two men (one of whom, Harry Belafonte, is African American) and a woman.[24] The film is actually a study of racial politics in the United States.

One early effort to take seriously the effects of a nuclear war was a television play entitled *Atomic Attack* (1954), which is centered on the lives of the Mitchell family in the aftermath of a hydrogen bomb attack.[25] While largely a curiosity, the film does help to highlight the evolution of understanding about a post–nuclear war world. The story is set in a household in Westchester, New York, about fifty miles outside New York City. Although the hydrogen bomb has destroyed the city, and there is some concern about radiation, the film is overly optimistic about the chances of a return to normal life after such a cataclysmic event. Many people do die in the attack, but most injured people are successfully treated even though they have been exposed to high levels of radiation. The message of the film is that civil defense planning before a nuclear war will help immeasurably after such a war, even allowing the United States to win a potential conflict.

These films reflected a desire among the public to believe—and the willingness of filmmakers to reinforce that belief—that while such a war would be very bad, it was ultimately winnable and afterward life would return to normal. Civil Defense films of the time often fed into that notion. Viewed today, some of the suggestions offered by films such as *Duck and Cover* (1952) and *Alert Today—Alive Tomorrow* (1956), like covering yourself with a picnic blanket as protection from a nuclear blast, seem absurd.[26] But these films were designed to reassure a public anxious about the dangers of an atomic attack. In contrast to films like this, the semi-documentary *The War Game* (1965) used evidence from Hiroshima and Nagasaki to demonstrate what a nuclear attack on Great Britain would look like. Made by the venerable BBC and scheduled to air on television, the film was so graphic and depressing that it was banned from British television.

One of the more interesting and well-known films of the genre is *On the Beach* (1959). Based on the novel of the same name by Nevil Shute,[27] the film follows the crew members of an American submarine that surfaces in Australia after a nuclear war. The submarine comes to Australia because that country seems to have the last traces of human life on the planet, but it is clear that as the winds circle the planet, eventually enough radiation will come to Australia to destroy human life there as well.

One of the critiques of *On the Beach* as a part of nuclear war cinema is that the film overemphasizes personal stories of love; however, all the love stories are ultimately doomed.[28] Everyone is going to die within weeks. If love is part of what being human is about, then a nuclear war that ends everything human will destroy that too. In one of the most transfixing scenes in the film, a young couple debates whether it is right to give their infant daughter cyanide to prevent her suffering if they die first. The question is not if their baby is going to die, but when. This sense of hopelessness had a dramatic effect on contemporary audiences.[29]

By the 1970s nuclear war films were becoming passé. Other threats (for example, environmental disaster, overpopulation) began to be prominent in American cinema. Video arcades were full of games like Missile Command and Space Invaders, which used images of mushroom clouds on a regular basis. Yet a growing antinuclear movement began to gain traction in its call for nuclear disarmament. Sting's hit "Russians" on his debut solo album was a message to both Soviet and American leaders. The song referred to the fallacy that nuclear war was winnable and appealed to common humanity with its refrain "The Russians love their children too." The song captured the growing antinuclear mood in Western democracies.[30]

Films during the 1980s began to reflect the antinuclear movement as well. There was an upsurge in the number of films warning about the dangers of nuclear wars by demonstrating the aftereffects of such a war. Unlike earlier films, such as *Five* and *The World, the Flesh and the Devil,* in which (although almost all the people are gone) the world remains largely intact and life goes on, postapocalyptic films in the 1980s portrayed a world that was hopelessly bleak and damaged. Perhaps one of the most famous and arguably the most influential was the made-for-TV film *The Day After* (1983). Set in Lawrence, Kansas, the film follows the lives of residents after a nuclear exchange between the United States and the Soviet Union. Although heavily edited by the censors at ABC, the broadcast had a dramatic impact on viewers. The airing of the movie was somewhat controversial because it purported to show the reality that would follow a nuclear attack. After it was shown, ABC aired special programs in which experts discussed issues surrounding nuclear weapons. Viewers' guides and discussions permeated the national airwaves. A national debate ensued. While *The Day After* brought a lot of attention to the issue of nuclear war, as Toni Perrine points out, the production values and script had the distinctive feel of a lower-quality American television enterprise. The movie followed many of the plot devices of what was known as "big-issues-of-the-day" television movies. Because it was set in rural America, some reviewers criticized the film because it did not address the devastation and conditions that would occur within large urban areas, the most likely targets of a nuclear exchange.[31] Although the film had some inaccuracies and shortcomings, there is no doubt that it impacted many people. *The Day After* produced a debate within the United States about the continued existence and potential use of nuclear weapons. Because roughly half of the adult population of the United States watched the film, it was a common point of discussion among many. In his autobiography, then president Ronald Reagan claimed that the movie was similar to scenarios developed by the Pentagon. He wrote that the film left him depressed and convinced that nuclear war had to be avoided at all costs.[32]

Much more cerebral, and less sensational, is the feature *Testament* (1983). The film is considered a more realistic alternative to *The Day After*. Produced on a small budget, the film does not rely on special effects to tell its compelling story of a family in the suburbs of San Francisco in the aftermath of a nuclear war.[33] The film relies on a technique similar to that used in *On the Beach,* but instead of a love story the plot focuses on a suburban mother (played by Jane Alexander, who was nominated for an Academy Award for her performance) caring for her three children as they succumb to radiation poisoning. The film adeptly depicts the deterioration of the family's quality of life and the emotional drama of their suffering.

Part of the impact of *The Day After* was the response it elicited from other filmmakers. What has been called the British answer to the film, *Threads* (1986), depicts the buildup to and aftermath of a nuclear war in Britain. Relying on a documentary-style narrative, the film follows the fate of two families in Sheffield. As time passes after the war, the threads of society become frayed: lawlessness emerges, radiation causes sickness, and birth defects become commonplace. In the final harrowing scenes, the long-term realities of nuclear warfare are manifested with horrifying effects. The film is considered by many critics to be the most successful of all such films in making the case against nuclear armament in the 1980s.[34]

When the Wind Blows (1986), a British animated feature, uses the plight of a retired couple living in rural England to illustrate misperceptions and misinformation about life after a nuclear war. As the Bloggs ready themselves for an imminent nuclear war, they consult government pamphlets and console themselves that if they survived the Second World War, they can survive this too. Hilda wants her comfortable life to continue; Jim romantically recalls the heroic days of World War II. They both assume that, as happened during the earlier war, the government will quickly reestablish order and provide basic services shortly after an attack. Jim dutifully follows government pamphlets on building a bomb shelter and stocking it. As the war comes to pass, the viewer becomes aware of how much misinformation the Bloggs and the general public have received from their government: the false hope, the inadequate preparations, the ignorance the people retain about the ramifications of a nuclear attack. Of course, this is the point of the film; the filmmakers hope to educate viewers about the dangers and threats we face.

Other non-American films encouraged viewers to think about the aftermath of a nuclear exchange as well. The Canadian film *23 Skidoo* (1964) is a short experimental film by Julian Biggs featuring normally busy urban settings around Montreal completely devoid of people. As the film progresses, there are hints as to what has occurred, but it is not until the action reaches a newsroom and the camera focuses on a partial news report about the first neutron bomb, a bomb designed to maximize radiation and minimize the blast,[35] that the viewer is aware of what happened.[36] The French film *La jetée* (1962) paints a devastating picture of the aftermath of global nuclear war.[37] In the ruins of Paris, after the Third World War, scientists believe that the only hope for the survival of humanity is time travel. Only thus can food and medicine be procured. To perfect the art of time travel, scientists experiment on prisoners of war, but the procedures and the actual time travel cause both pain and madness. The film is perhaps better known for the style of its filmmaker instead of its message; the entire film, with the exception of a few brief seconds, is a series of black-and-white photographs with a voice-over narrative.

Some Final Thoughts

What we could call the nuclear cinema encompasses a number of films that take widely different perspectives; however, the films do tend to fall into categories. Films about Hiroshima and Nagasaki almost always focus on the events that occurred and how innocents (human and nonhuman) were caught up in the atomic bombs. One could argue that early films offer an antiseptic depiction of nuclear war to those concerned about the prospect of a cataclysmic event—the general sense was that people would survive and eventually recover from nuclear war. The films of the 1980s offered a more alarmist attitude toward a nuclear war, emphasizing what was at stake. These films would often try to depict the unimaginable. Satirical films created an absurdist view to demonstrate what seemed to be an absurd situation. In the end, the films were, and are, a consistent reminder of the dangers faced, even if they are not always completely accurate.

Most political scientists assume, without much debate, that the development of the atomic bomb in 1945 created a new era in world politics. Judging from the cold war cinema and beyond, it would seem that the popular culture would agree. Yet, as Jerome Shapiro points out, there are other events in world politics that have a more direct and dramatic impact on people, such as the reliance on fossil fuels or famine.[38] It is clear that more people have been injured or killed between 1946 and 2013 by conventional warfare than by nuclear war. Yet the overwhelming and, perhaps, unimaginable destructive force of nuclear weapons, and the fear of their potential use, means that these weapons are a particularly important issue in world politics.

As we have noted, the prospect of a nuclear war seems remote today. The end of the cold war and the treaties that dramatically reduced the number of nuclear weapons have meant that very few seriously think about nuclear war between the United States and Russia. But concerns still exist about the potential that nuclear proliferation will increase the likelihood of nuclear war between other potential adversaries. The prospect that more countries could acquire the weapons—or that rogue elements, including terrorist groups, could acquire them—leads many analysts to consider the effects of proliferation.

With the end of the cold war there also has been a decline in the popularity and frequency of nuclear war films. The demise of the Soviet Union meant the demise of a theatrical villain for films in the West, particularly American films. Few other potential enemies have inspired the general fear produced by a coupling of animosity and nuclear weapons. Nevertheless, both the film *The Sum of All Fears* (2002) and the short-lived television series *Jericho* (2006–2008) were premised on the idea that the United States was targeted for terrorist attacks. While there has been growing concern about the possibility of a terrorist attack incorporating nuclear weapons, or at least nuclear material, there has not been a glut of films in the genre in the first decade of the twenty-first century.

That is not to say nuclear weapons have totally disappeared from screens across the world. For example, the television series *Battlestar Galactica* used nuclear warheads in its story of battles between humans and Cylons. But the psychological drama, and the traumatic impact of living under the constant prospect of nuclear war, is not a mainstay of early twenty-first-century films.

The much-publicized documentary *Countdown to Zero* (2010) touted the dangers of nuclear proliferation in the post–cold war era. Yet apocalyptic visions of the future usually employ other cataclysmic plot devices rather than nuclear weapons, including inanimate objects from space, such as meteors and comets (*Armageddon,* 1998, and *Deep Impact,* 1998), extraterrestrials (*Independence Day,* 1996, and *War of the Worlds,* 2005), disease (*I Am Legend,* 2007, *28 Days Later . . . ,* 2002, *Children of Men,* 2006, and *Contagion,* 2011), and zombies.[39] Like nuclear war films of the cold war period, post–cold war disaster films tell us a lot about ourselves. Not only do they express the fears of a culture—who might attack us or what dangers lurk in our minds—they also serve as a microcosm of what we believe are the essential characteristics of human beings.

7

INTRIGUE, ESPIONAGE, AND NUCLEAR SECRETS

Berlin on Film

During the cold war's nuclear standoff between the Soviet Union and the United States, the divided city of Berlin was the setting for many dramatic intrigues (both on film and off). The film portrayal of Berlin is instructive because the city has been at the center of many international events for well over a century. As the capital of Prussia, first, and then Germany, Berlin has been the epicenter of many political-historical events whose ramifications stretch far beyond central Europe. The rise of the Nazi Party in the 1930s and the start of the Second World War meant that many film actors and directors, such as Peter Lorre, Marlene Dietrich, Fritz Lang, and Billy Wilder, would leave the German film industry and become a major influence in Hollywood. Nevertheless, they would continue to tell stories about Berlin and Germany that resonated with American and global audiences.

Germany's defeat in World War I paradoxically led to a great cultural period in that country. During the Weimar period (1919–1933), named after the government known as the Weimar Republic, the German film industry was one of the most highly regarded in the world.[1] The film studio Universium Film AG (Ufa), located just outside Berlin in the Babelsberg district of Potsdam, produced many classic films in the style known as expressionism. Although the city is never mentioned specifically by name, Berlin in the year 2026, one hundred years in the future, is central to the classic film *Metropolis* (1927), directed by Fritz Lang and one of the most famous silent films ever made, a favorite of film aficionados. The city is the backdrop for a struggle between the elites and the workers of the city. Films of the Weimar period, such as the documentaries *Berlin: Die Sinfonie der Grosstadt* (Berlin: Symphony of a Great City, 1927) and *Menschen am Sonntag* (People on Sunday, 1930), celebrate the beauty and vitality of a city that would be destroyed by World War II. On the other hand, *M* (1931), a film also directed by Fritz Lang, deals with the problems of urbanization as a child murderer, played by Peter Lorre, terrorizes urban residents. The American film *Cabaret* (1972) captured the Weimar period in Berlin as it was coming to a close. In the film, singer/dancer Sally Bowles (Liza Minnelli) confronts changing public attitudes and politics as the Nazis coalesced power in Germany.

Certainly Berlin was an important focus during the Second World War, but the city—and its destruction—became the backdrop for many films afterward. The devastation was so complete that many filmmakers incorporated it into their work. For example, the television series *Flash Gordon* (1954–1955), which was filmed in West Berlin, worked a devastated city into its plotlines, giving a sense of how damaged the city was even a decade after the war. More concerned with the politics of war and occupation, *A Foreign Affair* (1948), a comedy starring Jean Arthur and Marlene Dietrich, pits the morality of occupying Americans against the deprivation of the Germans. More dramatically, the East German film *Ingendwo in Berlin* (Somewhere in Berlin, 1946) explores many of the same themes but focuses, albeit sometimes confusingly, on the psychological aftermaths of the war. As mentioned in chapter 4, *Anonyma—Eine Frau in Berlin* (A Woman in Berlin, 2008) captures the realities and horrors of war as the city is destroyed and residents, particularly women, are left to deal with the ensuing violence and deprivation.

During the postwar occupation, Berlin was divided into four zones of occupation (as was the entire country of Germany). As cold war tensions between the Soviet Union and the West grew, these zones became more permanent. The divide between West Germany (composed of the American, French, and British sectors) and East Germany (the Soviet sector) was mirrored and magnified in Berlin: the city itself was divided. Tensions between East and West were magnified in Berlin, culminating with the erection of the Berlin Wall in 1961. West Berlin was completely surrounded by Communist East Germany, and the western part of the city was seen as an outpost of freedom within the Communist world. The city became synonymous with spies and espionage as depicted in films such as *The Spy Who Came in from the Cold* (1965), *Funeral in Berlin* (1966), and *Torn Curtain* (1966).

The novel situation of a divided city led to a dramatic opportunity for filmmakers, although they did not need to rely on fictional stories; there were plenty of dramatic stories of people trying to flee into West Berlin. For instance, *Berlin Tunnel 21* (1981) and *Escape from East Berlin* (1962) are but two of the many stories of dramatic illegal crossings of the Berlin Wall. Billy Wilder, who had earlier directed *A Foreign Affair* and was a cowriter of *People on Sunday*, wrote and directed a scathing depiction of cold war politics in *One, Two, Three* (1961). The film is about a Coca-Cola executive (James Cagney) navigating not only the divided city but changing morals as well. While the film is a comedy, the tense situation of a divided city was not. Repeatedly, border incidents and provocations led to dangerous standoffs. The crises over the Berlin Wall had implications for global politics and were even a contributing factor to the Cuban missile crisis. Many scenarios for a war between the Soviet Union and the United States (and their allies) focused on Berlin. East Germany, formally known as the German Democratic Republic (GDR),[2] was seen as the most "Communist" of the Communist regimes. Its tactics are detailed in the film *Das Leben der Anderen* (The Lives of Others, 2006), a stunning film about how an East German writer slowly transforms from a supporter of the regime into an opponent. The film used the extensive surveillance techniques employed by the Stasi (secret police) and showed how suspicious, even paranoid, the regime had become.

It is against this background that the stunning events of 1989 occurred. Across Eastern Europe, partially motivated by Mikhail Gorbachev's policies of *glasnost* (openness) and *perestroika* (restructuring) in the Soviet Union, people began to challenge Communist regimes. Confronting the hard-line East German regime was daunting; very few could see a way to avoid bloodshed in bringing about the reunification of Germany without a major international crisis. Yet on 9 November 1989 East German leader Egon Krenz announced that the Berlin Wall would be opened without restrictions. A partylike atmosphere soon developed on both sides of the wall. People came to the Brandenburg Gate, scaled the wall, and openly greeted one another. Many brought hammers, chisels, and other implements to destroy the wall that for forty years had divided the city. Less than a year later, the two Germanies were formally reunited: the fall of the Berlin Wall represented a symbolic end to the cold war.

As joyous as the events of 1989–1990 were, change did not come without challenges. Berlin was a city that had been literally split into two; even buildings and the subway system (U-Bahn) were severed during the cold war. Wim Wender's follow-up to his successful *Der Himmel über Berlin* (Wings of Desire, 1993), *In weiter Ferne, so nah!* (Faraway, So Close! 1993), in which angels look over the residents of the city, employed Gorbachev in the film as a gesture of thanks for helping to reunite the city. Yet the difficulties of reunification began to seep into films. The American film *Hedwig and the Angry Inch* (2001), a film about the psychological dislocation of a transsexual punk rock singer, uses the Berlin Wall as a metaphor for the artificial divide that separates males and females. Like the fall of the wall, Hedwig's sex change removed a barrier between male and female, although Hedwig has difficulty negotiating life without the barrier. A much more direct film about the political implications of reunification, the German *Berlin Is in Germany* (2001) tells the story of a man who is arrested in East Berlin and serves time in jail, but when he is released finds himself in a reunited Germany. In a microcosm, he experiences what many East Germans felt; East Germany can be seen as a jail and upon release, the protagonist must navigate new neighborhoods and a different way of doing things.[3]

The most successful and popular film about the transition is no doubt *Goodbye Lenin!* (2003). Set during the transition in 1990, the mother of Alex (Daniel Brühl) experiences a heart attack shortly before the collapse of the East German government. When she awakes from a long coma, Alex is told that she must not suffer any shock or it could be fatal. Realizing the enormity of the change facing Berlin and Germany, Alex sets about remaking their apartment to reflect the days of Communism. He goes to great lengths to find products, clothing, and even people who have been discarded in the great rush to Westernize. The film is an homage to the GDR, a reminder that some little things in life were good and comforting even considering the overbearing Communist regime.[4] *Goodbye Lenin!* is an example of the phenomenon known as *ostalgia* (a German contraction meaning, roughly, "east nostalgia"), in which people remember products and ideas from the Communist days that were good. The film famously and fondly remembers such East German icons as cosmonaut Sigmund Jähn and the mother's favorite food, Spreewald pickles.[5]

In 1991, the German Bundestag (parliament) voted, by a slim margin, to move the capital of the Federal Republic of Germany from Bonn to Berlin. Since that time Berlin has undergone a transformation and has become one of the most important cities in Europe, ensuring that Berlin will continue to have a cinematic history as well as a political one. While there are a number of world cities that have a place in film history worth noting, Berlin represents the demonstrable changes of major power politics of the twentieth and early twenty-first centuries.

8

IS INTERNATIONAL COOPERATION POSSIBLE?

If we were to survey average people about international politics, no doubt they would believe that cooperation in world politics is almost nonexistent. Yet cooperation is an integral aspect of human life. For example, every time you go to a concert you are witnessing an act of cooperation among the musicians; most people think of marriage as an act of cooperation between two people. Every film, no matter how small and independent, is an act of cooperation among the director, producers, technicians, and performers. Because we see cooperation in everyday life, we should not be surprised to find evidence of cooperation in the international system. The very term *system* implies routine among the various components. The international system regularly has normal cooperative interactions. There is an old aphorism in journalism, attributed to Alfred Harmsworth, that goes, "When a dog bites a man, that is not news, because it happens so often. But if a man bites a dog, that is news." The meaning is that commonplace things, which happen on a daily basis, are not newsworthy. In international politics this could help to explain why most people believe that very little cooperation occurs in the world. Worldwide cooperation does occur regularly, but it is often under the radar. Every year millions of international tourists travel to various countries across the globe, billions of dollars in trade traverse international borders without incident, and most countries do not go to war with one another. All of which, we can argue, constitute acts of cooperation.

Cooperation can be defined as a situation in which two or more parties work together to achieve some benefit that would not be available to them if they worked alone.[1] Cooperation always contains at least some costs.[2] The way in which most people observe the most common form of cooperation in world politics is through international trade. If countries cooperate in trade, then there are some costs, such as opening your markets or reducing tariffs; however, the benefits to a country's economy can be substantial.

The question remains: What is the defining aspect of world politics? Realists would not deny that cooperation takes place; however, such cooperation is limited and exists only when the benefits are apparent.[3] The liberal perspective, on the other hand, is based in part on the assumption that humans are rational, calculating and, therefore, are capable of determining their own interests. Thus, liberals assume that humans are capable of understanding there are benefits, albeit at different degrees. These benefits have a long-term value, and people (and countries) recognize this. Liberals point to cooperation in terms of economic endeavors and shared tasks. By engaging in these endeavors and tasks we recognize the long-term benefits. This does not mean that everyone will participate in cooperation; the difficulty is that there might be significant barriers to cooperation.

This chapter will explore issues of cooperation in international politics and how it is (and is not) depicted on the screen. To begin a discussion of international cooperation we will consider different understandings of cooperation in the study of world politics. The chapter will explore why films and television programs do not regularly have cooperation as a major theme or story line. We also will examine how, although cooperation is not a primary message, acts and stories of cooperation still filter through many of the films audiences watch. Finally, the chapter will conclude with a consideration of whether sustained cooperation will result in a general peace.

The Study of Cooperation

Rousseau invites us to think about the nature of cooperation in the thought experiment known as the Stag Hunt (alternatively, the Stag and the Hare).[4] Briefly put, a group of hunters, armed with spears and knives, set off on a deer-hunting trip. The strategy of the hunters is simple: they will form a large circle around the deer, slowly moving closer to surround the animal, close off escape routes, and finally kill it. If each of the hunters cooperates and the plan is successful, then all of the hunters will secure enough food to feed themselves and their families for a long while. This act of cooperation benefits all who participate in the hunt. But Rousseau introduces a wrinkle, a potential problem. If, while lying in wait, one of the hunters sees a rabbit go by and leaves his or her post to chase it, then there is a gap in the circle providing an escape route for the deer. Now, the rabbit would supply enough food for that night's meal, but not nearly as much as a deer would provide. Does that hunter pursue the rabbit, ruining the trap that has been laid and leaving the other hunters empty-handed? Or does the hunter continue to cooperate with the other hunters in pursuit of the deer? The assumption is that humans are rational and are capable of determining their own interests and of calculating the costs and benefits of cooperation. The decision to cooperate (or not) is left to individuals and is based upon their own determination of interests. But because people are capable of understanding what the effects of cooperation and defections are, they will make their decisions accordingly.

When cooperation occurs, all who cooperate will benefit; however, this does not mean all humans will engage in cooperation with others. There could be significant reasons why people might defect from cooperation, including prejudices, past histories, and miscalculations. What theorists like Rousseau and Hume remind us is that this does not happen in a vacuum. Some hunters might decide to defect in pursuit of their own interests. Yet the other hunters will recognize this and learn from the information, because they are rational and calculating as well. Perhaps next time, the defecting hunter will not be invited on a hunt, or he or she will be shunned in the community. Additionally, hunting groups do not appear randomly; they are self-selecting. Thus, members of the group are chosen based upon a calculation of whether they might be good group members.[5] Therefore, cooperation is more likely to happen than we might initially think.

An alternative thought puzzle about the way in which human cooperation occurs in a world of anarchy is captured in the game theory known as the Prisoner's Dilemma. There are many variations; however, here is a simplified version. Imagine there are two people (Mary and John) who commit a crime—a bank robbery, let's say. They are arrested and interrogated separately. The police officer interrogating the two prisoners offers each a deal: if they give evidence against their coconspirator they will get a reduced sentence of only three years, while their accomplice will go to jail for seven years. Both Mary and John know the deal and will make a decision based on the following calculation: if Mary gives evidence to the police (and betrays John), then she will get three years and he will get seven years in prison. The same holds true if John betrays Mary. If they both give evidence against each other, they will both get five years in prison; however, if Mary and John cooperate with one another and do not give evidence to the police, they will both get off and serve no time in jail.

At first it looks simple: if the prisoners cooperate with one another, then they are free. But a careful analysis suggests that not cooperating with a partner might lessen your vulnerability. Consider Mary's position: if John betrays her, then she will go to jail for seven years. As a hedge against this possible betrayal, Mary might consider betraying John first. Then, if John does betray her, she will only get five years instead of the seven she would get if she were to cooperate with John and he betrayed her. Scholars point out that when the game is played, more than likely the two prisoners will give evidence against each other, and so the results will almost always be the "suboptimal outcome."[6] Simply meaning, the lack of cooperation among people leads to less than desirable outcomes.

Many films seemingly demonstrate the selfishness of human beings and, consequently, their inability to cooperate with one another. For example, *It's a Mad, Mad, Mad, Mad World* (1963) takes a comedic view of the problem. The premise is that a large amount of money is hidden, and the first person among a group of competitors who finds it gets to keep it. The chances of finding the cache would be greater if the competitors pooled their resources in the hunt, but that would mean sharing the prize—which each is reluctant to do. A more dramatic look at human selfishness is John Huston's masterpiece, *The Treasure of the Sierra Madre* (1948). Three less than prosperous Americans form an uneasy alliance to mine gold in the wilderness of Mexico. The harsh climate and suspicious nature of one of the miners lead to disastrous consequences.

It is difficult to overestimate the importance of the Prisoner's Dilemma for many scholars, yet others argue against applying this analogy to too many situations. While the Prisoner's Dilemma seems to model the real world, in actuality very rarely do we have only one opportunity to cooperate. In fact, we often see our potential partners for cooperation on a regular basis. Think about an organization to which you belong. If a person does not do what he or she is asked, that person is not invited to share in the benefits; however, the person will have future opportunities to cooperate. Whereas the Prisoner's Dilemma models cooperation on a onetime basis, in fact, most of the time cooperation occurs within an ongoing relationship.

In studying cooperation in world politics, we can apply Rousseau's Stag Hunt. States might find a task in which they are willing to cooperate, devise an approach to that task, create a plan, and begin the endeavor. It is possible that one country may defect from cooperation, however. Prisoner's Dilemma describes how defecting might occur. Think about a trade treaty: five countries may get together to eliminate tariffs (taxes) on shoes. This has several effects: there are more opportunities for shoemakers in each of the countries to sell shoes abroad; consumers in each of the countries have greater choices in their footwear; and it reduces the overall cost, through competition, of shoes, which is good for the economy. But let's say one country, Norway, for example, decides it wants to reinstate the tax on shoes and begins adding 15 kroner (about $3) on each shoe imported into the country. It is unlikely that the other countries will want to go to war over a shoe tax, but they will remember Norway's decision not to cooperate and take it into account the next time a beneficial cooperative opportunity occurs.

In his classic study of cooperation, Robert Axelrod seeks to understand why cooperation develops between people even in the most unlikely situations.[7] Axelrod uses computer games and simulations, biological interactions, and examples from politics to bolster his arguments. Among his most compelling arguments is an examination of trench warfare during the First World War. Axelrod describes how several soldiers in the trenches engaged in a "Live-and-Let-Live" system.[8] Simply put, German and English soldiers would engage in informal truces and understandings to allow each other specified times of guaranteed safety. This reciprocal exchange represented a degree of cooperation that allowed the retrieval and burial of the dead, ensured peaceful meals, or just facilitated a situation in which soldiers would not simply kill one another at will. This is the antithesis of the usual kill-or-be-killed mentality of warfare.[9]

The film *Joyeaux Noël* (2005) tells the story of one of these informal truces, the famous Christmas truce of 1914.[10] The film opens with what divides the countries at war: the scene switches between three classrooms, one German, one British, and one French. In front of each classroom stands a young boy reciting patriotic, jingoistic poems and songs about his country's enemies. Later, motivated by the spirit of Christmas, soldiers temporarily lay down their arms to celebrate the holiday. The film suggests that the soldiers, and the commanding officers, who did not authorize the events, have more in common than they initially realize.[11]

For cooperation to succeed, participants must overcome the barriers to cooperation. Among other things, barriers can be prejudices, biases, and a history between participants that makes it difficult for the participants to trust one another. For example, we would not expect two countries that have recently had a war to willingly jump at the chance of cooperation. We can see this tendency in the *Star Trek* franchise. In the original television series (1966–1969), the Federation and Klingons were constantly engaged in a series of conflicts and skirmishes. By the time the original cast begins to wrap up their tenure in *Star Trek VI: The Undiscovered Country* (1991), the premise is a proposed peace treaty between the Federation and the Klingon Empire. Premiering just a couple of years after the fall of the Berlin Wall, the film is a metaphor for the end of the cold war.[12] Throughout *The Undiscovered Country* characters struggle with their biases and prejudices in the face of a new cooperative reality.[13] Cooperation between enemies and the struggle against bias is depicted in several films, including *Enemy Mine* (1985), a science fiction film set in the late twenty-first century, and the cold war British film *Letter to Brezhnev* (1985), in which a young woman falls in love with a Russian sailor.

Motivations to Cooperate

Many advocates point to the material or financial benefits that can be derived from cooperation. Yet there can be other motivations to cooperate. Some would point out religious motivations for cooperation. For example, Psalm 133 reads, "Behold how good and how pleasant it is for brethren to dwell together in unity."[14] Cooperation is also a cultural value that many societies want to promote. The oft-used phrase "There is no I in team" posits that teamwork (cooperation) is more valuable and desirable than individual achievement. Popular culture and educational television programs aimed at children in North America, for example, try to teach and encourage cooperation as a part of being a good citizen. Programs like *Sesame Street* (1969–), *Mr. Rogers' Neighborhood* (1968–2001), and *Ni Hao, Kail-Lan* (2008–) emphasize good behavior through cooperation.

Proponents of cooperation argue that it is a course of strength, rather than an inherent weakness or a sign of vulnerability, as some see it. Political theorist Hannah Arendt argues that historically power existed only when human beings cooperated with one another. Her argument is premised on the idea that, although individuals may possess strength, without cooperation power cannot be exerted over others. Thus, in world politics the news media outlets, films, and the public at large concentrate on the physical resources a country might have (weapons or money, for example). But, as analysts, we take for granted the power of cooperation. As Arendt points out, there are many examples in history in which a small group of men, through cooperation, have ruled over vast amounts of territory.[15]

The idea of power through cooperation is expressed in Alfred Hitchcock's *Lifeboat* (1944). In the film, set during World War II, a group of survivors gathers on a lifeboat after a skirmish between a cargo carrier and a German submarine. The survivors are from different walks of life, including different socioeconomic classes, races, and political affiliations. Joining the lifeboat a little later on is a German man, Willy (Walter Slezak), who claims to be a sailor but in actuality is the submarine's commander. Willy proves to be more qualified than the others to survive at sea and thus appears stronger. Hitchcock was criticized by contemporary reviews for portraying the Nazi character as superior to those from democratic countries.[16] Yet, although Willy is the strongest, when the others cooperate with each other (by overcoming their differences), they can overpower Willy's strength. The metaphor for the audience was that if the other countries of the world cooperated, Nazi Germany could be defeated.

Finally, humans are social creatures and rely on each other for psychological and emotional support. Although we create political systems that emphasize independence, even radical independence, without other people humans can rarely achieve anything. Films such as *Robinson Crusoe* (1954), *Robinson Crusoe on Mars* (1964), and *Cast Away* (2000) all point to the need humans have for companionship.[17] Beyond that, film and television programs demonstrate that we have parts to play within society, and through cooperation we can build better towns and societies and thus prosper. *Our Town* (1940), the *Andy Hardy* film series (1938–1958), and *It's a Wonderful Life* (1946) portray communities in which people cooperate and produce a "good life." In *It's a Wonderful Life,* in particular, the theme of the film is that the life of a single individual, in this case George Bailey (James Stewart), is so profound that removing him from history would do irreparable harm. American television programs like *The Simpsons* (1989–), *Northern Exposure* (1990–1995), *The Gilmore Girls* (2000–2007), and even *Smurfs* (1981–1990) demonstrate a sense of community. Much of the drama in such stories is derived from a member of the community who is not fulfilling his or her job or role, or the plot revolves around determining who is a part of the community. Thus many of the problems in *The Simpsons* arise when Homer fails to adequately do his job or follow the rules of the community. This is illustrated in *The Simpsons Movie* (2007) when Homer, against the town's prohibition on dumping, drops his pig's excrement into the lake. On the other hand, determining who is a member of the community, and thus is entitled to work and enjoy the benefits of cooperation, is a point of dramatic interest as well. The Canadian television series *Little Mosque on the Prairie* (2007–), about a group of Muslims who open a small mosque in the Canadian heartland, comically but gently explores these issues.[18]

The Lack of Narrative and Drama in Cooperation

One of the problems of depicting cooperation on screens is that it is not particularly compelling. Nobody sits down to watch a YouTube clip of a person calmly giving detailed points about the good aspects of a politician or celebrity. However, let a person start ranting and raving against someone or some policy, and there is a good chance that the video will go viral. Classic storytelling always relies on conflict to heighten drama and make a good story. Shakespearean plays, for example, are based on some kind of conflict. The most compelling form of drama is one in which there is conflict. Almost all the films made today are based on some sort of conflict that must be ameliorated or overcome. There are rarely films about friendship, for example, because friendship typically does not have a beginning, middle, and end, a progression that is important in drama.[19]

The reason conflict is always present is that it has become a convention of human storytelling, including motion pictures. Drama consists of some basic elements: a lead character, an inciting incident, an objective, an obstacle, a crisis, the climax, and the resolution.[20] A dramatic work is premised on the idea that life is a constant struggle of trying to get what one wants, and to move a story along, characters must find motivation through complication and conflict.[21] Unlike most other art forms, drama requires an audience.[22] Thus, in attracting an audience, the filmmaker assumes that the audience will be familiar with the structure of storytelling as it has developed in drama and film and so constructs the film to follow those structures.

Despite the necessity of conflict for classic drama, films can demonstrate how conflict can be overcome through cooperation. This is the message of the 1931 film *Kameradschaft*. Directed by the famous German auteur G. W. Pabst, the film dramatized a 1911 disaster at Courrières, France, when German miners came to the rescue of trapped French workers. Pabst, who also directed *Westfront 1918* (1930), which was discussed in chapter 4, used the events to explore the idea of national identities among miners along the French-German border. The film's conclusion is that the miners have more in common with each other than they think, despite their national differences. In terms of the theme of cooperation, *Kameradschaft* picks up where *Westfront* leaves off. Toward the end of *Westfront,* the dying Karl is comforted by a wounded French soldier who takes Karl's hands and says, "Moi camarade . . . pas enemie, pas enemie" (My friend . . . not my enemy).[23] *Kameradschaft* takes this to the next logical step: if dying soldiers find that they do not have reasons to kill each other, the miners, who have more in common than not, should not have enmity between them.[24]

Quite often films use the three-act structure to tell a story of how cooperation can overcome obstacles, problems, or enemies. For example, in the American film *Our Daily Bread* (1934), a young couple flees urban life during the Great Depression to begin life on a farm. Not knowing how to farm, the couple organizes a group of people to share talents and resources. The drama in the film is whether the group will overcome obstacles to irrigate their crops and succeed in their enterprise. It also is a demonstration of how, although there are costs, cooperation ends up being beneficial for all.

It is interesting to note that some who study cooperation contend that cooperation does not exist without conflict.[25] Thus there are many films that use conflict as a background to cooperative efforts. The Czech film *Musíme si pomáhat* (Divided We Fall, 2000) tells the story of a childless couple who hide a young Jewish man in their apartment during the Nazi occupation of Czechoslovakia. Although comedic at times, the film explores the cooperation among members of the small town and their reliance on one another not only to survive, but to make life bearable as well. By the end of the film the interdependence of the townspeople saves most of them. It is perhaps instructive that although the English-language title of the film is *Divided We Fall,* the Czech title translates more literally as "We Must Help One Another."

Lest we think that this is simply wishful storytelling, the documentary *Stranded Yanks: A Diary between Friends* (2002) tells the story of Canadians who helped stranded Americans in the aftermath of the September 11, 2001, terrorist attacks. After the attacks, the United States closed its airspace to all incoming airplanes, so that many, particularly those from Europe, were forced to divert to Canadian airports. Passengers, mostly Americans, were forced to spend several days in Maritime Canadian cities and towns to wait for the reopening of American airspace. The documentary chronicles how several Canadians spontaneously and willingly helped Americans during their enforced stay.

In world politics, it is worth mentioning that Canadian-American cooperation is not limited to a few occasional dramatic events. In fact, cooperation is an ongoing process. The countries enjoy the world's longest unfortified border and a series of agreements that define their relationship.[26] One of those cooperative efforts, NORAD, was evident on September 11, 2001. NORAD, which allows for joint and integrated defense of the two countries, played an important part in safeguarding the airspace of the United States following the terrorists' attacks.[27] So well integrated are the two countries that the international border often runs through the middle of towns, which requires ongoing cooperation between local and national governments. The short documentary *Two Countries, One Street* (1955) visits the border towns of Rock Island, Stanstead, and Beebe, Quebec; and Derby Line, Vermont, to chronicle how those on opposite sides of the border cooperate. As the documentary points out, this case is not unique, as there are about seventy-five places along the border that have similar circumstances.[28]

This type of cooperation is not limited to the United States and Canada; other pairs of countries, like Australia and New Zealand and France and Britain, have extremely close and cooperative arrangements.[29] Of course this is not to imply that everything is perfect between these countries or that they never disagree. On the contrary, they do, quite often. But these countries have developed mechanisms and practices that allow them to solve their differences peacefully and efficiently.[30]

Cooperation in International Institutions

Although newspapers, cable television, and the nightly news do not often feature cooperation, world politics is full of examples of it. The previous chapters have been concerned with conflict, specifically wars and the threat of wars. After so much emphasis on war and conflict, it is difficult to convince people that wars are not very common. In fact it is far more likely for countries to engage in trade with each other than war. Nearly all the countries of the world belong to organizations such as the United Nations, the World Food Programme, the Universal Postal Union, and the World Meteorological Organization. All of these organizations help to facilitate cooperation and stability among states. Yet most people do not even know that some of these organizations exist, and if they do, they rarely hear of them.

It is similar to the complaint often heard about local media: Where is the good news? Think about what is shown during the nightly news: typically, the news leads with murder, mayhem, corruption, and vice ("If it bleeds, it leads"). Rarely do stories about people working together to build a playground or volunteering at libraries make the news, and certainly not the lead story. It is the same with international institutions. States create organizations to perform a task that the states believe need attention. Institutions, at their heart, are designed to minimize conflicts and maximize cooperation in world politics. The use of international institutions, such as the United Nations, is a relatively recent development.[31]

Cooperation in international institutions is not necessarily easy. In agreeing to cooperate with one another, there is a potential that one becomes more vulnerable, which is the cost associated with cooperation. If we think of marriage as a cooperative enterprise, then each participant begins to rely on his or her partner more and more. This does mean each is vulnerable to the other. In world politics, countries might cooperate, but they are increasingly sensitive to their partners. As cooperation endures, the impact is lasting and routine.

Organizing cooperation among many states offers specific problems that are vexing. The nature of sovereignty means that no outside force can compel a state to do anything against its wishes. This is designed to prevent states from being treated unfairly; however, it does give each state extraordinary power to control the agenda and actions of an international institution. Essentially, sovereignty implies that each state can exercise a veto over the decisions and actions of an international institution. Thus, what has happened in the development of international institutions is a move toward majority decision making in order to get things done.[32]

The process of cooperation is predicated on each participant working together with the others, and some mechanism must be worked out about how to make decisions for the group. If there are only two players in a cooperative enterprise, then the decision-making process is relatively easy: mutual consent. But the nature of organizations is that there are usually more than two participants. There are several methods to make decisions in international institutions: a single decider, majoritarian rule, or consensus.

The first method, allowing a single member of the organization to make a decision based on strength, expertise, or capability, is not often thought of as a cooperative process. Instead, the single decider might give a brief nod to cooperation, arguing that he or she is making decisions based on the needs of all. Yet, if not everyone has a say in the process, there is no guarantee that all concerns will be heard. The single decider could believe that he or she has the best interest of the group at heart; however, without the input of others, some individuals can feel left out of the process of decision making and therefore become alienated.[33]

The father in a "traditional" family in a Hollywood picture is typically depicted as a single decider. For example, Alonzo Smith (Leon Ames) in the musical *Meet Me in St. Louis* (1944), set at the turn of the twentieth century, decides unilaterally that he will accept a promotion and move his entire family to New York. While he has the family's financial interests at heart, his method of decision making is uncooperative because it does not include the desires or needs of the others, leading to alienation and anger. His daughter, Esther (Judy Garland), and wife, Anna (Mary Astor), have their own reasons for staying in St. Louis, not the least of which is the coming of the 1904 World's Fair. By not consulting others, Smith's actions seem overbearing, and he borders on being a bully. Although it is an option, sovereignty dictates that single-decider decision-making processes are uncommon in modern international institutions.

To overcome the problem of voices not being heard, states construct cooperative relationships in international institutions that take into account the voices of many. Democratic governments are often born on this principle. We generally accept that majority rule allows for concerns and problems to be heard and discussed. International cooperation can be arranged on a basis such as this. Yet one of the drawbacks is that a decision taken might not have the backing of all the affected members; in the worst-case scenario almost 50 percent could disagree. The minority is at risk of what de Tocqueville called suffering under the "tyranny of the majority."[34] On top of this, the concept of sovereignty rarely allows a simple majority decision to be the basis of a cooperative arrangement. Decision-making procedures in international organizations can take on complex processes because of sovereignty and past experiences. For example, the United Nations Security Council makes decisions by a super majority (nine of fifteen members), with the five permanent members, China, France, Russia, the United Kingdom, and the United States, having a veto over any action taken. This arrangement was arrived at because these countries were, at the end of the Second World War, thought to be the most powerful countries in the international system. Similarly, decision making in the European Union is notoriously complex and difficult to understand. On some issues, qualified majority voting (QMV), a practice of weighted voting based on the size of the population of each member state, is employed. On other issues consensus is required to make decisions.[35] The reason is because to make decisions, consideration must be given to relationships and history.

There are several films that remind the viewer about unheard voices or ideas not considered in democratic systems. Many of these films fall under the human rights paradigm (considered in chapter 13). For example, as depicted in *Mississippi Burning* (1988), the majority of people in Mississippi were in favor of denying African Americans their political rights prior to the civil rights movement of the 1960s. This is but one example of an instance in which a minority might have a good idea but the idea is not popular with the majority. A more humorous case of this is seen in the classic *Simpsons* episode "Marge vs. the Monorail" (1993). When the town of Springfield receives a windfall, Marge Simpson wants the money spent on fixing potholes in the city's streets; instead, the residents vote for the seemingly glamorous new monorail system—with disastrous results.

The final option is that all decisions must be made by consensus. Under such a mechanism, decisions can be slow to evolve and require much negotiation. In a process where decisions must be made by consensus, some participants might be impatient with the pace of decision making. Some might argue that consensus is a sign of a weak institution; however, others would contend that consensus satisfies everyone's needs, and the decisions agreed upon will be very strong. Yet consensus also means that everyone in the decision-making process essentially has a veto.

A prominent cooperative organization that requires consensus decision making is the North Atlantic Treaty Organization (NATO). Members of the organization pledge mutual defense with one another, in essence saying that a military attack on one member of the alliance is tantamount to an attack on all the members. Decisions at NATO on specific tasks or goals are subject to consensus: that is, all members must agree.

The comedy *Waking Ned Devine* (1998) illustrates the importance and complications of consensus decision making. The residents of a village on a small island in Ireland discover that a local man has won the national lottery. Unfortunately, the man who has won, Ned Devine, dies of a heart attack upon learning of this luck. If the lottery officials find out the winner is dead, then the money will be returned to the pot. Knowing this, two men in the village set out to convince the rest of the population to put up an imposter pretending to be Ned Devine and split the money equally among all the residents. Each of the villagers has a veto over the process because any one of them could tell the lottery agent of the fraud.

Some Final Thoughts

Sometimes cooperation occurs where we least expect it. As noted above, there are instances, such as during a war, where cooperation occurs between seeming adversaries. On occasions there is cooperation between groups that, at first glance, appear to be hostile toward one another; however, if they have a common purpose or desire, then it is logical to assume that they might overcome their differences to participate in a cooperative enterprise. *Pray the Devil Back to Hell* (2008) is a powerful documentary that explains how Christian and Muslim women worked together to bring about peace in Liberia. The film features the activism of Leymah Gbowee, who organized prayer meetings and eventually a sex strike among the women of Liberia to achieve peace. At first there was suspicion among the women, but ultimately they worked together, using peaceful and imaginative means, to force a peace settlement between the warring factions of the country. Eventually, the women worked to elect Ellen Johnson Sirleaf as president of Liberia in 2005—she became the first female to be elected as head of a government in Africa.

With the success of the film, the election of Sirleaf, and worldwide publicity, many took notice of the nonviolent tactics employed by the women of Liberia. Both Gbowee and Sirleaf made television appearances in the United States on programs such as *The Daily Show with Jon Stewart* and *The Colbert Report*. In 2011 the two women, along with activist Tawakul Karman of Yemen, were awarded the Nobel Peace Prize for their work. The award was in recognition not only of the peace process that helped to end the war in Liberia, but of the cooperative efforts the women employed to ensure peace instead of confrontational measures.

Does cooperation lead to peace? Maybe. There are a number of theorists and thinkers who have argued that the two things are related. David Mitrany argues that if cooperation could exist on a technical level, then it would have a spillover effect into other realms. He suggests that states should cooperate on technical, noncontroversial issues as the basis of beginning other cooperative ventures. By focusing on technical issues, removing "political" considerations from cooperative ventures, then peace can be established.[36] Indeed, some political scientists have pointed to evidence that the more emphasis there is on interdependent and shared joint memberships in international organizations, the less likely two states are to go to war.[37]

Based on a novel by H. G. Wells, the film *Things to Come* (1936) imagines overcoming nationalist differences to allow people to cooperate, eventually eliminating the need for war. Wells (and the film) believed in a strategy similar to Mitrany's functionalism, that focusing on technical issues that would benefit all humans would eventually eliminate the need for war.[38] The film argues that war was fought not on behalf of people, but for crude political ends instead. By the end of the film, although war nearly destroys human civilization, people create a future where they can live wealthy, peaceful, and secure lives—and scientists lead society rather than politicians.

Whether this is merely utopia-inspired thinking or actually possible is a matter of some debate, but the evidence clearly demonstrates some positive attributes to international cooperation. It is important to note that there are two forms of cooperation: that between antagonists and that between friends.[39] During the cold war, at a time when both the Soviet Union and the United States were ready to engage in a devastating nuclear war, the two countries cooperated on occasion if it was in their mutual interest to do so. For example, there were spy swaps[40] and cooperation in nuclear proliferation and safety. As another example, despite the animosity and frequent name-calling between the two, Cuba and the United States cooperate on a myriad of issues, especially migration, drugs, and terrorism.[41] These are instances of cooperation between antagonists.

On the other hand is cooperation between friends. There are some countries, like the United States and Canada, that have developed such highly complex and cooperative relationships that it is virtually unimaginable they would ever resort to war. While this relationship may be an anomaly, several other countries continually cooperate with one another in several areas. In fact, global cooperation in trade is ubiquitous. It is also worth noting that despite the media reports to the contrary, far more countries cooperate with one another than go to war. Yet it depends on one's perspective which is the more dominant force in world politics: cooperation or conflict.

Part 3

CHALLENGES IN MODERN WORLD POLITICS

9

IRANIAN CINEMA

Iran has been viewed, from the perspective of most people in the West, as perhaps the least cooperative country in the world. The actions of the government appear erratic and nonsensical, especially to those not familiar with Iran's recent history. Yet Iran's history with major powers, its flirtations with democratic rule, and the role of political repression in various Iranian governments have played significant roles in creating modern Iranian politics.[1] Examining the national cinema of a single country can be helpful to understanding the politics and political culture of that country. That being said, it is simply fallacious that watching a single film, or even a handful of films, from a certain country will allow you to understand the politics of that country. Viewing films from a country allows us to glimpse conversations and perspectives—we do not always understand the context of the conversations, but it provides a starting point for further appreciation.

It is probably no surprise that cinema in Iran is political. This applies to the making of films as well as the subject matter of particular films. Even under the shah, prior to the Islamic Revolution of 1979, films were subject to censorship, and overt criticism of the government was not allowed. Filmmakers in the country began using techniques and stories to convey their political views without expressing them directly.

Iranian cinema tends to focus on common people, unlike the case of Western films, whose characters are often the best, bravest, or brightest. The story in a typical Iranian film takes place in a rural village or on nondescript city streets, instead of the imagined worlds or unrealistically idealized versions of reality popular in the West.[2] At first glance, many of the stories appear to be simple tales; however, upon scratching the surface, one finds they make larger points about universal themes.[3] Because the number of people who speak Farsi is relatively small, the target audience is not as widespread, and the budgets of Iranian films are typically not very big. Nevertheless, the stories are often mesmerizing and complex despite the focus on everyday people.

As Iranian directors gained the attention of international critics in the early 1970s, more and more Iranian films began to be screened internationally. The release of the highly acclaimed *Gaav* (The Cow, 1969), directed by Dariush Mehrjui, which examined the close, some might say obsessive, relationship between a farmer and his cow, was delayed by the government of the shah because it accurately depicted the poverty of the country.[4] Despite the international success of *The Cow,* audiences in Iran largely ignored the film, preferring to buy tickets to see American or Indian films.[5]

Since the 1979 revolution that brought the Islamic theocracy to power, filmmakers have had to adapt to specific regulations and rules that promoted the regime's religious views. For example, women, who are required to be veiled only in public in Iran, were required to wear veils in films regardless of whether the scene took place in public or at home. There can be no fraternization between men and women, and definitely no sexual situations.[6] The restrictions mean that Iranian cinema has a different look and feel from Western cinema.

A theme expressed in many Iranian films is the tension between modern culture and Islam as understood by the revolutionary regime. The controversial film *Adam Barfi* (The Snowman, 1994) is a comedy that follows the attempts of a man to get a visa to work in the United States. During his adventures and travails to obtain the visa, he dresses as a female, something deemed decidedly un-Islamic. Although the story has the protagonist fall in love with an Iranian woman, and he eventually decides to stay in Iran, the film was initially banned. Once *The Snowman* was released in 1997, it was very popular in Iran, although it was not without controversy.[7]

Other films directly challenge the current standards of the society. The disarming comedy *Offside* (2006) follows women who dress as boys in an attempt to watch the World Cup qualifying game between Iran and Bahrain in June 2005.[8] Since women are forbidden to attend men's sporting matches, their attempts to gain entrance are illegal. After a group of women is detained by guards, all the characters seem to perform their duties stoically, albeit halfheartedly. At one point a woman who has been detained asks one of the guards if he would allow a Japanese woman to enter the stadium. He says he would, but his logic for doing so becomes very contorted. As one reviewer put it, all the soldiers really want to do is have some peace to enjoy the game.[9] As the women, and the soldiers who guard them, celebrate the success of the Iranian team, the story establishes a clear dilemma. Ultimately, all—men and women—are proud of their homeland and they support their football/soccer team with patriotic zeal, but the rules of the society make it hard to do so.[10] Other films, such as the drama *Jodaeiye Nader az Simin* (A Separation, 2011), examine how complexities of Iranian society manifest themselves in different groups of people and the conflicts emerging from these differences.

Still other films are veiled critiques of the regime. *Raye Makhfi* (Secret Ballot, 2001) illustrates the process of holding an election in a rural underdeveloped region, the politics of gender in a theocratic state, and the promised benefits of democratic rule. The story is of a female election agent (Nassim Abdi) who is sent to the remote islands off the coast of Iran to collect votes on election day. Her guide is a soldier (Cyrus Abidi) who has been assigned to protect the area from smugglers. One of the subtexts of the film is that it is clear the soldier does not like working with a woman. The message of the film is that the elections do not matter and that the immediate concerns of people (their jobs, their lives, and their survival) outweigh their interest in voting. At one point the soldier asks why there are elections every four years; because it is the law, replies the agent. When they are driving through the desert their jeep comes to a stoplight in the middle of the desert. The solider waits until the stoplight turns green even though there are no cars within miles. The agent asks him to drive on because it is ridiculous to have a traffic light there, but the soldier reminds her that it is the law. This is the way the soldier demonstrates the arbitrary nature of the law and of how little use it is to the people.

Some films help to demonstrate the diversity of Iran. Approximately 10 percent of the population of Iran is Kurdish. Films like *Zamni barayé masti asbha* (A Time for Drunken Horses, 2000), *Gomgashte dar Aragh* (Marooned in Iraq,[11] 2002), and *Lakposhtha parvaz mikonand* (Turtles Can Fly, 2004), all of which were directed by Bahman Ghobadi, offer stories about a distinctive minority whose people live not only in Iran but in Iraq, Turkey, and Syria as well. These three films focus on a people who manage to survive persecution, poverty, and war while maintaining a distinct cultural life.

While technically not Iranian cinema, films from the Iranian diaspora also help to shape an international view of Iran.[12] The very popular *Persepolis* (2007) tells the story of the Iranian revolution from the point of view of a young girl who grew up during it. Based on the graphic novel of the same name by Marjane Satrapi, this animated film depicts the excesses of the Iranian revolution and catalogues the experiences of a young woman living in Iran at that time. But the film is not a complete indictment of Iran: Marjane, who spends time in the West, finds it narcissistic, and she continues to celebrate Iranian culture as well.

These films give the viewer a more complex view of a country that appears difficult at best. The combination of understanding the context of films and the history of Iran serves to better understand the country. Regardless of the Westerner's own interpretation or view of Iran, these films assist in analyzing the perspective of the Iranian people, if not of the government. As noted in previous chapters, there are often significant barriers to cooperation between different political and cultural entities; understanding the culture of a country through its art—in this case films—can help all sides overcome those barriers.

10

PATTERNS OF CONSUMPTION AND POVERTY

Economics is an important and vital part of world politics. As international trade has flourished, the citizens of many developed countries have enjoyed an ever-increasing standard of living. A great deal of this growth has depended on a consumer-driven economy in which the health of the economy is linked to consumer spending.[1] At the other end of the spectrum there are places on the planet in which people live in desperate poverty. Both ends of the spectrum of economic development have implications for world politics. This chapter explores some of those implications. Certainly, different theoretical perspectives view the implications differently. Nevertheless, one can observe that regions of poverty and wealth can foster transnational issues such as immigration, an illegal drug trade, and human trafficking. It is also likely to highlight the disparity of consumption between rich and poor.

The Consumer Society: Yesterday and Today

During the cold war period there was a focus on a highly intrusive government in films of the future. As examined in chapter 3, several films examined the possibility of severely reduced freedom for humans. During the first decade of the twenty-first century, it seems that there was much more of a focus on intrusive corporations, ubiquitous advertising, and a breakdown of civil society in films.[2] Benjamin Barber has examined the likely effects of growing globalization in today's world and concluded that there are imperatives that make developed parts of the world's economy reach for more standardization and homogenization. The effect, Barber argues, will be a backlash from both within and outside and a reduction of choices for consumers.³ Barber believes that there will be a reaction against this sameness; people will fight on behalf of localized identities.

Barber's assertion that the more corporations and globalization grow, the fewer choices consumers will have seems paradoxical and counterintuitive at first. When modern consumers walk into a store, they are inundated and overwhelmed with choices. In supermarkets, there is a veritable cornucopia of food and food products. But, especially with products, consumers are asked to spend their money in certain ways. Technological innovations mean that consumers spend more money getting the latest gadget; new innovations mean that iPods replaced MP3s, which replaced CDs, which replaced records, and Blu-ray has begun to replace DVDs, which replaced VHS. In each case, the consumer buys new hardware to use the technology and eventually repurchases much of the software (movie and music collection).

Or consider the automobile industry: there are literally dozens of automobile types and models for the consumer to choose from. However, for most people in North America, not owning an automobile is unthinkable. Public transportation is not readily available or convenient for most of the population. The automobile industry has been accused of driving public transportation out, buying passenger train and subway lines so that they would be eliminated as competition and people would be forced to buy automobiles as transportation. The idea that the automobile industry would buy up public transportation options in the United States to increase its market share forms the mystery of the film *Who Framed Roger Rabbit* (1988). The film is probably best known for its mixture of live action and animated characters, drawing on famous cartoon characters of Hollywood's past, including Mickey Mouse, Bugs Bunny, and Betty Boop. While the live-action detective Eddie Valiant (Bob Hoskins) works to determine who is behind the framing of the animated character Roger Rabbit for murder, he uncovers a plot to destroy Toontown (where all the animated characters live) in order to build a brand-new modern highway. Early in the film, when asked why he does not have a car, Eddie replies he has no need for a car because Los Angeles has the best public transportation system in the world. In explaining his plan to redevelop Toontown, Judge Doom lays out a vision of a freeway where there are detours along the way for people to shop, fill their cars with gas, and eat fast food. Since he is acquiring Toontown, he stands to make a fortune from the home of the cartoon characters.⁴

The corporate culture, in which employees are socialized to work and act in ways that benefit the corporation, as opposed to self or community interests, has often been a target of filmmakers. *Local Hero* (1983) is a film delving into the effects of corporate culture and the oil industry on people, business, and the environment. The film establishes a classic culture-clash story in which an American executive, Mac MacIntyre (Peter Riegert), is sent to Scotland to buy up a town along the North Sea so that his company can build an oil refinery. Mac is eager to please his bosses and clearly relishes his corporate lifestyle; however, his visit to the small Scottish town of Ferness changes his outlook on life, even though the townspeople seem inclined to accept the offer of being bought out. Environmentalism is one of the themes of *Local Hero:* the local residents live close to the land and are more aware of the impact of nature.[5]

A strange occurrence throughout the film is that from time to time military jets fly overhead on the way to bomb an empty beach for target practice. One can hear the bombs going off in the background. Townspeople take this as normal; Mac is a little surprised by the random bombings, at one point commenting, "The jets spoil a really nice area." He does not seem to realize that his corporate mission will facilitate the same thing: if he is successful in buying the town, this "really nice area" will become an oil refinery. More subtly, the filmmakers are reminding us of a more obscure point, the relationship between oil and the military. The military does not work without oil, and the military needs to secure and protect oil supplies. The corporate protagonists and the villagers of *Local Hero* find some happiness with a return to nature and to a consideration of factors other than money as important.[6]

After the collapse of Communism in Eastern Europe in 1989, many citizens wanted something that had been in short supply in the days of Communism: consumer goods. Some have worried that the pendulum has swung to the opposite extreme; instead of having no consumer items, perhaps people are now too focused on having consumer goods. *Ceský sen* (Czech Dream, 2004) is a final student project by two students from the Czech Film Academy. Their goal in the film is to explore how the onset of Western-style consumerism affected the citizens of the Czech Republic. The filmmakers create a fictitious hypermarket (superstore) called the Czech Dream, hiring a consulting firm to make their enterprise seem real, and begin an advertising campaign to alert the public to its existence. Image makers begin to transform the two film students into real managers, complete with business clothes and professional headshots.

In watching the film, it is difficult not to have some sympathy with those who show up looking for free gifts and incredible prices on items such as steaks. Nevertheless, the filmmakers' point is to demonstrate the effects of advertising on people. They are making the argument that shopping has become a pastime for many Czechs. Instead of pursuing hobbies such as hiking, music, and gardening, people are turning to shopping as a distraction from life.

The film demonstrates how advertisers lead people to think that they need material items to fulfill their lives, or to stress how they are getting a good bargain. The advertising theme song is not overly subtle; its intent is clear

> It will be a nice big bash
> And if you got no cash
> Get a loan and scream
> I want to fulfill my dream!

The song is clearly a parody designed to mock how much people are willing to go into debt to acquire stuff. But the point of the film is that consumers are so caught up in the trappings of perception and lifestyle that they do not consider the implications of overconsumption.

The pursuit of commodities takes on interesting dimensions in Eastern Europe. If *Czech Dreams* documents the way in which consumer goods are status symbols in post-Communist countries, the Polish film *Galerianki* (Mall Girls, 2009) demonstrates the length to which some will go to acquire those goods. In the film, teenage girls provide sexual favors for men in mall restrooms in exchange for jewelry and clothes. Although the film is fictional, it is based on an actual phenomenon in Poland: young women prostitute themselves for cell phones and shoes. The "Mall Girls" do not consider themselves prostitutes, arguing that in order to live in an expensive city like Warsaw and to be accepted as cool, they must have those things.[7] The film raised a national debate in Poland about the nature of consumerism and the role of parents in post-Communist Poland.[8] Sex as a commodity is seen in the dark film *Lilya 4-ever* (2002) as well. Set in Estonia, the film follows sixteen-year-old Lilya, who has been abandoned after her mother leaves her to seek a better life in the United States. Left alone with nothing, Lilya relies on her good looks and body to make her way. She is persuaded to go to Sweden, where she dreams of a better life in the West; however, she falls into the trap of sex slavery, drug and alcohol use, and a tragic fate.

Of course the problem of overconsumerism is not limited to former Communist countries. A consumer economy is the basis for most advanced Western economies in today's world. For example, consumer spending accounts for two-thirds of the American economy; therefore, for the economy to grow consumers must spend more. This feeds into a scenario in which the culture of the society is to acquire "things." This has the effect of creating a culture dependent on convincing more and more people to buy more and more items. Advertising becomes ubiquitous—and so does the urge to spend.[9]

Films as Consumerism

Films, especially in the United States, are often seen as promoting certain lifestyles and consumer products. The practice—discreet but deliberate—of placing recognizable product brands in films to heighten their market appeal has become common. Thus, the use of Reese's Pieces in *E.T.: The Extra-Terrestrial* (1982), Diet Pepsi in *Back to the Future* (1985), and Mac computers in *Independence Day* (1996) is not mere coincidence but a designed attempt to connect the products with the emotions the audience experiences during the film. The pressure to spend, and to have, has created what some have called a consumer culture in which promotion comes easy. It has led some to argue that the propaganda of the twenty-first century is not a political propaganda, but propaganda to spend.

A slew of documentaries in the 1990s and 2000s questioned the effects of consumer culture in the United States and beyond and took aim at corporations that were thought to promote this culture, even to the detriment of the American people. One favorite target of documentary filmmakers is Wal-Mart. The film *Wal-Mart: The High Cost of Low Price* (2005) chronicled the perceived detriments of opening Wal-Marts across the United States, including elimination of business taxes for local communities, an unsafe work environment, and negative environmental consequences. Even the venerable public television program *Frontline* produced "Is Wal-Mart Good for America?" (2005), which argued that the chain's reliance on China for low-cost products had a negative effect on the American economy. The American fast food company McDonald's came under scrutiny in the documentary *Super Size Me* (2004) in which the director Morgan Spurlock spends a month eating nothing but food from McDonald's. By the end of the month Spurlock, an otherwise extremely healthy individual, is advised to revise his diet because his life is potentially in danger. Over the course of the film, Spurlock examines how advertising impacts patrons.

The message of these films is that society is cheapened as consumers pursue ever-increasing amounts of products and goods at ever-lower prices. The pursuit of such things inevitably has consequences, undermining local economies, producing higher levels of consumer debt, damaging the environment, and making people unhealthy. Does the attainment of material goods make consumers happy? Typically, the way the world assesses success (or development) is by measuring how much money the society produces. But economic wealth does not readily translate into economic happiness. During times of economic stress, films sometimes make the claim that money does not bring happiness. Thus, during the Great Depression, American films would pose happy poor people against discontented and cynical wealthy people. The 1938 film *You Can't Take It with You* explored the themes of wealth versus happiness, ending with some indeterminate conclusions. In the film Jimmy Stewart plays the son of a wealthy tycoon interested in acquiring the home of an eccentric family that cares little for money. The message at the end of the film seemed to suggest that both wealth and happiness are good; however, you are likely to be a better person if you are poor.

Consumption and the Future

If people are overly concerned with acquiring status through the accumulation of goods, then an argument could be made about the eventual coarseness of society. This argument forms the basis of the little-regarded film *Idiocracy* (2006). Director Mike Judge, who also wrote and directed *Office Space* (1999) and the television series *King of the Hill* (1997–2009), presents a dystopian view of the world five hundred years in the future in which the average intelligence of people has declined precipitously. The film is a satire of the current culture of immediacy, lack of depth, and conspicuous consumption.

The premise of the film is that a completely average man, Joe Bauers (played by Luke Wilson), and a prostitute, Rita (Maya Rudolph), are recruited by the military to be kept in suspended animation for a year. Through a series of unlikely events, the pair is awoken in the year 2505. Rita and Joe's chambers are dislodged when garbage stacked for centuries creates the great garbage avalanche of 2505.

The future, according to the film, is vulgar and rude. While this may seem an exaggeration, some would contend that there exists a celebration of the uninformed, particularly in American culture and cinema. Films such as *Forrest Gump* (1994) and *The Curious Case of Benjamin Button* (2008) suggest that characters do not need to be intelligent to survive and even thrive in the modern world.

Eventually Joe is brought to the White House because it turns out he is the smartest person in the world. He joins the White House staff, which is composed of several not very bright people. The world is facing a food-shortage crisis and Joe is enlisted to figure out why the plants will not grow. The problem largely lies in the materialistic culture, which through advertising hypes artificial ingredients as more beneficial than natural products (similar to the marketing techniques exposed in *Super Size Me*)—therefore people erroneously think the unnatural is preferable.

The world painted by director Mike Judge is a stark and stinging indictment of current cultural trends, particularly the traits of an overconsumptive society inundated with ubiquitous advertising. The puerile flatulence and sex jokes are not meant to be funny to the audience; they are supposed to be a demonstration of what the people of the twenty-sixth century would likely find funny.

The story of the distribution of *Idiocracy* is perhaps as telling as the message itself. After seeing a preview of the film, 20th Century Fox, the production company, stopped production, refusing to release it for two years. In fact, the film that now exists on DVD and is shown on cable television is an incomplete version. When the studio did release the film, it appeared on very few movie screens and then Fox sent it for DVD release very quickly. This has raised questions about the motivations of 20th Century Fox. Some writers point out that advertisers were probably unhappy about the portrayal of their products in the film. If this is true, companies mentioned in the film must have contacted Fox to demand that the film be withdrawn. Others have pointed to the portrayal of Fox News in the film, anchored by a shirtless male wrestler and a vacuous, big-haired, big-bosomed female anchor. Since Fox News Channel and 20th Century Fox are owned by the same parent company (News Corporation), some wonder if the film was downplayed by intra-corporation politics. Yet others have claimed that the message of the film is such a serious indictment of American culture that no studio would want to take a chance on offending the common people in the United States.[10] Nevertheless, the film developed a cult following and frequently airs on cable television.

The world in *Idiocracy* is not too dissimilar from the future imagined by the Disney-Pixar feature *Wall-E* (2008). Set several hundred years in the future, the film opens with the protagonist, a tiny and lone robot called Wall-E, routinely sorting the trash and cleaning up the detritus of a decadent world. The little robot's mission is to mop up after humans because they have so polluted the planet that it has become unlivable. Wall-E has developed a habit of sorting through the trash for interesting and useful items. Wall-E manages to maintain himself by stripping defunct robots of useful parts; he also collects intriguing items for his own amusement, including a videotape copy of *Hello Dolly!* which he plays frequently throughout the film.

Futurama, a television series created by Matt Groening (who also created *The Simpsons*), uses a similar technique to explore issues of overconsumption in the episode "A Big Piece of Garbage" (1999). New (New) York is under threat of a big ball of garbage sent into space centuries ago. When the characters land on the ball in an effort to destroy it, they discover the garbage is made up of worthless movie tie-in items, including Bart Simpson dolls. It is instructive that filmmakers understand the pointlessness of product tie-ins, yet the economics of the system help to drive the creation of productions and faux memorabilia.

An examination of the background shots of Wall-E's Earth reveals that most of the trash comes from an overconsumptive society.[11] There are very few signs of government in the film; instead, the Buy-N-Large Corporation takes an omnipresent role. Wall-E's existence on Earth is juxtaposed with scenes of the surviving humans who live on the space cruise liner *The Axiom.* The thousands of humans on the cruise liner use their all-access hover chairs to float around the ship. The hover chairs were originally designed for elderly people who were having trouble walking, but in the film everyone uses them, just as everyone is waited on by robot servants.[12] Much as in *Idiocracy,* intellectual curiosity has dropped precipitously on *The Axiom.* People spend their days roaming around on their hover chairs, talking to each other on computer screens (instead of face-to-face) and constantly imbibing smoothie-type drinks. At one point a passenger looks up from her computer screen and says that she has been too busy to notice that the ship has a pool.

This is a theme that has become more prevalent in film and television. For example, the episode "eDork" (2004) from the adult animated series *Aqua Teen Hunger Force* pokes fun at the trend of having more and more functions on cell phones. It seems the drive for new products is a matter of status rather than of function; consumers are motivated by a desire to acquire gadgets regardless of their ability to afford the items or even whether the technology is useful.[13] As Robert Putnam has pointed out, the increase in technology inevitably leads people to become more and more isolated.[14] While consumers might crave more technology, there are studies suggesting that the more "connected" we are, the less happy we become.[15]

Wall-E ends on an optimistic note; once humans leave their hover couches and begin to exercise, disengage from electronic communications, and reconnect with other humans, they can solve their problems. It is important to notice some of the other messages in the film, such as Wall-E continuing to operate for centuries because of solar power, and that cooperation and friendship can overcome a number of problems. Perhaps a more obscure reference in the film is the name of the space cruise liner, *The Axiom*. The word *axiom* is derived from a Greek word meaning "authority," suggesting that the story being told has some authority. Further, in logic and mathematics, an axiom is a statement whose truth is so obvious there is no need for proof. The filmmakers are pointing to serious issues they believe should not be overlooked.

The impact of *Wall-E* was substantial, and there have been several interpretations of the film. The film was released during the 2008 American presidential election; some pundits quickly latched onto the seeming most obvious message of environmentalism:[16] Many saw the film as pro-environmentalism and politically progressive; however, at least a few conservative commentators in the United States saw the film as an indictment not only of big business but of big government, which drives consumerism. The repeated viewings of *Hello Dolly!* by Wall-E represented a harkening back to "old fashioned and wholesome entertainment."[17] Although widely acclaimed, *Wall-E* was not universally praised; some considered the film a cop-out, letting humans off too easy and not taking consumers to task for the havoc they are creating.[18] It is interesting to note the contradiction between the message of the film and its marketing, which used crass consumerism methods (such as toys, games, and tie-ins) to promote the film, all of which would contribute to the amount of garbage created in the world and harkens back to the *Futurama* episode.

There are few films that explore cultures disengaged from consumer-driven mentality. Exceptions are films such as *Witness* (1985) and *Dances with Wolves* (1990), which celebrate cultures that are not a part of mainstream Western life. However, it is not as easy to disengage from the Western lifestyle and consumerism as one might think. The documentary film *No Impact Man* (2008) begins as a simple experiment of a family trying to have

no environmental impact whatsoever. What begins as a self-indulgent publicity ploy to sell a book proposal evolves into a thoughtful piece of cinema
in which one realizes how embedded American lives are in consumptive
patterns (the same could be said of *Food Inc.* [2008] as well). While the film's
participants, and the project itself, have been criticized for what seem to be
self-promotion measures, the documentary is a fascinating consideration
not only of humans' impact on the environment but also of the effects of
lifestyles on individuals.[19]

Missing from the Future?

Czech Dreams, Idiocracy, and *Wall-E* all examine the effects of consumerism
and a declining interest in things intellectual. The films specifically focus
on those of us who tend to overconsume, but most people on our planet
today do not live a life in which they are able to engage in the behaviors
that would lead to the problems depicted in the films. While at first glance
it might be easy to say that people who live in these regions have no effect
on international politics, the poorer areas of the world are often those where
problems such as political instability, the illegal drug trade, and increased
occurrences of diseases emerge. There are few, if any, films concerned with
the plight of people at the other end of the spectrum. But if the predicted
results of overconsumption come to pass, those who are desperately poor
would also suffer the fate shown in the films we have been examining. It is
interesting that the poor seem to be invisible in these films. For example,
we do not see the fate of people who are too poor to afford a luxurious life
aboard *The Axiom* in *Wall-E*. Left unstated is whether these people were left
to perish in a polluted world.

No doubt those who live in parts of the world that are extremely poor
would like to engage in the consumer society if given the opportunity.
And no doubt people from across the globe would prefer to consume the
food Westerners do and to enjoy their comforts and leisure activities as
well; however, most people are concerned with the day-to-day challenge
of merely surviving.[20] With widely available communication technologies,
the lifestyles of the more developed countries become advertisements for
poorer societies. Western cinema, particularly American film, has a broad
audience in lesser-developed countries and often has a detrimental impact.
Films that glorify the consumer society and overconsumption, like *Confessions of a Shopaholic* (2009) and *The Devil Wears Prada* (2006), are widely

available around the world through DVD. It is not unreasonable to assume that those who do not have that lifestyle might seek it through whatever means available, even if we consider those means illegal, whether through unauthorized immigration or other methods.[21]

There have been a number of classic films dealing with poverty in American cinema. Even some of the earliest American films explore the issue of poverty. In *The Kleptomaniac* (1905), a wealthy woman has a habit of stealing but is acquitted because she is rich; meanwhile a poor woman who steals bread to feed her two hungry children is convicted. The film concludes, not so subtly, that there is one law for the rich and another for the poor. American films of the 1920s were often concerned with poverty, especially when it came to dealing with young people who might find love across class lines.[22] The adaptation of John Steinbeck's novel *The Grapes of Wrath* (1940) is considered a classic of American cinema. Yet, it is not often that we see extreme poverty portrayed on film and television, at least in narrative stories.[23] Films usually do well if they accurately portray the lives of the audience, or if they encompass the audience's aspirations. Since most people who live in extreme poverty do not have the means to see films and television, it is uncommon to have films that focus on extreme poverty. On occasion, however, there are some fine examples of films that portray poverty and its effects on individuals and society.

While some who are reading this book may have known difficult times, it is safe to assume that most readers' lives are radically different from those in extreme poverty.[24] In 1999, 189 countries adopted eight Millennium Development Goals to achieve by 2015. The first goal was to eradicate extreme poverty and hunger. Members of the United Nations agreed to halve the number of people who live on less than $1 a day by the target date.[25] At the present writing, it appears the targets will not be met. People who live in extreme poverty face an uphill battle in escaping what has become known as the "poverty trap."[26] The more academic term for the poverty trap is *structural poverty,* the idea being that the structure of society, or people's lives, makes it extremely difficult to escape adverse circumstances. It has been argued that structural poverty is not a temporary problem that income alone will fix. The poor suffer from malnutrition and poor health care, and live in urban slums, all conditions difficult to escape. In addition, the structural poor are marginalized and have very little voice politically.[27]

Two films that explore the lives of those who live in severe poverty, and the implications of poverty, are *Cidade de Deus* (City of God, 2002) and

Slumdog Millionaire (2008). Both films have found a modicum of success at the box office, especially on the art-house circuit. *Slumdog Millionaire,* in fact, was well regarded enough to garner an Academy Award for Best Picture at the 2009 ceremonies. Likewise, *City of God* has won numerous awards and was nominated for four Oscars, including one for Fernando Meirelles for directing.

City of God takes place in a housing development outside Rio de Janeiro. The film opens with an armed standoff between a gang and the police, with the film's narrator, Rocket (Alexandre Rodrigues), caught between the two. Rocket, a photographer, recounts the story of the housing development, known as City of God, and how he came to be in his position. The story begins in the 1960s when three unemployed teenagers turn to petty crimes and eventually drug dealing. City of God becomes a war zone; the police are outmanned and outgunned. The situation is not dissimilar to that in northern Mexico in 2009–2011; drug money buys better weapons than those possessed by the police. The message of the film is clear: the circle of violence and poverty will continue and only a lucky few can escape.

The lives in *City of God* are so desperate that violence and crime seem almost natural to some as a way to escape the hardship of life. Reliance on drugs, even the marijuana smoked by Rocket, helps the characters in the film deal with the realities of their lives. In a paradox, the thing that provides people relief from their misery also fuels the misery of the housing complex and its inhabitants. Poverty, lack of education, and urban slums are particularly difficult to escape; drugs add another barrier to the mix. One of the taglines for the film, "If you run you're dead . . . if you stay, you're dead again," seems appropriate when discussing *City of God* and serves as a reminder of the difficulty of the poverty trap.

One could argue that *Slumdog Millionaire* is a more upbeat film, one that celebrates the survival of the human spirit in the face of overwhelming odds; others might say that it is overly romantic. Yet there are some very serious issues explored in the film, including the treatment of children and the use of torture in order to gain a confession. The film takes place in India and oscillates between the present and the past. What at first might be a little confusing to the viewer begins to reveal its importance as the film progresses. Jamal (Dev Patel) is a contestant on the Indian version of the game show *Who Wants to Be a Millionaire.* Each time he answers a question correctly he wins more money, but a wrong answer will leave him with nothing. Jamal is considered a "slumdog" because he grew up in the slums of Mumbai, where people's lives are considered to be no better than those of dogs.[28] As Jamal begins to win more and more money on the program, questions begin to arise over how someone with such limited opportunities and relatively little education is able to answer the increasingly difficult questions. Jamal is arrested on suspicion of cheating. After Jamal is unsuccessfully tortured for a confession, the investigating police officer begins to ask how he knows the answer to each question. As Jamal explains, each answer reveals a part of his past, and the sergeant—and the audience—begins to understand his story.

The film has a happy ending, albeit with some tragedy and self-sacrifice, but it might be more instructive to consider the plight of the child actors who played the younger versions of the protagonists after the film was released. Within two months of the Academy Award ceremony, ten-year-old Azharuddin Mohammed Ismail, who played one of the characters as a young child, had his shanty home destroyed by government officials in an effort to clean up the slums and get rid of illegally built homes. Then, in September 2009, Ismail lost his father to tuberculosis, a disease that is often successfully treated in the developed world. A few months earlier, the *News of the World*, a British tabloid, reported that the father of child actress Rubina Ali, who played Latika as a young child, had tried to sell the actress for approximately $300,000 to a journalist posing as a buyer. Reports surfaced to suggest that the father was willing to sell his daughter because he was too poor to take care of the young actress. Although the veracity of the story has been questioned, it did focus attention on the miserable conditions in which these actors lived despite the great international success of the film. Several media outlets carried the story of Rubina Ali's family when the young star was found to be living in a one-room shack flooded with ankle-high sewage water filled with rats and scorpions.[29]

Slumdog Millionaire is a compelling story, albeit a highly improbable one; however, the reality of poverty, child exploitation, and gangs is indisputable. Many have argued that *Slumdog Millionaire* gives people unrealistic hope for escaping the bonds of poverty. *City of God* is probably much closer to reality than *Slumdog*. Nevertheless, both films allow us to glimpse a part of the world that few of us experience.

Some Final Thoughts

The implications of these divergent patterns of consumption might play a significant role in twenty-first-century world politics. If the consumption patterns of those in the developed parts of the world lead to environmental degradation and resource scarcity, the effects of environmental disasters and resource competition will be felt worldwide. If crass consumerism leads to a decline in intellectual curiosity, the ability to solve major world issues becomes problematic. If, on the other hand, extreme poverty continues in many parts of the world, the associated effects (including increased drug trade, political violence, and disease) are equally likely to spill over into the rest of the world.[30] A final point to consider: What might be the reaction of those who do not enjoy the consumption of many goods to those who do? Will those who do not have, who find life a constant struggle, envy or resent those who live in luxury? Although the effects might be debatable, the difference between extreme poverty and mass consumption will no doubt help to shape the future of world politics.

11

HUMAN MIGRATION

Immigration, Emigration, and Refugees

While media accounts might give a different impression, migration in world politics is not new, nor is it limited to a single set of destinations. In fact, migration has happened as long as humans have inhabited the Earth. With globalized travel, levels of immigration currently are at historically high levels, so much so that immigrants constitute a substantial portion of the world's population.[1] Since it lends itself to dramatic and cinematic depiction, migration has been a topic that has been explored many times throughout the history of film.[2] In the classic days of Hollywood film there were several actors who posed as "immigrants" who would occasionally show up on the screen in familiar roles that ingrained themselves into the imaginations of the picture-going audience. Some were actual immigrants. The first superstar of the global film industry, Charlie Chaplin, was an immigrant from Great Britain. His tramp character would become iconic and is still recognized a century later. Others, like El Brendel and Chico Marx, would use faux accents and attire to create the illusion of being an immigrant. El Brendel, who is largely forgotten today, used a broken Swedish accent to create humorous situations but was actually born in Philadelphia. Chico Marx, born in New York and part of the famous Marx Brothers, used a fake Italian accent to create mayhem in several films. For example, in *Monkey Business* (1931), Chico purposely misconstrues some words in order to confuse Groucho. The situation leads an exasperated Groucho to remark, "That's the problem with immigration." The line reflects one of the fears that lay behind the issue.[3]

Before beginning our survey of migration issues, it is important to define a few terms. *Immigration* usually refers to the movement of people into a territory that is not their own, primarily for economic purposes. *Emigration* refers to the process of leaving a country to go elsewhere, also usually for remunerative purposes.[4] As we will see, emigration can create difficulties for the sending countries, most notably the condition known as "brain drain." Because the persons most likely to emigrate, and in some instances most likely to be recruited to emigrate, are often the most educated and successful, many would argue that sending societies will lose their best and brightest in current migration practices.[5] A different category is encompassed in the term *refugees,* people forced to leave their home for fear of political reprisal if they remain, including loss of their lives.[6] Under international law, a refugee carries legal status, and states are obliged to act in a particular manner to protect those seeking asylum.

The political challenges of immigration in modern times are daunting. In the modern international system the concept of sovereignty means that counties create borders to define where a state's exclusive jurisdiction begins and ends. Theoretically, states are self-contained, and what passes across international borders—people and materials—is monitored and controlled; however, the amount of people and goods crossing the borders has burgeoned because of an increasingly interconnected world and economies, making monitoring and controlling difficult. Technology has changed how immigration occurs as well. A century ago, immigrants who left their country knew the chances were remote that they would ever see the friends and family they left behind again.

The topic of immigration has implications for states and individuals. How we define ourselves is a matter of identity politics. Our identity is shaped by our birth, our family, and our experiences. Immigration leads to interesting philosophic questions: Are our identities changeable? What is the effect around the world of identity politics? The film *The Infidel* (2010) explores some of these issues in a comedic way. It centers on a devout Muslim living in London who unexpectedly learns he is adopted and that his birth parents were Jewish. The protagonist spends the rest of the film questioning his identity and his place in society.[7] One of the reasons that immigration politics is salient is that current economic, migration, and business trends challenge notions of community, identity, and politics. This chapter will explore some of these issues. On the other hand, from an economic perspective, there are several motivating factors that help create immigrants and circumstances to facilitate their migration.

For many countries, questions about immigration have increased in recent times. Issues of migration and immigration test the boundaries of society. While modern technology and transportation make migration more common, the problems and feelings associated with immigration are nothing new. Many of the complaints about immigration focus on the perceived dilution of culture. This argument makes the case that newcomers will substantially change the politics and/or culture of the host country and adversely affect the social cohesion of a society. For instance, the influential political scientist Samuel Huntington argued that increasing immigration from Mexico is linguistically, demographically, and culturally changing the United States in ways that threaten to create new divisions within the country. He further argued that unlike previous waves of immigration, twenty-first-century migrants are not assimilating and this will have the effect of creating a bilingual society, which he believes is unsustainable.[8] Other voices that oppose immigration argue that immigrants create economic stress on the host society. Those who support immigration counter and refute these arguments. For instance, some analysts contend that immigration helps to keep inflation in check and that there is a positive economic impact.[9] To be sure, illegal immigration both in North America and Europe creates hostilities and leads to complex politics that seemingly pits due process and humane treatment against the observation of law and rules.[10] What makes the politics of immigration, and even illegal immigration, more complex is that there might be many hidden interests that would support the continuation of current policies.[11] Suffice it to say, the issue of immigration does not fit well into a single category and is a very sensitive issue in many countries because charges of xenophobia and racism often tinge the debate.

In order to explore the issues of immigration in modern world politics this chapter will first examine the Hollywood depiction of immigrants and American society. Because so many of the people who worked in Hollywood in the early days were émigrés, films about immigration had an important impact on American cinema. Next, the chapter will consider the issue of immigration in modern-day politics, focusing first on the United States and then considering immigration to Europe. The chapter will then turn to a discussion of the effects of emigration on those who are leaving their home countries. Before concluding, the chapter will also consider people who flee their country because they fear for their lives: refugees.

Hollywood, History, and Immigration

The development of cinema coincided with a major wave of immigration to the United States. In fact, many of the original Hollywood pioneers were immigrant entrepreneurs who created an industry that began attracting a migrant community. These "Hollywood Moguls," as they would come to be known, would emphasize the strategy of assimilation, meaning that immigrants should and would adopt the customs, practices, and language of American culture.[12] Doing so would ensure that the immigrant met with success and prosperity. Whether this was actually true is open to debate; however, many of the films in the first half of the twentieth century emphasized this conception.

In the early days of moviemaking, the new medium of the cinema facilitated the assimilation of newly arrived immigrants by attempting to educate them about American political culture. Alice Guy Blaché, a female pioneer in American cinema, directed one such film. *Making an American Citizen* (1912) opens in a foreign country (presumably Russia) where Ivan and his wife decide to move to the United States. Upon arriving, Ivan beats his wife on the docks in New York City (with the Statute of Liberty in the background); an upstanding American witnesses this abuse and stands up for the just treatment of women. The film encourages migrants to throw off their cultural traits of the past in favor of new, presumably better, American traits. By the end of this short film, a title card reads, "Completely Americanized!" and Ivan begins his new life in an American way.

The not-too-subtle message Blaché is conveying is that immigrants may have practices and habits that are distinctly not American, but once educated and trained these new immigrants will see the value of the American way of life. There is also a deeper message: as a female pioneer in the industry of cinema, Blaché is also arguing that equal rights for women, or at least the fair treatment of them, is patriotic. The Nineteenth Amendment to the Constitution, granting women's suffrage, would not be ratified until eight years after this film was released (in 1920).

Blaché was engaging in the debate about the values of the United States, and how immigrants should be introduced to those values. Often these early films cast the traditions and practices of other countries as barbaric and backward, contrasting them to American traditions, which were seen as progressive and enlightened. This theme can be observed in films such as *Sold for Marriage* (1916), in which a young Russian girl (Lillian Gish) is nearly forced to marry against her will upon arriving in the United States. The message of these films was that immigrants who had come seeking a better economic life were, as a bonus, finding a more enlightened culture as well. Note that this had the effect of privileging American culture and tradition over others.

Not only were new immigrants educated about American culture and practices in these early films, they would also be warned of potential dangers. In the film *Traffic in Souls* (1913), directed by George Loane Tucker, young Swedish immigrant women are warned about traveling alone for fear that they will be captured by white slavers, what is called today enforced prostitution or human trafficking. The film was produced in a pseudo-documentary style and warned both immigrants and the American public how thousands of young girls would disappear into prostitution.[13] Another popular film of the genre was *Inside the White Slave Traffic* (1913), which was filmed covertly and depicted how women were lured into enforced prostitution.

Perhaps the most famous immigration film of the early twentieth century was not a film lesson for immigrants but instead a mild critique of how American society treated them. Charlie Chaplin's *The Immigrant* (1917) merged the struggles immigrants faced with the pathos and comedy that became the hallmark of the filmmaker's career. Many filmgoers of the day were familiar with Chaplin's knockabout and roughhouse comedies. During this period Chaplin was under contract to produce twelve films for the Mutual Film Company, and he was beginning to experiment with social commentary through the use of comedy and pathos. His films were well produced and easy for audiences to understand and appreciate. While most of *The Immigrant* is a comedy about misplaced money and mean waiters, the story is established with Chaplin's tramp character joining a group of immigrants coming to the United States. Chaplin, himself an immigrant from Britain, wanted to point out the irony of the immigrants arriving in the "land of liberty" and the immigration authorities throwing a rope around them as if they were cattle.[14] During the rest of the film Chaplin does not engage in fantasies of immigrants getting rich and finding success—rather, the protagonist faces struggles, personal loss, and affronts from Americans. The immigrant does eventually find happiness in love, but not necessarily the financial windfall that many stories on the theme promised.

The Immigrant stands in contrast to many classic Hollywood films in which the immigrant and his or her experience are somewhat romanticized. For instance, in *I Remember Mama* (1948), the Norwegian Hanson family is depicted as scrupulously saving their money for any eventuality. At the same time their honesty and hard work demonstrate to the audience why they are invaluable to American society. Norwegian immigrants were also depicted favorably in *Our Vines Have Tender Grapes* (1945), in which the values of hard work and community are central.[15] *Yankee Doodle Dandy* (1942) depicts real-life Irish immigrant George M. Cohan and his wholehearted adoption of American culture, which was so thorough that he wrote many patriotic songs, including the film's namesake and the World War I anthem "Over There."[16] In *A Ship Comes In* (1928) a Russian family struggles, but through their honesty, earnestness, and work, they too are able to become good, upstanding Americans.[17]

The films above suggested that the lives of immigrants were difficult, but with hard work, acculturation, and good values the immigrant would persevere and prosper. Yet some films of the period did acknowledge that at times immigrants were mistreated, exploited, and had nowhere to turn for legal justice. It is interesting to note that several issues central to concerns over immigration today were also true fifty-plus years ago. For example, in the drama *I Cover the Waterfront* (1933), when a smuggler is about to be caught illegally bringing Chinese immigrants into the country, he throws them overboard to drown. In *Human Cargo* (1936), starring Claire Trevor, immigrants are killed by being thrown out of an airplane when the traffickers are in danger of being captured by the authorities. Currently, human traffickers and so-called coyotes take advantage of migrants and even kill in order to prevent capture. The taut drama *Border Incident* (1949) also portrays many themes today's audiences would recognize. The long wait to achieve legal American citizenship and the economic desperation of Mexican workers drive many to cross the border illegally. At the same time, there are criminal elements on the American side willing to take advantage of the illegal migrants. Ricardo Montalban stars as a police detective who joins a group of Mexican immigrants looking for work. A gang of American traffickers makes money on the illegal immigrants both ways, first by charging them to go across the border and then by robbing and killing them when they cross back into Mexico. Because the migrants are illegal, they cannot appeal to the police or other authorities for help.[18] Other films of the period tell similar stories. *Illegal Entry* (1949) is about a group that illegally smuggles immigrants into the United States. In one of the most stunning scenes of the film, the smugglers kill all the immigrants by dumping them out of an airplane over the Pacific Ocean when they believe they are being pursued. The short film *Forbidden Passage* (1941), part of MGM's Crime Does Not Pay series, warns of many of the same issues. Again, migrants who are desperate to enter the United States are taken advantage of by nefarious human traffickers who willingly kill the migrants, this time through drowning, rather than be captured by the police and authorities. The film won the Academy Award for Best Short Subject Film.

These films created an image of the immigrant as desirous to participate in American culture as well as take advantage of the economic opportunities of the United States. A common theme was that for the immigrant who assimilated as much as possible, life would be better. Those who did not assimilate could, and probably should, be viewed with suspicion. Elements of this conception can be seen in later classic films such as *The Godfather* (1972), in which old-world Sicilian traditions lead to violence and crime. The failure to acculturate is a common complaint among those who oppose immigration, such as Samuel Huntington.[19] The lack, or perceived lack, of acculturation is a persistent theme in the politics of immigration, not only in the United States but in Europe as well.

Immigration as a Modern-Day Issue

In the twenty-first century, as in the past, there is ambivalence about immigrants and immigration in many countries. The concerns expressed, ranging from xenophobia to worries about the economic impacts of immigration, shape political discourse and are therefore a rich subject for films. The dramatic circumstances that many migrants face, including hardship and personal sacrifice, are tailor-made for film. Society's debates over immigration are mirrored on screens. We rarely see pure anti-immigration films; however, we do see some of the concerns expressed by those who oppose immigration show up in different genres.

The Simpsons has turned to the question of immigration in several episodes, most notably in "Much Apu about Nothing" (5 May 1996). After the city of Springfield institutes a "bear tax," citizens begin to blame rising taxes on immigrants. A movement emerges to drive all immigrants out of Springfield, including the character Apu, who owns the local Kwik-E-Mart. In another episode, "Coming to Homerica" (2009), *The Simpsons* revisits the sensitive question of immigration, this time when calamity strikes the barley industry of the neighboring town of Ogdenville, which was settled by Norwegian immigrants more than a century ago. Ogdenville sees its economy collapse, prompting several residents to move to Springfield. At first the people of Springfield welcome the newcomers; the respectful Norwegians of Ogdenville prove to be good workers, and the townspeople are pleased that they fill the day labor jobs Springfield residents do not want.

Homer is happy to have help working on his roof.[20] But when community services, such as the hospital, become overburdened because of the increase in population, the new arrivals become easy scapegoats. Faced with a shortage of officers because of budget cuts, Police Chief Wiggam enlists private citizens "who would agree to do our jobs for the adrenal rush that comes from the tiny taste of authority over your fellow man."

The writers of *The Simpsons* are clearly drawing on the issue of immigration (both legal and illegal) between the United States and Mexico. Immigration advocates argue that, much like the Ogdenvillians, Mexican immigrants have come to the United States to perform jobs that Americans do not want to do.[21] In many cases, immigrants are entrepreneurial in order to make a living—the Ogdenvillians helping people with their lawns and home repairs are not taking jobs from Springfieldians. But when services are stretched because of increased population, the local population is unwilling to pay for the new residents to use the services; they vote to deny them benefits.[22]

Likewise, the *South Park* episode "Goobacks" (2004) has immigrants from the year 3045 travel back to the present because the future is so "crappy" they cannot get jobs. Using a variation of a racial slur to point out that the writers are actually referring to Mexicans, the episode encourages the viewer to think about the implications of poverty and lack of opportunities driving migrants to find a better life. The answer to the problems of the Goobacks is interesting: making the current world better so that the future will not be so awful will keep the migrants in the future. The answer seems to suggest that to control immigration, people should work for a better life in places (countries) that face emigration, thus reducing the impetus to leave.

Scholars of immigration refer to the phenomenon of push-pull factors. That is, there are forces that lure migrants (pull factors) to a destination, such as more money and better opportunities. On the other hand, there are push factors, forces such as declining economic opportunities or changing business environments, that send people abroad.[23] While many of the destinations might be romanticized as places of incredible opportunities, migrants might not appreciate the difficulty of finding work or the long hours or desperate working conditions they might find, a theme in films such as *La noire de . . .* (Black Girl, 1966), *El Norte* (1983), and *Moscow on the Hudson* (1984)[24] and depicted in the documentary *Food, Inc.* (2008).

While the United States, Canada, and Australia have been the traditional destinations for migrants, Europe, particularly since the Second World

War, has been a destination as well. Films like *Dirty Pretty Things* (2002), *Beautiful People* (1999), *Reise der Hoffnung* (Journey of Hope, 1990), *Das Fräulein* (Fraulein, 2006), and *Welcome* (2009) document the immigrant experience in Western European countries. Many of these films tell stories similar to those told about migrants immigrating to the United States. The stories focus on the hopes and aspirations of people coming to Europe, a "promised land" of sorts, but here, as elsewhere, the immigrants find hard work, menial jobs, and sometimes tragic consequences.[25]

The prevalence of undocumented immigration (illegal immigration) has created new controversies in the debate about immigration. There is nothing particularly new about undocumented immigration, even in the movies. Hedy Lamarr, for example, played a woman who proposes a marriage of convenience with Jimmy Stewart in *Come Live with Me* (1941). Similarly, famous French actor Gérard Depardieu proposes the same to Andie MacDowell a half century later in *Green Card* (1990). It is worth noting that in both of these films the undocumented person is European, whereas most current controversies about undocumented workers are about people from other parts of the world.[26] Furthermore, in both of the films, the acquisition of proper documentation leads to a love story between the main characters. In real life, of course, undocumented migrants face a perilous journey just to get to their destination and then often face discrimination and exploitation, as depicted in the Slovenian film *Rezervni deli* (Spare Parts, 2003).[27] The danger of undocumented migration often goes unobserved by the general public; thousands die in remote locations attempting to reach their destinations.

Those who have spent time in a foreign country can attest to the difficulty in navigating different language and cultural practices. With immigration comes a sense of not knowing the rules and thus constantly risking misadventures. This can lead to comedic consequences. An African friend once told me of the first time he arrived in the United States in the early 1980s. He got off the airplane in Houston to visit his brother; initially he felt a sense of dislocation and confusion. To get his bearings he sat down and watched people for a few minutes to decide what he should do next. He was amazed to note that people walked up to a glass door and "magically" the wall would slide open for them. Feeling confident, he decided to try it for himself—and promptly walked into a glass window, hurting his head. There is a long history of films about immigration taking this form: a fish-out-of-water story to make larger points. For example, the film *Delicious* (1931) follows the trials and tribulations of a group of immigrants bound for America. Immigration comedies such as *At Sea Ashore* (1936) allowed comedians such as Patsy Kelly and Lyda Roberti to use miscommunication between cultures as a source of comedy. More recently, we see this kind of story in films such as *Coming to America* (1988) and *My Big Fat Greek Wedding* (2002), both of which tell the story of immigrants confronting the difficulty of their cultural misunderstandings of modern American life. As such, these films seemingly help to overcome a tendency toward stereotyping and offer explanations about how cultural mix-ups can occur. These films try to humanize both the new and old cultures by giving the viewer a cultural reference point so that one can understand the sources of misunderstanding.

The tendency to treat a single incident as a cultural trait has important consequences in world politics. What we normally refer to as *stereotyping* happens when a society assigns overly broad attributes to a whole group of people based upon the actions of a few. Throughout the history of films, groups that are not considered part of mainstream culture have been stereotyped. In the early days of Hollywood some of the most egregious stereotypes have involved African Americans;[28] however, others have been targeted as well. Take, for example, Italians, Jews, and East Europeans during the early days of Hollywood.[29] Later, particularly during World War II, Japanese, and even Japanese Americans, were the target of stereotypes. During the Korean and Vietnam wars, American films created disturbing characterizations of Asians.[30]

One group that has been consistently stereotyped throughout the history of Western films is Arabs. Positive or neutral portrayals of Arabs in films made in Western countries are exceedingly rare. Although Western audiences have become sensitized to the portrayal of many groups, stereotypes of Arabs and Muslims often pass without comment. In the 1990s, and certainly in a post–September 11 world, the question of Muslim and Arab immigrants living in Western societies has raised a number of fears. Many television series and films have seemingly fed into these concerns. More often than not, Arabs are depicted as villains, sheiks, or gratuitous exploiters. Jack Shaheen points out that rarely are Arabs portrayed as normal individuals with common lives; the stock villain in many films has become the Arab or Muslim terrorist, with very few counterimages to challenge these portrayals.[31] This situation has been exacerbated by a few incidents. The Dutch filmmaker Theo van Gogh made a film titled *Submission* (2004), which criticized the treatment of women in Islamic societies. Van Gogh was assassinated in 2004 by a Dutch-Moroccan Muslim claiming desecration of his religion. The assassination sparked a wave of vandalism and reprisals across the Netherlands. Situations such as this worsen tensions between communities.[32] Do they represent the real relationship between communities? Do the acts of individuals or a few individuals overshadow the reality of multiple communities living side by side in relative peace? Film and popular culture can and do give meaning and context to incidents such as these.

In response to stereotypes and in an effort to develop a sense of community, the Canadian sitcom series *Little Mosque on the Prairie* (2007–) portrays a small group of Muslims living in small-town Canada. The diverse group, with different practices, outlooks, and understandings of their faith, presents a picture of Muslims that many in the West would not recognize. The group is not monolithic; there are varying degrees of faith among the congregation, and they face discrimination and misunderstanding from the local population. Similarly, the Christians of the town are not monolithic either. Some embrace their neighbors, while others, particularly a local talk-radio host, fan the flames of bigotry and misunderstanding. *Little Mosque on the Prairie* serves a community-building purpose as well. Produced and aired by the Canadian Broadcasting Company (CBC), the series also helps to educate non-Muslim Canadians by using plotlines to explain the religious and cultural practices of many Muslims. Similarly, the BBC documentary series *Women in Black* (2008) explores many of the issues that confront Muslim women both in the Middle East and Europe. The series provides interesting insights about the conflict between cultures and expectations of the individual while at the same time explaining cultural practices to outsiders.

Different cultural practices are a source of anxiety for many people and can mar relations within a society. A technique filmmakers use to discuss immigration in a less threatening manner is to employ extraterrestrial aliens as an alternative to human immigrants (note that the use of the words *alien* and *immigrant* are sometimes interchangeable). Comedic television series such as *My Favorite Martian* (1963–1966)[33] and *Mork & Mindy* (1978–1982) used the otherworldly behavior of extraterrestrials as both a source of comedy and as a metaphor for the practices of non-Americans. The premise of both series was that the alien had to give up his own cultural habits in order not to be detected by Americans. Later, *Men in Black II* (2002) would use a similar premise. In this film the metaphor is taken a little further: immigration would require all Americans to forget their past in order for assimilation to work in the United States.[34] More recently, the South African sci-fi feature *District 9* (2009) features aliens, derogatorily referred to as prawns, living in a fenced-in compound known as District 9. Without directly referring to immigrants in a traditional sense, the film is a statement about how migrants are treated in some countries.[35]

The Immigrant and the Effects of Migration

One of the important aspects of emigration is its impact on the individual and his or her family.[36] Often migrants are forced to leave behind families (including spouses and children), which might have dramatic effects on them. For instance, separation of parents from children can result in trauma to the children.[37] Increasingly, females immigrate abroad without their children in an effort to provide a better life for their families financially.[38] This is the theme of the Mexican-American coproduction *La misma luna* (Under the Same Moon, 2007), in which Rosario (Kate del Castillo) migrates to the United States to help provide for her son, who remains in Mexico with his grandmother. Rosario faces constant threats of deportation, and on a whim an employer refuses to pay her. Meanwhile, her son, in an effort to join his mother, makes the dangerous trip across the border. Similarly, a father tries to raise his son as an undocumented worker in *A Better Life* (2011), facing the added pressure of not being able to utilize the services of police officers for fear of deportation. The situation faced by undocumented workers is not unique to the United States. As depicted in the Belgian film *Illégal* (2010), many people from Eastern Europe and North Africa illegally enter European Union countries. Deportation can mean the splitting up of families, including, most dramatically, separating children from parents.

The strain of evading immigration agents and living in the shadows of a legal system can have a psychological impact on undocumented migrants as well.[39] Set in the present-day United States, *The Visitor* (2007) offers a story of how immigrants can enrich the lives of the host country while also documenting the difficulties of being a migrant in a new country. The film offers a glimpse of how despair overcomes those who find themselves without legal recourse or options. In the film, a bored college professor finds new meaning in life when he is confronted with a young undocumented couple squatting in his apartment. After an incident, the young man is arrested and deportation proceedings are begun against

The life of irregular (or illegal) migrants is one of constant fear of detection. The film *Illégal* illustrates this point and the potential of families being divided as a result of modern immigration policies. (Courtesy Film Movement)

him by immigration authorities. Because he is a Muslim from Syria, he is treated with suspicion, which is common in the post–September 11 atmosphere. Ultimately, *The Visitor* suggests that despite differences between immigrants and Americans, there is a shared humanity between the two cultures.

Even for those individuals who immigrate through established and legal channels, there can be emotional and psychological challenges. This is depicted in the Canadian short film *Arrival* (1957). Another example is *Inch'Allah Dimanche* (2001), in which the protagonist, Zouina, moves from her home in Algeria to northern France.[40] The background of the film is that Algerian workers were brought to France because of a labor shortage after the Second World War; after 1974 the French government allowed the guest workers to bring their families. Zouina and her children leave Algeria to join her husband in France. Over the course of the film she tries to make sense of the world around her, finding the cultural differences difficult to understand, including next-door neighbors who are obsessive about their backyard garden. Because she is dislocated from the culture she knows, feeling isolated, Zouina spends her limited free time trying to make contact with

Immigrants such as Zouina in *Inch'Allah Dimanche* face isolation, depression, and confusion as a result of the pressures of new cultural expectations and dislocation. (Courtesy Film Movement)

another Algerian woman in town she has yet to meet. Meanwhile, she must contend with racist neighbors who find her cultural practices threatening.

Today's immigrants quite conceivably could return to their home country for several visits, make telephone calls, and even use streaming video over the Internet to keep in touch.[41] But this does not solve issues of isolation and loneliness. The difficulty of living a life with a limited understanding of the language and cultural habits of the dominant culture can be very isolating. In *Amreeka* (2009), a Palestinian mother and son (Muna and Fadi) initially view American culture as frustrating and hostile, particularly because their arrival coincides with the 2003 American invasion of Iraq. Muna opines at one point that immigration is like transplanting a tree: you can move it but it does not grow. The anthropologist Kalvero Oberg used the phrase "culture shock" to describe the dislocation people feel when they spend a significant amount of time in a strange culture.[42] Oberg argued that everyone who travels abroad for any extended period of time, especially for the purposes of work, feels isolated and has a negative reaction to the new surroundings, which are difficult to comprehend at times. When traveling abroad, almost everyone initially enjoys a sense of adventure at the newness of situations, sights, sounds, and food. However, the longer one stays in unfamiliar surroundings, the more discomfort one feels. One of the initial phases of culture shock is rejection of the new culture, followed by a regression to the person's home culture. Thus, for those suffering culture shock, everything about the new culture seems bad and reminiscences of the home culture become romanticized as good. A person who suffers culture shock may become irritable and hostile; it may seem that no one understands or cares about his or her problems. As Oberg writes, most people get over culture shock eventually.

The significance of culture shock with respect to migration is the perceptions that can be created. If an individual does something peculiar or antisocial in his or her homeland, it is considered purely an individual act. Perhaps the person is having a bad day or perhaps the person is just not very nice. Yet if a person performs a peculiar or antisocial act in a foreign country, then the act is construed as a national trait.[43] For example, suppose an American is traveling abroad and a retailer does not wait on him or her quickly enough. In response, the American begins to rant and rave about the inconsiderate shopkeeper. For those who witness the event, according to Oberg, the behavior can be seen as a trait of all Americans. Thus, in the minds of the locals, all Americans rant and rave when they do not get their way. We can see this in the film *Crash* (2004), in which a lack of understanding means cultural biases and stereotypes develop.

As immigrants begin to interact with a new culture, misunderstandings can occur within families as well. As the film *Avalon* (1990) indicates, subsequent generations of immigrants are likely to abandon traditional practices and change family traditions.[44] Sometimes there are conflicts between immigrants and their children over how far they should assimilate and what form their cultural accommodation should take. A film such as *Bend It Like Beckham* (2002), in which the daughter of Sikh immigrants living in London would rather play soccer (football) than submit to cultural ideas of female respectability, demonstrates this tension.[45] In *Amreeka*, the relationship between a Palestinian mother and her son is tense because of their immigration. The son is not accepted by his American classmates and he is alienated over the course of the film. Throughout the entire extended family there is a difference between the generation that immigrated (the parents) and the next generation (the children), which is increasingly acculturated into American society. The German film *Gegan die Wand* (Head On, 2004) takes this even further, exploring the sexual practices of immigrants in Western society as a young woman of Turkish descent (Sibel Kekilli) rebels against the restrictions of her conservative family.[46] In real life, Kekilli faced trouble from her family after the film's release when it was revealed that she had once acted in pornographic films.[47]

Refugees and World Politics

While the main factor pushing and pulling voluntary immigration tends to be economic, another category of migrants face a different type of motivation. Refugees are people who must flee their home because remaining would result in injury or even death. According to the United Nations High Commissioner for Refugees, in 2010 there were 10.5 million refugees around the world.[48] The word *refugee* is primarily used to designate a person who stands in opposition to government or dominant culture practices. Although the migration to another country for an immigrant is thought to be voluntary, and for a refugee forced, refugees face many of the same issues as immigrants, including isolation, culture shock, and difficulty finding employment. These are the themes of the autobiographical film *Desert Flower* (2008), which tells the story of Somali-born supermodel Waris Dirie, a victim of female circumcision. On top of these challenges, refugees, such as Dirie, can often suffer from trauma and post-traumatic stress brought on by the experience of violence.[49]

There are many organizations to help refugees adjust and acculturate to the host society, but the sheer number of refugees has been an increasing problem.[50] *God Grew Tired of Us: The Story of the Lost Boys of Sudan* (2006) helps to explain the challenges that refugees face leaving their home and coming to a place like the United States. In the film, which follows four young men from Sudan who were housed in a refugee camp in Kenya, the cultural loneliness and isolation is apparent. Settled in Pittsburgh and Syracuse, the young men work to send money home and seek to obtain an education. Their isolation and grief affects not only the young men but the families they left behind as well, which is apparent when one's mother comes for a visit toward the end of the film.

While many refugees would probably rather stay in their home countries, the next destination of choice is not always a developed country like the United States, Sweden, or Germany. Most of the time refugees escape to a neighboring country. These countries are chosen because of their proximity, the likelihood that the refugees will encounter a similar culture, and because relocating closer incurs the least amount of cost.[51]

The desire of refugees to remain close to home is represented in films such as *Gomqashtei dar Aragh* (Marooned in Iraq, 2002) and *Hævnen* (In a Better World, 2010). Bahman Ghohadi's *Marooned in Iraq* is set during the Iran-Iraq War of the 1980s and vividly depicts the lives of the Kurdish population living in Iraq in the aftermath of the attacks on their villages by the Iraqi government of Saddam Hussein. The Danish film *In a Better World*, which is not exclusively about refugees, depicts the conditions many refugees face as a Swedish doctor tends to the residents' needs in a Sudanese camp.

The current legal definition of refugees does not include a category that seems to be increasing and is likely to continue to do so in the future: environmental refugees.[52] There are individuals who are forced to flee their homes and countries because of environmental threats, including hurricanes, tsunamis, earthquakes, floods, industrial pollution, and climate change. While these migrants are not recognized as refugees in a legal sense, their growing number poses a potential challenge to world politics in the future.

Some Final Thoughts

As noted several times in this chapter, a complaint that is often leveled at immigrant communities is that they do not integrate or assimilate into the host culture, causing concerns that immigration represents a threat to the cohesiveness of a society. In many countries around the world people become upset that immigrants retain their own language, music, and popular culture rather than adopting those of the host country. Foreign-language books, newspapers, and radio stations represent physical manifestations of lack of assimilation to which opponents to immigration object. It is easier to argue against such tangible manifestations of immigration than it is to make an economic case about the negative effects of immigration on the labor market. Films, television, and newspapers engender visceral reactions. For example, the recording of a Spanish-language version of the "Star-Spangled Banner" caused quite a controversy in 2006.[53]

Many people express consternation about the number of Spanish-language television networks, radio stations, and newspapers in the United States. Given the loneliness, culture shock, and isolation that many feel, it is perhaps not surprising that migrants will seek out items that are familiar and remind them of home and families.[54] Thus the consumption of news and popular culture from the home culture is a booming business—but not a new one. The history of American cinema is littered with films made in the United States in a language other than English for domestic immigrant audiences. For example, Yiddish-language films such as *Yidl mitn Fidl* (Yiddle with His Fiddle, 1938) and *Zein Weib's Liebenik* (His Wife's Lover, 1931), and the Ukrainian-language film *Natalka Poltavka* (1937), directed by Hollywood's Edgar G. Ulmer, are examples of film that once played to immigrants in the United States. With advances in technology, films are easier to produce and distribute abroad in the form of DVDs and Internet-streaming media and have been a feature of the globalized media market.

Immigration creates the challenge of people of different cultures and faith living side by side in a community. Some countries, like Canada, have tried a strategy of multiculturalism, a policy of equal coexisting cultures with one country.[55] Yet, given difficulties between communities in Europe, some European leaders, like Angela Merkel in Germany and David Cameron in Britain, have suggested that multiculturalism has failed in their countries and that different strategies should be employed.[56] Attempts to reconcile various communities take many different shapes. In 2011, the French National Football (Soccer) team introduced a new uniform that has a patch sewn inside so that players and fans wear it across their hearts. It reads: *Nos Différences Nous Unissent* (Our Differences Unite Us).

Given the increase of international travel and communication, high levels of migration will no doubt continue into the foreseeable future. An increase in different push factors (such as the environment) might also contribute to increased migration. On the horizon there may be newer forms of immigration that will elicit charges of neocolonialism. While immigration to richer countries has proven to be controversial, emigration from richer countries to poorer regions of the world is not as well known. As depicted in the documentary *Paraiso for Sale* (2011), there are an increasing number of middle-class Americans who are buying oceanfront and luxurious property, which they could not afford in the United States, in places like Mexico and Panama. Many retire to these communities. These immigrants continue to see themselves as American citizens rather than adopting the local language, customs, and citizenship of their new homes.[57] Whether this will create new controversies in immigration politics remains to be seen. Suffice it to say the politics of migration is likely to remain contentious and high profile for the foreseeable future.

12

A Primer on Human Rights

Human rights might be one of the most provocative and interesting topics in world politics today. With the growth in the number of democratic regimes around the world, the topic of human rights has gained more salience. Because democratic governments posit that the fundamental basis of government is premised on respect of the rights of individuals, they argue that democracies promote human rights around the world. Despite this argument, there is not a clear definitive agreement about what does, and does not, constitute human rights. Nevertheless, debates about what constitutes human rights often punctuate several other debates in world politics.

There are compelling issues that make human rights an intriguing issue in world politics. First, we instinctively empathize with the victims of human rights abuses because of our sense of justice and because of the drama involved. On the other hand, scholars have pointed out that the focus on human rights represents a challenge to the concept of sovereignty. If we insist that other countries adhere to certain standards of how they treat their citizens, it can be argued that the principle that states may run their domestic matters free from outside influence has been violated.

Principles of Human Rights

Defining what actually constitutes human rights has been a vexing topic not only in world politics but among academics as well. Generally, human rights are considered those circumstances required to, at a minimum, live a life of dignity.[1] What constitutes a life of dignity is a matter of debate in the study of human rights.

One of the important debates in the study of human right is whether rights are universal or culturally specific. Do basic rights apply to every single human being in the world, regardless of sex, creed, race, or ethnicity? This would be the universal perspective: human rights apply to all humans. The alternative perspective is that human rights are particular, meaning that rights are applied differently depending on the cultural standards of a given society. For example, article 16 of the Universal Declaration of Human Rights, which is discussed below, provides that people have the right to marriage and that this "shall be entered into only with the free and full consent of the intending spouses." In Western cultures the right might be interpreted to mean that people can choose their own spouses; however, in many cultures around the world, arranged marriages are the norm, so that an arranged marriage cannot be considered a violation of a basic right.[2]

The Universal Declaration of Human Rights

In the aftermath of the Second World War, many people were horrified by the scale of the major human rights violations during the war. At early meetings of the United Nations, member countries agreed to draft a nonbinding international declaration to establish the importance of human rights for all people on the planet. The chair of the UN Human Rights Commission, Eleanor Roosevelt, widow of the wartime American president Franklin Delano Roosevelt, became a leading advocate and important player in this process.[3] The Universal Declaration of Human Rights, adopted on 10 December 1948, contained a comprehensive enumeration of human rights.

Comprising thirty articles, the declaration lists a series of rights to which all nations were to aspire. One of the difficulties involved in negotiating and writing the document was the need to incorporate different philosophic and religious traditions—not just those from the West. While representatives from Western democracies tended to emphasize the political and civil rights of individuals during the negotiations, representatives from socialist countries tended to emphasize social and economic rights. Some Asian representatives argued that social order and harmony were the only way to guarantee rights for the entire society. Still others emphasized the necessity for decolonization as a prerequisite for the enjoyment of rights. Consequently, the declaration reflects several backgrounds and its negotiation was a source of friction between members of the commission.[4] The first twenty-one articles focus on civil and political rights; articles 22–27 are concerned with economic and social rights; and the final three articles are a recognition of group rights.[5]

The declaration has been translated into several languages in hopes that awareness of the document will prompt people to pressure their governments to observe the rights enumerated.[6] The declaration also has served as the basis for many subsequent international treaties concerning human rights. As such, the Universal Declaration is a foundational document, but it is also an aspirational document—a goal—toward which the international community strives.

Primary International Human Rights Treaties

While the decision to make the articles of the Universal Declaration nonbinding has been chastised as soft, the drafting of the document led to a much more formal process of creating treaties to secure human rights worldwide. Today there are a number of human rights treaties that attempt to shape relationships between states based upon a mutual respect for shared standards of human rights.[7] The topics of modern international treaties vary, and their provisions have evolved over time. Table 12.1 on the following page lists human rights treaties that have been created through the United Nations system.

Recently there have been attempts to create international courts, such as the Caribbean Court of Justice and the International Criminal Court, to help secure rights and to punish those who engage in the most egregious violations of human rights. Additionally, there are a number of regional human rights treaties, including the Council of Europe's Convention for the Protection of Human Rights and Fundamental Freedoms (1950) and the American Convention on Human Rights (1969).

Genocide?

Genocide has come to be seen as the most dire of human rights violations. The term *genocide,* coined by Raphael Lemkin, is defined in the Genocide Convention as the commission of acts with the "intent to destroy, in whole or in part, a national ethnical, racial or religious group."[8] Many scholars have argued that this definition is too narrow and restrictive. Frank Chalk has proposed that genocide constitutes a one-sided mass killing designed to eliminate a group, as defined by the perpetrators.[9] The use of the term *genocide* can be very controversial; to label an act genocide has serious ramifications in world politics. Nevertheless, there is common agreement that

Table 12.1. Major human rights treaties negotiated through the United Nations

Treaty	Open for signature	Entry into force
Convention on the Prevention and Punishment of the Crime of Genocide	1948	1951
International Convention on the Elimination of All Forms of Racial Discrimination	1966	1969
International Covenant on Economic, Social and Cultural Rights	1966	1976
International Covenant on Civil and Political Rights	1966	1976
Optional Protocol to the International Covenant on Civil and Political Rights	1966	1976
Second Optional Protocol to the International Covenant on Civil and Political Rights, Aiming at the Abolition of the Death Penalty	1989	1991
Convention on the Elimination of All Forms of Discrimination against Women	1979	1981
Optional Protocol to the Convention of the Elimination of Discrimination against Women	1999	2000
Convention against Torture and Other Cruel, Inhuman or Degrading Treatment or Punishment	1981	1984
Convention on the Rights of the Child	1989	1990
Optional Protocol to the Convention on the Rights of the Child on the Involvement of Children in Armed Conflicts	2000	2002
Optional Protocol to the Convention on the Rights of the Child on the Sale of Children, Child Prostitution and Child Pornography	2000	2002
International Convention on the Protection of the Rights of All Migrant Workers and Members of Their Families	1990	2003

certain atrocities are true examples of genocide: the Holocaust (1933–1945), Burundi (1972 and 1993), Cambodia (1975–1979), Rwanda (1994), and Darfur (2003–2010). This is far from a complete list, but it does indicate that genocide has happened several times in recent history.[10]

13

HUMAN RIGHTS AND MODERN WORLD POLITICS

The topic of human rights is a relatively new consideration and cuts across some of the most basic assumptions of world politics. Because the principle of sovereignty is so closely associated with the rights and privileges of states, what occurs inside the borders of a state traditionally has not been a concern of those outside; however, with the incidence of mass atrocities, genocides, and political violence spilling over international borders, the post–World War II period has seen a focus on the achievement of international human rights as an important aspect of world politics. There are more films directly concerned with human rights, both domestically and internationally, than films about any other topic covered in this book. Thus, it is impossible to cover them all, or even to provide an adequate sample. Instead, this chapter will review a representative sample of issues in human rights, highlighting some of the most famous international films about the topic as well as some highly acclaimed but lesser-known films.

One of the challenges of writing about films and human rights is an issue that is similar to that of cooperation discussed in chapter 8. While there are a number of excellent films about "lesser" human rights violations, most films tend to focus on the most horrific instances for dramatic effect. Thus there are far more films about genocide than child soldiering. That being said, as those who experience violence and human rights abuses can attest, there are no "lesser" human rights violations.

A Brief Survey of Civil and Political Rights in Film

Perhaps one of the most prominent rights violations displayed in American cinema is discrimination. Discrimination can take many forms, including

EMBASSY
NEWSREEL THEATRE
46th St. & Broadway · PEnnsylvania 6-3200

STARTS
THURSDAY
6:00 P. M

MAY 3rd

FOR
ONE
WEEK

SEE !   *SEE !*

NAZI
ATROCITIES

History's most shocking record. Real life pictures
revealing the unbelievable atrocities committed by
the Nazis in their murder camps. Official U. S.
Army films will shock all Americans—
But it must be seen

HELD OVER !
NAZI DEATH FACTORY

"MAIDANEK" Near Lublin, Poland, where 1,300,000
Humans were put to death by the Nazis

SEE NAZI SS GUARDS EXECUTED

Plus MANY OTHER LATE WORLD WIDE NEWS EVENTS

Latest Issue March Of Time

"MEMO FROM BRITAIN"

Learn what Briton's are really thinking today. How will
Britain's post-war plans affect America

•

Notice: Program subject to change without notice

Films have become a significant method to inform the public about human rights violations. This postcard, sent to advertise upcoming films to cinema patrons, highlighted the discovery of concentration camps by Allied forces in 1945. Subsequently, such films were used to help build the case against perpetrators in proceedings such as the Nuremberg Trials. (Postcard from the author's collection) the denial of jobs, educational and social opportunities, housing, and political rights based on characteristics such as ethnicity, race, or religion. The rights enumerated in the Universal Declaration of Human Rights, according to article 2, apply to all people without regard to any kind of distinction, including race, sex, language, or national origin. Because of the legacy of slavery, Jim Crow laws, and racial discrimination in the United States, American cinema has often been a source of films that deal with racial injustice.[1] Classic films and novels, such as *The Defiant Ones* (1958), *A Raisin in the Sun* (1961), *To Kill a Mockingbird* (1962), and *Black Like Me* (1964), detail the hardships and difficulties faced by African Americans in racially segregated America.[2] Many of these films chronicle the economic disadvantages, political discrimination, bigotry, and personal affronts suffered by American citizens simply because of the color of their skin.

Many times this bigotry and racial discrimination has turned violent. Groups that favored continued racial segregation, such as the Ku Klux Klan (KKK), used violence and intimidation to deny African Americans their political rights and often to hinder their economic opportunities as well. A good example is *Mississippi Burning* (1988). The film is loosely based on the June 1964 disappearance and murder of three civil rights workers in Philadelphia, Mississippi. The film's director, Alan Parker, fictionalized the account because he believed a documentary film about the incident would fail to capture the public's attention.[3] *Rosewood* (1997), based on a 1923 incident that took place in Rosewood, Florida, tells the story of white vigilante justice carried out on an African American man falsely accused of rape.[4]

The violence directed toward African Americans is the subject of the documentary film *Strange Fruit* (2002), a film that links politics with both film and music. It relates the story of how the song "Strange Fruit," written by a white man and performed by Billie Holiday, helped to give voice to African Americans in the United States who thought they had no defense against mob rule, especially in the South. The song is about lynching, the practice of extrajudicial hanging of African Americans by white mobs. The mobs would demand immediate justice, without trial, for blacks accused, often unjustly, of various crimes.[5] Many times charges of rape would be applied to black men romantically involved with white women. The lyrics of "Strange Fruit" are haunting:

Southern trees bear strange fruit
Blood on the leaves and blood at the root
Black bodies swinging in the southern breeze
Strange fruit hanging from the poplar trees.

Radio stations across the United States refused to play the record because of its controversial topic. Despite this, it was one of the most popular songs of 1939. The lyrics were written by Abel Meeropol, who wrote it under the pseudonym of Lewis Allan.[6] The song is most closely associated with African American jazz legend Billie Holiday, whose haunting rendition captivates the listener.

Despite highlighting of the issue in the 1940s, lynching and other extra-judicial killings of African Americans remained a problem for several more years. As the civil rights movement gained momentum in the 1960s, high-profile films began to explore the politics of racial discrimination in more depth. Perhaps the most famous of those films is *Guess Who's Coming to Dinner* (1967), starring Hollywood legends Katharine Hepburn and Spencer Tracey. The film explores racial issues through the proposed marriage of a white woman and a black man (Sidney Poitier), and was considered groundbreaking at the time.[7] The film was released just six months after the important U.S. Supreme Court decision *Loving v. Virginia* (1967), in which the court struck down a law in Virginia that outlawed interracial marriages.[8] The decision did not prompt the film, which was already in production at the time, but the coincidence of case and film speaks to the atmosphere of changing race relations in the United States in the 1960s.

American films on occasion explored the ethnic and racial discrimination concerns of other groups. Historically, during the classic Hollywood period, the treatment of Native Americans, regularly referred to as "Indians," was typically negative.[9] Discrimination against other groups, such as Hispanics and Asians, has been the subject of American films as diverse as *West Side Story* (1961) and *Gran Torino* (2008).

Sidney Poitier starred in another high-profile film in 1967, the British film *To Sir, with Love* (1967), set in the East End of London. Poitier plays a Caribbean engineer who has trouble finding work and begins teaching white, working-class students. The film explores the racial differences of the teacher and his students, focusing on the bigotry and biases faced by people of African descent in Britain.

Other films made outside the United States have examined ethnic discrimination as well. The Russian film *12* (2007), a remake of the American film *12 Angry Men* (1957), is a story in which a young man from Chechnya is accused of killing his Russian stepfather. The jurors, who represent Russian society at large, are faced with the biases and stereotypes they hold toward people from the breakaway region of Chechnya. The French film *Chocolat* (1988) adds another layer to the issue of racial discrimination by exploring the legacy of colonialism as well. The protagonist, Aimée, contemplates her relationship with a young African during Cameroon's colonial period under French rule.

In addition to racial discrimination, religious discrimination has been a consistent theme in American cinema. Although founded on the idea of religious tolerance, the United States, like many countries in the world, has struggled with religious issues from time to time. After directing the racially insensitive *The Birth of a Nation* (discussed below), the first important American film director, D. W. Griffith, made a plea for tolerance in general with his epic *Intolerance* (1916).[10] The film is a series of four interlocking stories detailing "man's intolerance toward man"; one story focuses on the St. Bartholomew Day's massacre of 1572, in which a wave of assassinations and mob attacks marred relations between Protestant and Catholic communities in France.

Anti-Semitism has been a persistent issue in history. Discrimination against Jews because of their religious beliefs was a persistent phenomenon across Europe, dating back to the Middle Ages and culminating in the Holocaust of the mid-twentieth century. Because many of the early film moguls in Hollywood were Jewish, there was less overt anti-Semitism in American films than in other forms of popular culture. Hollywood tended to downplay Jewish themes in films.[11] Yet some American films, such as *The House of Rothschild* (1934), *Gentleman's Agreement* (1947), and *Fiddler on the Roof* (1971), have examined the effects of anti-Semitism on both Jews and the wider society. Television series in the United States such as *Seinfeld* (1989–1998) and *Friends* (1994–2004) have helped make Jewish characters mainstream in popular culture around the world. Nevertheless, even after the Holocaust, anti-Semitism remains a phenomenon in society. Even the extremely popular Mel Gibson film, *The Passion of the Christ* (2004), which recounts the crucifixion of Jesus, faced charges of anti-Semitism because of its depiction of Jews.[12]

Religious discrimination and bias is not limited to Jews. In fact, it can take many targets. For instance, Professor Jack Shaheen has pointed out that Islam has frequently been a target of misrepresentation and deleterious depictions.[13] Likewise, Mormonism, too, has been subject to erroneous and exaggerated depictions in popular culture. The first Sherlock Holmes novel, *A Study in Scarlet* (1887), written by Arthur Conan Doyle, incorporates an anti-Mormon storyline into its plot. Several films of the early twentieth century portrayed Mormons as lecherous and possessing hypnotic power. Despite the religion's founding in the United States, many of these films came from Europe, such as the Danish *A Victim of the Mormons* (1911) and the British *Trapped by the Mormons* (1922), although the United States contributed *A Mormon Maid* (1917).[14] Increased migration and a globalized media market have meant that, increasingly, discussion of various religious beliefs and misperceptions are a part of entertainment television. Thus, reality programs (*17 Kids and Counting* [2008–] and *All-American Muslims* [2011–]) and situation comedies (*The Simpsons* [1989–], *Little Mosque on the Prairie* [2007–], and *The Big Bang Theory* [2007–]) regularly invoke religious practices and customs in a way to help demystify beliefs.[15]

The largest demographic targeted by discrimination worldwide has historically been women. It is difficult to encapsulate the discrimination against women as it has been depicted on screen because discrimination has been so ingrained within the practices of various cultures. For example, many classic American films depict women as subservient to men and incapable of working outside the home. In these films, marriage means that women give up their careers and begin a life as a homemaker. When married women do work outside the home in films, such as *Young Man of Manhattan* (1930), it often leads to marital difficulties and even divorce.

The birth of the cinema predates the acquisition of women's right to vote in most countries. This means we have some interesting examples of films that both advocate and argue against women's suffrage: for example, *What Eighty Million Women Want* (1913) and *Les femmes députés* (Women Deputies, 1912).[16] Such films are not limited to century-old films; the issue of women voting is a central theme in the Iranian film *Raye makhfi* (Secret Ballot, 2001). Today women around the world face different types of discrimination and oppression. Whether the issue is access to opportunities and enjoyment, as depicted in *Offside* (2006) and *Persepolis* (2007); economic exploitation, as in *Nine to Five* (1980) and *My Brilliant Career* (1979); or sexual exploitation, as found in *The Magdalene Sisters* (2002) and *Hope in Heaven* (2005), films continue to explore the denial of rights around the world.

Human Rights and Violence

While the right to political dissent is often taken for granted in many democracies, the practice of criticizing a government can be dangerous in many parts of the world. Amnesty International and Human Rights Watch, two prominent human rights organizations, continually chronicle people who are jailed, injured, tortured, or even killed for their political beliefs. One of the practices used by political regimes to stifle criticism is a technique known as extrajudicial executions and/or killings.[17] Simply put, individuals who are critical of the government are killed. Because the execution happens outside the legal framework, meaning that no trial is held and there is no chance for the accused to offer a defense, the act is illegal. Films have proved a useful medium to detail these events.

Missing (1982), starring Sissy Spacek and Jack Lemmon, chronicles the aftermath of the 11 September 1973 coup d'état in Chile, notorious because it brought Augusto Pinochet to power, where he would remain until 1998. The film reenacts the efforts of Ed Horman, a conservative American businessman, to find his left-leaning activist son, Charlie, who was arrested by the military after the coup. *Missing* chronicles the human rights abuses that were suffered by the Chilean people as well as a handful of Americans. In a powerful scene toward the end of the film, Ed Horman and his daughter-in-law are led through a prison morgue containing the bodies of hundreds (perhaps thousands) of people who have been tortured and executed. In the end, Charlie Horman is one of the victims of the coup, a coup that many, including the film's director, believe was organized and carried out with the complicity of the American government. Although most critics disagree with the director's conclusions that Horman's death was the result of American intervention in Chilean politics, they still regard the project as powerful filmmaking.[18] While the debate about the role of the United States in the coup remains controversial, in investigating the veracity of the film, Robert Toplin concludes that there is a significant degree of truth to Thomas Hauser's account, the book on which the film is based, and that Chile was one of the ugliest examples of American interference in another country's affairs.[19]

In human rights parlance, *disappearance* is a phenomenon or practice that is used to silence political protest. It involves the tactic of abducting people who are perceived to be political opponents, torturing the individuals for information, and eventually, more than likely, killing them and hiding the bodies. The friends and family of the disappeared are never notified—the person simply disappears. The tactic has the effect not only of eliminating political opposition but of intimidating others who oppose government policies. Leaving the fate of the disappeared to the imagination is a powerful deterrent.[20]

La historia oficial (The Official Story, 1985) is set in Argentina during the so-called dirty war, similar in circumstance to the coup in Chile.[21] This film takes a different approach, examining the long-term aftereffects of disappearances. Although the story is fictitious, it draws upon many facts.[22] The film is centered on a high school teacher (Norma Aleandro) who is trying to learn the background of her adoptive daughter. Her search leads her to meet the women of the Plaza de Mayo, the main square in central Buenos Aires, because she suspects the girl is the daughter of a *desaparecido* (disappeared). In real life, the plaza became the center of an amazing protest held nearly every Thursday beginning in 1977. Women (known as the Mothers of the Disappeared), wearing white scarves, would walk around the square holding photographs of their children.[23]

A human rights violation that has garnered increasing attention of late is the plight of child soldiers. Although at first it might seem intuitive, defining a child soldier has been difficult. The international treaty that prohibits child soldiering defines a child as anyone under the age of eighteen; however, in many societies around the world adulthood commences when a child goes through an initiation ceremony or begins to take on adult jobs, which could occur before the age of eighteen. Thus, coming to an agreement about when childhood becomes adulthood is difficult.[24] Nevertheless, there is a general agreement that the tactics and intimidation used to secure and maintain an army of children set these minors apart from regular soldiers.[25] For instance, Uganda's Lord's Resistance Army (LRA) has abducted children and uses violence and intimidation to force them to commit heinous acts. The LRA has come under increased scrutiny in recent years because of its widespread use of child soldiers and the viciousness of its attacks. Led by Joseph Kony and espousing a pseudo-Christian philosophy, the group has used drugs, violence, sexual exploitation, and mysticism to cause fear and havoc in northern Uganda, ostensibly in opposition to the government.[26] Several reports have chronicled how groups like the LRA force abducted children to kill their families, causing untold psychological trauma. The goal of these groups is to desensitize the children to violence so that they can kill without thought or regret. In 2000, in reaction to child soldiering in general, the international community adopted a treaty to combat the practice.[27]

The depiction of child soldiers on film has been rare and limited to a number of documentaries, although the use of child soldiers in the diamond conflicts of Sierra Leone is a central element of the film *Blood Diamond* (2006). The documentary *Children of War* (2009)[28] is a high-profile film that had its world premiere in the chambers of the United Nations General Assembly and is a part of the Zero under 18 Campaign.[29] The film documents the lives of former child soldiers who have been freed from the LRA and are undergoing therapeutic rehabilitation. Dramatically, the film also considers the point of view of the spiritual leader of the LRA, Abonga Papa, who was captured and interviewed about his understanding of the conflict. The independent film *Invisible Children* (2003), made by a group of novice filmmakers, explores the fear caused in the Acholi region of Uganda by the Lord's Resistance Army. The film offers a novel account of the phenomenon because the filmmakers admit they were unaware of the plight of children in Uganda when they began making the film.[30] In March 2012 the same filmmakers released *Kony 2012*, an Internet video that called for the international community to arrest Joseph Kony, the leader of the LRA. Although there is a paucity of films that feature child soldiers, online content as a method of advocacy has flourished.[31]

Genocide: The Ultimate Crime

There is one human rights violation that holds fascination in its sheer enormity of effect and scale: the crime of genocide. Genocide encompasses the deliberate attempt to eliminate an entire group of people. Probably the most famous case of genocide is the Holocaust, when the German state under Nazi rule in the 1930s and 1940s attempted to destroy the Jewry in Europe, killing approximately 6 million Jews. But the Holocaust was neither the first nor the last genocide.

There is no doubt that films have contributed to the prominence of the Holocaust, but there are other genocides and stories told through film as well. A common misunderstanding is that genocide is a spontaneous act of violence. The truth is quite the opposite: genocidal events are meticulously planned prior to the actual event. Professor Gregory Stanton has argued that there are eight distinct stages of genocide, of which six come before the actual killing of individuals. Included in these stages are the processes of organization, preparation, and dehumanization.[32] Through the use of film, television, and even Internet content, we can trace the patterns of behavior outlined in Stanton's thesis.

A film that helps to demonstrate the planning of a genocide is *Wann-seekonferenz* (Wannsee Conference, 1984). Basing its script on the detailed transcript of the actual meeting of high-level Nazi officials, the film is a real-time recounting of the conference that ultimately decided on the "final solution," the extermination of the Jews. Another version of the same event is presented in the HBO Film *Conspiracy* (1992), which clearly had a much higher budget. Both of these films have their strengths. *Wannsee Confer-ence,* named after the town where the event took place, concentrates on the jovial and glib nature of the proceedings. On the other hand, *Conspiracy* presents an air of opulence: the conference participants are using expensive china and crystal and eating fine foods while discussing plans for wholesale murder of millions of Jews.

What the films above do not address is how so many could participate in such abhorrent crimes. Because most humans have an aversion to killing other humans, perpetrators must convince others to overcome their cognitive barrier to killing.[33] Occasionally film and other forms of popular culture have played a role in the dehumanization process. Prior to and during the Holo-caust, German cinema was geared toward segregation and dehumanization of Jews. German propaganda films during the Nazi period would often use overdrawn characterizations to paint Jews and other groups as undesirable and duplicitous. For example, *Jud Süss* (1940) uses a historical event from the dukedom of Württemberg in the 1730s to make accusations against all Jews. The director of the film, Veit Harlan, would later stand trial for "crimes against humanity, complicity in persecuting others on racial grounds, and . . . [collaborating] in the planning of such crimes."[34] Although Harlan was acquitted because the prosecution failed to provide evidence of a direct link between *Jud Süss* and the actual killing of Jews, the trial did open questions about the legal position of those who engaged in such filmmaking.[35]

Likewise, *Der Ewige Jude* (The Eternal Jew, 1940) used a documentary style to depict Jews in the most unfavorable light. Cobbling together film fragments from other sources, the film accuses Jews of being dirty, deceitful, corrupt, and a drag on society. Although after the war the film's director, Fritz Hippler, would deny that he played a significant role in creating the film, there is substantial evidence to the contrary. Like Harlan, Hippler stood trial but was acquitted. Hippler maintained during the trial that Propaganda Minister Joseph Goebbels was responsible for the film.[36]

German cinema under the Nazis is probably the best example of films that used stereotypes to undermine the humanity of a group of people. However, there are many examples of films that help to classify and symbolize people, each a prerequisite to dehumanization, according to Stanton. Even American films have engaged in this practice from time to time, although not to the extreme to which Japanese and German cinema did during the Second World War. American films have taken the opportunity to create an impression that certain groups of people might not be quite human. For example, World War II–era cartoons in the United States, such as *You're a Sap Mr. Jap* (1942), *Tokio Jokio* (1943), and *Bugs Bunny Nips the Nips* (1944), depicted Japanese people in extremely exaggerated form, using images and verbal references to refer to them as monkeys.

While not having the intent of specifically targeting the group for destruction, many films, particularly in the silent and early sound period, showed African Americans in such a negative and unflattering light that the portrayals verged on robbing African Americans of their humanity. Although undoubtedly one of the most important films in American cinematic history,[37] *The Birth of a Nation* (1915) depicts African Americans as drunkards, lazy, and incapable of complicated thoughts. In one shocking scene, a group of African Americans in the Mississippi state legislature are shown as uncouth and inconsiderate, taking their shoes off and resting their feet on the desk, eating fried chicken and drinking whiskey during the debates. Even worse is the depiction of mixed-race individuals, so-called mulattos, who, according to the film, are duplicitous and violent. It is the mixed-race men in the film who impose sexually on white women, even to the point of attempted rape. By convincing people that these are the attributes of African Americans, the director D. W. Griffith (and the author of the novel on which the film is based, Thomas J. Dixon) were arguing that African Americans were morally, socially, and intellectually inferior to whites and therefore not deserving of the same privileges. While neither man advocated the genocide of African Americans, the two were part of a large segment of society that advocated the denial of voting rights to blacks and the segregation of the races because African Americans were not considered fully human.[38]

Other forms of popular culture and media have been used to dehumanize ethnic groups. During the Rwandan genocide, radio programs were used to undermine the humanity of the Tutsi. Radio-Télévision Libre des Mille Collines (RTLM) had a Western-style talk-show format, in which very little field investigation was conducted, but radio personalities (disc jockeys) led discussions of public interest, conducted long interviews, fielded listeners' calls, and staged, or participated in, comic interludes. Sometimes the language on the broadcasts would be somewhat crude, which offended some listeners but was designed to attract a specific audience: young people, and particularly males under the age of twenty. RTLM adopted street language that resonated with youths and made them more sympathetic to the station's propaganda. RTLM's agenda was to convince people that Rwanda was surrounded by enemies who planned to return Rwanda to a colonial system in which the Tutsi would be privileged. Commentators would claim that Rwanda would be better off if certain segments of the society were eliminated and persuaded people that the target groups (Tutsi and moderate Hutu) were either subhuman or guilty of crimes that warranted elimination. If these commentators were called on such outrageous statements, they would claim they had been misunderstood or were only joking.[39]

When covering the actual extermination phase of genocide, filmmakers have a difficult time encapsulating all that happens. In order to tell a story, a filmmaker must concentrate on specific events. There is a quote, often attributed to Soviet dictator Joseph Stalin: "A single death is a tragedy, a million deaths is a statistic."[40] Very large numbers are numbing and incomprehensible to most people. Thus, the difficulty for a filmmaker is that it is nearly impossible to encapsulate millions of deaths into a single story or piece of artwork. Consider making a film about the Rwandan genocide of 1994, in which approximately eight hundred thousand people died in about three months—it is impossible to capture the entire magnitude of the event. The genocide is not about eight hundred thousand people dying, it is about a murder occurring, then another, and another—repeated eight hundred thousand times. Imagine a filmmaker devoting just one second of footage to each victim: that portion of the film alone would constitute nine and one-quarter days of footage. Telling stories about genocide has one of two effects: either the film reduces the event to the stories of a tiny fraction of the victims, or it uses such huge numbers it is difficult for audiences to comprehend the enormity of the tragedy. While neither approach is satisfying, a combination of the two gives us a better picture of what occurs during genocide. The first approach has been to offer a broad overview of genocidal events. These films, which often take the form of documentaries, use a long view in the hopes of informing the audience about genocides. The drawback is that, as the quote above suggests, the sheer numbers become overwhelming and the audience often misses that genocide affects the lives of individuals. Simply using statistics misses the point that these stories are about real people.

As another approach, some artists try to personalize the stories of a genocide so that the audience understands the impact of what happened. For example, the Memorial to Murdered Jews in Berlin, which is located adjacent to the Brandenburg Gate, attempts to personalize the stories of the victims of the Nazi period. In one room of the information center, there is a voice narration (in German and English) that gives a brief biography of several of the victims. This is how many films treat the subject as well. The problem with this strategy is that it runs the risk of making the film about the individuals portrayed in the script rather than the broader incident of genocide. One can imagine that in the minds of the uninformed, the Holocaust is simply the tragedy of Anne Frank.

Finding a balance between these two approaches can be difficult. Documentaries can often utilize a broad perspective to capture the total score of a genocidal event or to provide context. The four-part series *The Genocide Factor* (2000) covers a broad range of incidents from biblical times through the end of the twentieth century. This perspective allows the viewer to consider the commonalities between the different genocides; however, it leaves many of the details out. As the most famous example of genocide in Western culture, the Holocaust is the subject of a multitude of films. It is difficult to capture the scale of the events that left 6 million Jews (as well as Roma and others) dead; however, there have been numerous attempts to do so. Among the more well known are *Genocide* (1982) and *Shoah* (1985). The American-made documentary *Genocide* used Hollywood star power (Orson Welles and Elizabeth Taylor are narrators) to chronicle the lives of Jews before and during the Nazi period. The French documentary *Shoah* (the title is the Hebrew word for *calamity*),[41] was originally released as an eight-and-a-half-hour documentary tracing the effects of the Holocaust across Europe. The film's director, Claude Lanzmann, conducts numerous interviews with ordinary people about their experiences during the Holocaust. It is difficult to summarize such a film in just a few words. In fact, the film is broken into segments that facilitate its viewing. For instance, one segment concerns the testimony of Filip Müller, a Czech Jew, who describes his experiences on "special detail" at Auschwitz. The description of his experiences focuses on prisoners being taken from the trains to the gas chambers and afterward the dead bodies being sent to the crematoriums. Müller describes the conflict experienced by the workers of the special detail: whether or not to tell people going to the gas chambers of their impending death. Another segment is a description of how the Jews of Corfu (Greece) were rounded up

Jewish children who left Germany in the late 1930s as a part of the Kindertransport are commemorated in this statue outside the Friedrichstrasse station in Berlin. On the opposite of this memorial, titled *Trains into Life—Trains into Death,* Jewish children are depicted waiting for trains that will take them to concentration camps. (Photograph by the author)

and shipped to Auschwitz. Of the 1,700 people who were taken, only 122 returned after the war.

Other documentaries are good at examining additional events and effects of the Nazi period. For example, *Paragraph 175* (2000) is an explanation of the persecution of homosexuals by the Nazis. *Into the Arms of Strangers: Stories from the Kindertransport* (2000) examines the voluntary transfer of Jewish children to Great Britain. The goal was to save the children but had the effect of breaking up families. Such documentaries, of which there are many, focus on specific aspects of the genocide, which helps the viewer understand the sheer enormity of the events.

There is one shocking and interesting piece of film history, dedicated to chronicling the effects and results of the Holocaust, that was locked away in the archives of the British Imperial Museum for forty years. The rediscovered film, originally titled *F3080*, was uncovered and aired in the United States in 1985 as part of PBS's *Frontline* series, retitled *Memory of the Camps*.[42] The footage was shot in 1945 as Allied troops liberated concentration camps such as Dachau, and it uses a documentary approach to demonstrate the atrocities of the camps. In preparing to air the film, PBS hired British actor Trevor Howard to read the script, which was written in 1945. At some point during the process, British officials brought in famed director Alfred Hitchcock to edit the film. As presented in 1985, the film is a gritty and unflinching examination of German concentration camps, with ghastly images of thousands of dead bodies and dozens of emaciated living (if just barely) inmates. The images presented in this film are raw and difficult to watch at times, but of course were exponentially more difficult to experience and even to film. Often the experiences of those who witnessed the camps were so horrific that their moral underpinnings were shaken.[43]

Narrative films have filled in where documentaries leave off. Where a film like *Memory of the Camps* can horrify the viewer with gruesome sights of emaciated bodies, narrative films can tell the emotional story of the victims of genocide. Interestingly, several narrative films about the Holocaust are American made. It has been noted that events that occurred in the 1930s and 1940s in Central Europe have become a major genre in American cinema. This has been termed by some film scholars the Americanization of the Holocaust. A film like *The Diary of Anne Frank* (1959) personalizes the Holocaust for many, particularly young, viewers because so many American students read Anne Frank in school; it is often an introduction to the Holocaust in American public education.[44] There is an argument that this, and other forms of popular culture about the event, has placed the Holocaust into American history in the minds of the public. It is as if American film-makers have used their craft to explain to Germans, Poles, and Jews what occurred in *their* history.[45] It is clear, though, whatever the motivation, that the killing of millions of Jews during the Second World War had a profound effect on the American psyche.

Although the Holocaust had been the subject of films and television before, the 1978 miniseries *Holocaust* set a new standard in television for its depiction of the event. Focusing on two German extended families, one Jewish (Weiss) the other not (Dorf), the story follows both the perpetrators and the victims through the turbulent years. As the Weiss family is destroyed, its members ending up in various concentration camps, the Dorf family enjoys a relatively good life. One, Erik Dorf, rises through the ranks of the Nazi Party. The miniseries takes in a grand sweep of history and played to some of the biggest television audiences in history to that point.

The impact was immense, not only in the United States but in Europe as well. The miniseries had a significant impact in the United States in that it created a narrative of what happened, even if it did rely somewhat on a soap-opera formula. Film scholar Judith Doneson has argued that the series helped cement the notion that the Holocaust was a metaphor for contemporary evil and also helped bolster American support for the state of Israel. The airing of *Holocaust* in West Germany proved to have profound consequences. It provoked a national conversation and even resulted in a cancellation of the statute of limitations on war crimes, set to expire at the end of 1979.[46] The film prompted a reevaluation of German attitudes toward the Holocaust and resulted in a number of public discussions and memorializations.[47]

Perhaps the most famous American film about the Holocaust to date is director Steven Spielberg's *Schindler's List* (1993). Both highly acclaimed and extremely influential, the film recounts the story of Oskar Schindler, who saved many Jews by employing them in his factory during the war. Schindler created a list of workers who were deemed essential to his factory, which supplied material to the Germany army. In doing so, Schindler was able to save many from concentration camps and eventual extermination.[48] The film's high profile is evidence of the power of film. There were a number of people who helped Jews during the Holocaust, but *Schindler's List* makes Oskar Schindler a common reference point for the public.[49] Yet another major English-language film about the Holocaust is Roman Polanski's *The Pianist* (2002), the story of musician Wladyslaw Szpilman's (Adrien Brody) survival of the Holocaust. The film not only captures the brutality of the Holocaust, but helps to demonstrate how victims were dehumanized and how random violence demoralized people. Considered a modern classic and directed by a Holocaust survivor, the film paints a picture of the fear and deprivation that seized even those victims who survived.[50]

Immediately after the Holocaust, a handful of films from Central and Eastern Europe tried to make sense of the events. Not a particularly coherent film, but nonetheless very intriguing, the German *Die Mörder sind unter uns* (Murderers among Us, 1946) is set in the aftermath of the Second World War. The film is an examination of "decent" Germans coming to grips with the reality of what the state had done in their name. Of course, this approach would later be criticized. *Murderers among Us* assumes that those responsible for the atrocities are the Nazis. One can see how this approach would appear to absolve the average German from the crimes. It would take a generation to redress the issue.

The so-called Generation 68ers began asking what their parents and grandparents had done during the war. *Das Schreckliche Mädchen* (The Nasty Girl, 1985) tells the story of a German girl who writes an essay about her hometown's complicity during the Holocaust, causing much consternation in the town. The film beautifully demonstrates the ongoing denial of responsibility even decades after a genocidal event. Of course, it was the Nazis who committed genocide during the 1930s and 1940s, but successive German leaders do note that most Germans either actively or passively supported the Nazi regime—thus it is impossible to completely distinguish between the two. In a speech marking the fortieth anniversary of the end of the Second World War, German president Richard von Weizsäcker said that it was Germany's duty to continue to acknowledge the crimes of the Nazi period and to acknowledge the past, even if those who actually witnessed or participated in the crimes were passing from the scene. To do so was Germany's legacy and responsibility.[51]

The countries that were occupied by Germany during the Second World War have revisited the topic several times. In many cases these films focus on questions about guilt and responsibility. For example, *Romeo Julia a tma* (Romeo, Juliet and the Darkness, 1960), a film that has been referred to as a Czech *Anne Frank* because in it a student conceals a Jewish girl in the garret of his house, examines the effects of the Holocaust on a community.[52] *Daleká Cesta* (Distant Journey, 1948), a Czech film shot on location at the Theresienstadt concentration camp, uses the reality of the camp to help the audience understand the experience of the camp and the cruelties of the Nazis. The Polish film *Ostatni etap* (The Last Stage, 1948), filmed at the Auschwitz concentration camp, used survivors as extras in the film and is an important early film focusing on the cruelty of the Holocaust. The film is based on the experiences of director Wanda Jakubowski during her time at the camp. *Obchod na korze* (The Shop on Main Street, 1965) is a Slovak film in which a poor young man, Tono, is offered the shop of an elderly Jewish woman. At first the young man sees it as an opportunity to succeed, but in reality the shop is kept open by the kindness and generosity of the Jewish community. In time, Tono comes to care for the woman and finds himself torn between his hopes for the future and his sense of loyalty to the woman.[53] *Die Fälscher* (The Counterfeiters, 2007), an Austrian production filmed on location at Sachsenhausen concentration camp just outside of Berlin, recounts the true story of an attempt to disrupt the Anglo-American economies by using counterfeiters from the prison population to print enough currency to have an adverse effect. *Ambulans* (Ambulance, 1961) is a stark short film from Poland that helps to explain the exclusion and subjugation of people, particularly children, during the Holocaust. There are no words contained in the film; but none are needed to convey its message. The film ironically uses an ambulance as an instrument of death to help highlight the cruelty of the concentration camps.

Since France was occupied during the war, many French films have examined the Holocaust as well. *Nuit et brouillard* (Night and Fog, 1955) makes the point that people pretend the events of the Holocaust only happened at a certain place within a given time frame, rather than being actions that occur, on a smaller scale, over and over again. The film opens with a question: "What hope do we have of truly capturing this reality?" As an early documentary on the subject, it set a distinct tone for future documentaries on the subject.[54] *Le chagrin et la pitié* (The Sorrow and the Pity, 1969) examines the role of the collaborationist Vichy government, which not only helped the Germans fight the war but also deported Jews to concentration camps. This was in contradiction to the prevailing notion of French political culture, which suggested that most French actively worked against the occupation. Yet films like *Au revoir les enfants* (1987) and *Elle s'appelait Sarah* (Sarah's Key, 2010) demonstrated that many French citizens actually participated in the deportation of Jews. Even the sentimental *Le vieil homme et l'enfant* (The Two of Us, 1967) depicts the savior of a young Jewish boy as anti-Semitic.[55]

Some filmmakers have chosen to fictionalize stories to make a larger point about the effects of genocide. But we can ask, is there a need for reality? The Italian film *La vita è bella* (Life Is Beautiful, 1997) employs the comedic talents of Roberto Benigni, who also wrote and directed the film, to highlight the plight that many Jews faced in Europe. Benigni's character, Guido, uses humor and cunning to protect his son in the face of great sorrow and misery; the danger with this film, of course, is that students will focus on the film's comedic interludes rather than the serious subject at hand. However, the end of the film, although somewhat sentimental, hits home as Benigni sacrifices himself to save his son. Without giving away the plot, it seems improbable that a child could be hidden inside a concentration camp and avoid detection for a period of time. Furthermore, the ability of Guido to do various acts inside the camp (for example, use the loud speaker and secure food for his child at a party) seems to argue against the film's authenticity. And the comedy does raise questions about the seriousness of the subject matter.[56] Nonetheless, its form of storytelling has made the film one of the all-time highest-grossing foreign-language films in the United States. Criticisms aside, the film is immensely popular with the public, which means more people have learned about the Holocaust. More recently, *The Boy in the Striped Pajamas*[57] (2008) is the evocative story of the son of a concentration camp commandant who befriends a Jewish boy who is interned at the camp. Based on a young adult novel of the same name by Irish author John Boyle, the film is controversial because many of the details do not correlate to reality. Some find this effective because the lessons learned can be transferred to other incidents, a reminder that the Holocaust has become a metaphor for larger evils.[58] On the other hand, the film does not accurately tell the story of what actually happened and therefore might cheapen and exploit the victims of the Holocaust.[59] There seems to be no doubt that the story is effective in eliciting an emotional response; however, it does not accurately portray the realities of concentration camps. The question remains as to what role these films play in telling the story of the Holocaust and educating the general public about genocide.

There have been several genocides that go unnoticed by the public at large and which do not generate many films. Genocidal events have occurred in Burundi, Cambodia, and the former Yugoslavia. While some films have been produced about various genocides, none have gained the attention or accolades accorded to films about the Holocaust or the Rwandan genocide.

The film *The Killing Fields* (1984) recounts the murder of millions of individuals in Cambodia during the 1970s and the plight of one man to escape the regime responsible, the Khmer Rouge. The film tells the true story of Dith Pran, a journalist and translator for the *New York Times* reporter Sydney Schanberg, after the takeover by the Khmer Rouge. The regime killed an estimated 1.7 million people beginning in 1975. The actor who portrayed Dith Pran, Haing S. Ngor, was a surgeon in Cambodia before escaping to the United States. With very little acting experience, Ngor won the Academy Award for Best Supporting Actor for his role in *The Killing Fields*. In 1996, Dr. Ngor was murdered outside his home in Los Angeles. Some of his friends and family believed it was in retaliation for his opposition to the Khmer Rouge.[60] In 2010–2011, trials began to try the surviving members of the Khmer Rouge regime in Cambodia.[61]

The 1990s saw two genocidal events that shook the conviction that a genocide like the Holocaust would never happen again. The breakup of the country of Yugoslavia led to a wave of "ethnic cleansing" that resulted in thousands of people being killed. Films such as *Pred dozhdot* (Before the Rain, 1994), *Bure baruta* (Cabaret Balkan, 1998), and *Welcome to Sarajevo* (1997) are set during this time period and help to tell the stories of the conflict between the groups.

The events in Rwanda in 1994 helped to reopen an international conversation about genocides and the world's ability (and willingness) to do anything about them. In 1994, long-simmering ethnic tension spilled into genocide when radical Hutus began a systematic extermination of Tutsis and any Hutus suspected of working with, or aiding, Tutsis. The killings took place between April and June 1994, approximately ninety days, and claimed the lives of about eight hundred thousand people. The rate of killing was faster than that of the Nazis during the Holocaust.[62]

The events in Rwanda were so dramatic that they inspired a number of well-regarded films, though not reaching the level of films about the Holocaust. Perhaps the most detailed documentaries have been aired on the PBS series *Frontline*. *The Triumph of Evil* (1998) and the subsequent *The Ghosts of Rwanda* (2005) detail not only the events of the genocide but also the unwillingness of the international community to do anything about it. Narrative films such as *Hotel Rwanda* (2004), *Sometimes in April* (2005), and *100 Days* (2001) tell individual stories of the genocide and have garnered international recognition and awards, including Academy Award nominations for two actors (Don Cheadle and Sophie Okonedo) in *Hotel Rwanda*. These films have begun a process of raising consciousness about genocide while not focusing solely on the more well-known example of the Holocaust.

Nevertheless, many genocides (such as Darfur) remain underreported and unknown by the public at large.

Justice for Human Rights Victims?

One of the reasons the Holocaust remains salient today is because of the response by the international community. After the Second World War, the Allies in Europe established a special court to try those responsible for the worst human rights crimes committed. The mission of the Nuremberg Trials was to gather, present, and disseminate evidence related to the events surrounding the Holocaust. The Nuremberg Trials are the subject of the film *Judgment at Nuremberg* (1961), a dramatic narrative film that explores not only the trials but the politics behind them, particularly in a cold war setting. The Nuremberg Trials created a precedent, and subsequently a number of courts have been established to seek justice for the victims of human rights, including, in 1998, the establishment of a permanent court, the International Criminal Court, to provide a place to try those who commit the worst human rights violations.[63] Thus, in the late twentieth century, trials have been seen as an essential part of the recovery process and search for justice. Therefore, the International Criminal Tribunal for Rwanda, located in Arusha, Tanzania, plays a central role in the film *Sometimes in April*, which is concerned with the legacy of the Rwandan genocide.

As depressing as the subject of human rights violations might be, there are signs of hope. The global community has remained remarkably united, at least rhetorically, in its effort to highlight the importance of human rights. It is important to remember that human rights violations are not committed by single individuals; the crimes outlined in this chapter require accomplices. Although responsible for the deaths of millions of people, the political leaders of regimes very rarely actually kill individual people themselves. Instead, they direct, entice, and order subordinates to do it on their behalf. Government violation of human rights requires many hands and accomplices.

Human rights violations are caused not only by those who actively direct and commit them, but by those who stand by and allow them to happen. Many films, such as *The Diary of Anne Frank, Romeo, Juliet and the Darkness,* and *Divided We Fall,* depict people who try to save the victims of genocide. Unfortunately, these people are the exception, not the rule. In the film *Shoah* there is a stunning segment in which the film's director confronts a group of Polish villagers about what was occurring during the Second World War at a local concentration camp. The villagers in Chelmno claim that there was nothing they could do about the fate of the Jews, although everyone realized they were to be killed. A group of women even suggested that many Polish women saw Jewish women as competitors because Polish men preferred making love to them. Some people expressed happiness that there were no more Jews in the town.[64]

Many times people turn their heads away from human rights violations; no doubt it is hard to watch and comprehend the implications of such events. When people are confronted with uncomfortable information, they avert their eyes and choose to look away; humans have a "normalcy bias."[65] Columnist Nicholas Kristof, desperate to figure out how to make people more concerned with the genocide in Darfur, lamented that people will pay more attention to a single homeless animal than to millions of homeless people. He satirically proposed that Darfur should be represented by a puppy with large soulful eyes and floppy ears. Then, maybe, people would empathize with the victims.[66]

Conclusion

MESSAGES AND WORLD POLITICS

Art and politics frequently intersect in many ways. This book has focused on the intersection of film and world politics. Films have the ability to shape the ways in which we view the world. In the previous chapter it was noted that an excellent film about Oskar Schindler, *Schindler's List* (1993), created a cultural touchstone by which people could make common references. People who performed similar acts are now known as alternative Schindlers, or they are at least compared to him.[1] An episode of the television series *Seinfeld*, "The Raincoats" (1994), highlighted the importance of the film to both the Jewish community and society at large, comically signaling why the film should be treated reverently. Given the power of cinema to establish the framework of discussions, to inform people, and to create a narrative, it should be no surprise that film and television are important in understanding world politics today.

For as long as there have been films (and popular culture), there have been disagreements, controversies, and arguments over their influence. Film is a place where there are ongoing conversations, where battles occur over what is, or should be, culture.[2] At times the struggle has been about what is shown on the screen. Some boycotts are concerned with how certain individuals or groups of individuals have been portrayed,[3] while other protests about films are concerned about the messages, content, or visions portrayed. For example, in the early 1930s the Legion of Decency, a Catholic organization, routinely called for boycotts of films that were deemed morally objectionable.[4] Religious groups, particularly in the United States, have often advocated protests or boycotts of films that they find offensive.[5] *The Last Temptation of Christ* (1988), a film that depicted Jesus as a human racked by doubts and fears, resulted in a firestorm of protests from religious leaders.[6] Other protests have been organized against films that run counter to an accepted political message. Thus, films like *Our Leading Citizen* (1939) were boycotted because of perceived anti-union sentiments.[7] Suffice it to say, films and television programs are contested forms of art precisely because of their ability to set and shape political agendas and attitudes.[8]

Political Messages

This book has attempted to demonstrate that there are messages in most films produced throughout the history of moving pictures. Some of these messages are overt; many are presumably unintentional or simply a part of the culture that produces the work.[9] As the twentieth century progressed, it became apparent to many that being able to control and manipulate media was a potentially important power to be acquired. The prospect of being manipulated, especially by governments, was something that a number of writers worried about in the middle of the twentieth century. There is no doubt that world events helped to shape many writers' fears. The ability of Soviet and Nazi propaganda to mobilize people concerned a number of writers. Perhaps what is interesting, and what makes propaganda still relevant, is not that writers necessarily feared individual regimes, but that these regimes demonstrated how easily people could be manipulated. Thus George Orwell demonstrates how propaganda shapes politics in his novels *1984* (filmed in 1956 and 1984) and *Animal Farm* (filmed in 1954 and 1999); Ray Bradbury speculates how the manipulation of people could have dire consequences in novels such as *Fahrenheit 451;* Aldous Huxley examines the effects of brainwashing in *Brave New World.*

Moving images have become a sophisticated art in the modern world; however, the moving image is not limited to art and entertainment. It has become an essential tool of advertising and marketing (in fact, some would call it manipulation). The goal of many television advertisements is to create lifelong customers. Television advertisements, for example, rely on pathos, sentiment, and vanity to encourage consumers to purchase their products—and to do so again and again. As such, television advertising has become a major industry, one that, some have argued, has the ability to shape cultures and habits.[10]

Given the success of commercial enterprises, we should not be surprised that there will be people who attempt to modify or sway the public's opinion about world politics. There is nothing new about this. Films that attempt to persuade date back to the very early days of cinema, and the practice

This closed cinema in Wexford, Ireland, is symptomatic of the changes in watching films. No longer are people apt to share the experience with others; viewing has increasingly become a solitary experience. (Photograph by the author)

has evolved and become more sophisticated. What has changed in recent times is the ready availability of films and television programs. On-demand streaming through the Internet has made films available virtually anytime, anywhere. It makes it much easier to see films and to consider the diverse examples in a book such as this. Yet this personalization of film viewing means that most people see films alone, rather than in a theater. While filmmakers might be concerned about the aesthetics of small screens versus big screens and other artistic concerns, we might consider the impact on politics. Does seeing films in a theater create a sense of shared experience? Do witnessing and hearing the reactions of other people help us gauge the political messages that might be delivered in a film? Political scientist Robert Putnam has speculated that the development of technology has increasingly made us more isolated from one another. The result, he argues, is a loosening of the social trust and bonds that make democratic governance possible.[11] The rise of VHS, DVD, Blu-ray, and online streaming has meant that people are less likely to have a communal experience when they watch a film.

Newer relatively inexpensive methods of creating films have meant some monumental changes in the messages delivered to people. In the aftermath of the September 11, 2001, terrorist attacks on New York and Washington, a number of conspiracy theory films and websites emerged to challenge the prevailing interpretation. The primary contention was that the events were part of an official cover-up.[12] Another example of the effectiveness of amateur filmmaking is an Internet video released in September 2012, *The Innocence of Muslims,* which sparked worldwide protests. At the same time, *Kony 2012* created a sensation, albeit a short-lived one, demanding the arrest and trial of Lord's Resistance Army leader Joseph Kony for employing child soldiers. Yet the techniques that allow for easier film and video making also make it easier for films to be manipulated. Do the patina and polish of motion pictures make it harder for the average person to distinguish between fact and manipulation?

While many who study film are aware of the techniques that help to persuade people, many viewers are not. A disturbing trend in journalism is the use of video news releases (VNR). A VNR is a short film made by a company to appear as if it is a news story, when in fact it is a promotional story designed to highlight the benefits of a product so that consumers will buy it. Local television stations routinely use VNRs as a part of their news-cast, often without any indication that it is an advertisement.[13] Although studies indicate that most viewers are unaware of this practice, people who watch the news reported that they want to be informed when a television station uses VNRs as a part of its newscasts.[14] The ability of corporations and others to get their message into the news, and accepted as fact, is stag-gering. Moreover, journalists have resorted to using information distributed by corporations in what has been termed "churnalism." Rather than going out and finding news, there has been a trend to simply sift through press releases and scour the Internet to find stories that can be reprinted, often without fact-checking or even rewriting.[15]

As related to film, the difficulty with such practices is that a well-made film often becomes history for many people in the audience.[16] The public's interpretation of events is filtered through the lens of media. This is why it is hard to imagine moving images taking the place of the written word when it comes to research and in-depth understanding of important historical and political events. This book is premised on the idea that film provides alternative information and data, but that it is *not* a substitute for the research and rigor of a true news source or a reliable history book.

Traveling without Leaving the Couch

Despite the limitations and drawbacks of using film to understand politics, it is still an invaluable tool for glimpsing the world. Films and television programs, especially those made in other countries, provide alternative understandings of the world, allow us to see cultural differences, and give us the chance to appreciate history from another perspective. Films and television programs allow us to glimpse a cultural conversation. Cinema is not a substitute for travel, but it is the next best thing. We can sit, be comfortable, and observe the experiences of others. Often we can listen to conversations in other languages and, through subtitles, understand them. Film and cinema open doors to understanding—understanding the world and its diverse politics, and understanding ourselves as well.

ACKNOWLEDGMENTS

It is a time-honored tradition for the author of a book to acknowledge a debt of gratitude to several people. This author is no different. It is gratifying to know that I have had the support of so many people in producing this labor of love. I appreciate all who have offered suggestions, let me discuss ideas, and helped me along the way. It is impossible to mention everyone individually, for the sake of brevity. To those not specifically mentioned here, I apologize for the omissions, but do thank you.

I want to begin by thanking the faculty and staff of Shippensburg University. In particular I want to mention the staff members of Ezra Lehman Memorial Library who cheerfully tracked down materials and books essential to completing this manuscript. The members of the political science department of Shippensburg University have been consistently supportive and encouraging throughout my tenure at the university, not just while I was working on this project. Specifically, I would like to acknowledge Dr. Alison Dagnes and Dr. Nielsen Brasher for hearing me out and offering support and advice.

I am also appreciative of everyone at the University Press of Kentucky, especially Anne Dean Watkins, Bailey Johnson, and the anonymous reviewers whose suggestions made this manuscript much better. I extend my gratitude to Robin DuBlanc for her excellent copyediting of the manuscript.

Finally, thank you to my family for love and support. Miranda and Liam Sachleben helped me understand the finer points of children's television, and to Angie, my sounding board and draft reader, I owe very much—more than I can express. Thank you.

My father, Charles Sachleben, was not really a film aficionado; however, he was always interested in understanding the world from different perspectives. As a child of about six or seven, I remember him telling me about an interesting film being shown on our public television station that night, *Alexander Nevsky*, complete with a description of the Battle of the Ice at Lake Peipus. Not many fathers would entice their young sons to watch a subtitled Soviet film from the 1930s. Also, one of his favorite films was the obscure and these days rarely screened *Colossus: The Forbin Project*. He is the reason why both of these films appear in the book. Unfortunately, my father died as I was in the process of working on the manuscript that came to be known as *World Politics on Screen*. To him I dedicate this book.

NOTES

Introduction

1. "D'oh! More Know Simpsons Than Constitution. Study: America More Familiar with Cartoon Family Than First Amendment," MSNBC, 1 March 2006, http://www.msnbc.msn.com/id/11611015; McCormick Tribune Freedom Museum, "Americans' Awareness of First Amendment Freedoms," 1 March 2006, http://www.forumforeducation.org/node/147.

2. See Benedict Anderson, *Imagined Communities: Reflections on the Origin and Spread of Nationalism,* rev. ed. (New York: Verso, 1991), 59–65.

3. Karl W. Deutsch, *Nationalism and Its Alternatives* (New York: Knopf, 1969), 14.

4. Anderson, *Imagined Communities,* 6.

5. Consider our friend Sally; she could read a newspaper from a small town in central Ohio. She could read wedding announcements, information about local businesses and what is happening in local churches, but because she has no reference to the town, the information about events probably has little impact on her.

6. Anderson, *Imagined Communities,* 61–63.

7. This is not dissimilar from the approach taken in Iver B. Neumann and Daniel H. Nexon, "Introduction: Harry Potter and the Study of World Politics," in *Harry Potter and International Relations,* ed. Daniel H. Nexon and Iver B. Neumann (Lanham, MD: Rowman & Littlefield, 2006), 6–9.

8. Benjamin R. Barber, *Jihad vs. McWorld: Terrorism's Challenge to Democracy* (New York: Ballantine Books, 2001), 88–99, 307–9.

9. Raymond G. Gordon Jr., ed., *Ethnologue: Languages of the World,* 15th ed. (Dallas: SIL International, 2005), online at http://www.ethnologue.com/.

10. For a more in-depth discussion of film, film construction, and film criticism, see James Monaco, *How to Read a Film: Movies, Media, Multimedia,* 4th ed. (New York: Oxford University Press, 2009); and David A. Cook, *A History of Narrative Film,* 4th ed. (New York: Norton, 2004).

11. Richard Meran Barsam, *Filmguide to Triumph of the Will* (Bloomington: Indiana University Press, 1975), 27.

12. *Memory of the Camps* will be discussed in more detail in chapter 13. The program website, which includes a link to watch the entire film, is available at http://www.pbs.org/wgbh/pages/frontline/camp/index.html.

13. For more details about the history and background to the film, see Elizabeth Sussex, "The Fate of *F3080,*" *Sight and Sound* 53, no. 2 (1984): 92–97.

14. For an update on one of the men made famous by the photograph, see Ed Vulliamy, "'I Am Waiting. No One Has Ever Said Sorry,'" *Observer,* 27 July 2008, 24.

15. Ed Vulliamy, "Poison in the Well of History," *Guardian,* 14 March 2000, G2-2.

16. Robert D. Putnam, *The Comparative Study of Political Elites* (Englewood Cliffs, NJ: Prentice-Hall, 1976), 384.

17. See Will Kaufmann, *The Civil War in American Culture* (Edinburgh: Edinburgh University Press, 2006), 18. Abraham Lincoln is apocryphally reported to have said on meeting Harriet Beecher Stowe, "So you're the little lady who started this great war."

18. Judith E. Doneson, *The Holocaust in American Film,* 2nd ed. (Syracuse: Syracuse University Press, 2002), 190–96. Doneson also argues that the miniseries has the effect of Americanizing the Holocaust. This process of discussing what individuals did during the Second World War has sparked a number of films, notably *Das schreckliche Mädchen* (The Nasty Girl, 1990) and *Le chagrin et la pitié* (The Sorrow and the Pity, 1969).

19. Doneson, *The Holocaust in American Film,* 195–96. Doneson elaborates on European reactions, including those from France and Switzerland. For a further discussion of the impact of the miniseries *Holocaust,* see Tom Driesbach, "Transatlantic Broadcasts: *Holocaust* in America and West Germany," *Penn History Review* 16, no. 2 (2009): 76–97.

20. The speech was given to the Bundestag to commemorate the fortieth anniversary of the end of the Second World War (8 May 1985).

21. Dennis Broe, "Fox and Its Friends: Global Commodification and the New Cold War," *Cinema Journal* 43, no. 4 (2004): 98. Broe claims that the program, a major rating success for Fox Television, helps to facilitate the political agenda of the parent company the News Corporation.

22. For a more detailed discussion of so-called enhanced interrogation, see Mark Bowden, "The Dark Art of Interrogation," *Atlantic Monthly,* October 2003, 51–76.

23. Dahlia Lithwick, "But Jack Does It: Two New Books Suggest the Bush Administration Based Its Torture Policy, in Large Part, on the Exploits of a Fictional Action Hero," *National Post* (Canada), 31 July 2008; see also Joan Biskupic, "Scalia's Comments on Torture Latest Taste of Bluntness," *USA Today,* 14 February 2008.

24. This can take many forms. In the documentary film *Vote for Me—Politics in America* (1996), congressional candidate Maggie Lauterer faces a voter concerned that a curtailment of gun rights will make the United States more vulnerable. The voter references the movie *Red Dawn* (1984) as a potential of what could happen if the United States is not vigilant. (The film's website is http://www.cnam.com/voteforme/about.htm.) Famously, Senator James Inhofe used Michael Crichton's novel *State of Fear* as evidence that the science behind climate change is a worldwide fraud. See Jamie Wilson, "Comment: Michael Crichton Testifies on Global Warming," *Guardian,* 29 September 2005, 1.

25. Adrian Blomfield, "Russia to Ban *Simpsons* and *South Park,*" *Telegraph,* 24 September 2008.

26. David Ignatius, "Think Strategy, Not Numbers," *Washington Post,* 26 August 2003, A13.

27. Dan Quayle, "Speech to the Commonwealth Club," 19 May 1992.

28. Ernest Giglio, *Here's Looking at You: Hollywood, Film and Politics,* 3rd ed. (New York: Peter Lang, 2010), 21–29.

29. Jody Baumgartner and Jonathan S. Morris, "The Daily Show Effect: Candidate Evaluations, Efficacy, and American Youth," *American Politics Research* 34, no. 3 (2006): 341–67.

1. The Modern World and Those Who Try to Explain It

1. The film *Juan de los muertos* (Juan of the Dead, 2011) is a thinly veiled critique of the Cuban government masking as a zombie film. Victoria Burnett, "Socialism's Sacred Cows Suffer Zombie Attack in Popular Cuban Film," *New York Times,* 11 December 2011, A6.

2. Thus, for example, President George H. W. Bush, in a speech to religious broadcasters, said that the country should resemble the 1970s American television series *The Waltons* more than the satirical animation series *The Simpsons*. Chris Turner, *Planet Simpson: How a Cartoon Masterpiece Documented an Era and Defined a Generation* (Cambridge, MA: Da Capo, 2004), 225–26. This phenomenon is not limited to the United States; see, for example, Declan Walsh, "For Many in Pakistan, a Television Show Goes Too Far," *New York Times,* 27 January 2012, A4.

3. Mike Chopra-Gant, *Cinema and History: The Telling of Stories* (New York: Wallflower, 2008), 2.

4. Opinions about the episode, entitled "The Puppy Episode" (1997), varied. Some thought it was a milestone for the advancement of rights; others saw it as evidence of the degradation of American cultural values. Influential cultural and political commentator Rev. Jerry Falwell labeled DeGeneres "Ellen Degenerate." Frank Rich, "The *Ellen* Striptease," *New York Times,* 10 April 1997, A29; Charlie Patton, "Any Speculation about the Sexual Orientation of ABC's 'Ellen' will End Wednesday Night When Character Played by Ellen DeGeneres Comes out of the Closet," *Florida Times-Union,* 27 April 1997, E1; Frank Rich, "Family Values Stalkers," *New York Times,* 13 January 1999.

5. We see a similar trend in North America with the inclusion and recognition of the rights of Muslims, especially in the aftermath of the September 11, 2011, terrorist attacks. Television programs such as *All-American Muslim* (2011–) and *Little Mosque on the Prairie* (2007–), which will be discussed in subsequent chapters, are examples. We can also observe how films and documentaries that portray a group in unflattering ways can be a source of friction as well. In January 2012 it was revealed that during a training session for New York City police officers, a film depicting many American Muslim leaders as extremist was shown. Later the same year, coinciding with September 11 commemorations, a video insulting Islam and the Prophet Muhammad, *The Innocence of Muslims,* surfaced. The violent reaction around the world, resulting in many deaths, was linked to the assassination of the American ambassador to Libya, J. Christopher Stevens. Joseph Goldstein, "Kelly Says Anti-Muslim Films Shouldn't Have Been Screened," *New York Times,* 28 January 2012, A21; Rick Gladstone, "Anti-American Protests Flare beyond the Mideast," *New York Times,* 15 September 2012, A1.

6. Moisés Naím, "Dangerously Unique: Why Our Definition of 'Normalcy' Can Be Costly for Everyone Else," *Foreign Policy* 150 (September/October 2005): 112–11.

7. For background to the rise of Hollywood as a film capital, see Kristin Thompson, *Exporting Entertainment: America in the World Film Market, 1907–1934* (London: British Film Institute, 1985).

8. Lane Crothers, *Globalization and American Popular Culture* (Lanham, MD: Rowman & Littlefield, 2007), 56–58.

9. A number of British television comedy series have found success in the United States as well, including *The Benny Hill Show* (1969–1989), *Monty Python's Flying Circus* (1969–1974), and *The Office* (2001–2003), which was remade as an American series of the

same name (2005–2013). This is further evidence that comedy is dependent on language and culture and finds difficulty traversing cultural lines.

10. Gerald Vizcaur, *Interior Landscapes: Autobiographical Myths and Metaphors* (Minneapolis: University of Minnesota Press, 1990), 197–98, 262.

11. See "Politics Aside, Iranians Love American TV shows," *Middle East Online,* 2 March 2009, http://www.middle-east-online.com/english/?id=30702; and Hiedeh Farmani, "US Television Shows Give Iranians a Friendlier View," *Middle East Times,* 2 March 2009.

12. Barber, *Jihad vs. McWorld,* 100–151.

13. Benjamin R. Barber, "More Democracy, More Revolution," *Nation,* 28 October 1998.

14. Jack G. Shaheen, *Reel Bad Arabs: How Hollywood Vilifies a People* (New York: Olive Branch, 1994), 5.

15. George F. Custen, *Twentieth Century Fox: Daryl F. Zanuck and the Culture of Hollywood* (New York: Basic Books, 1997), 3, cited in Stanley Corkin, *Cowboys as Cold Warriors: The Western and U.S. History* (Philadelphia: Temple University Press, 2004), 6.

16. Jens Ulff-Møller, "The Origin of the French Film Quota Policy Controlling the Import of American Films," *Historical Journal of Film, Radio and Television* 18, no. 2 (1998): 167–82; Jens Ulff-Møller, *Hollywood's Film Wars with France: Film-Trade Diplomacy and the Emergence of France Film Quota Policy* (Rochester, NY: University of Rochester Press, 2001); Roger Cohen, "France and Spain Import Quotas," *New York Times,* 22 December 1993. The issue of creating quotas on the number of films is not new. In France, the creation of a quota system was a political debate in the late 1920s and early 1930s; see, for example, Carlisle MacDonald, "French Again Seek 3-to-1 Film Quota," *New York Times,* 18 May 1929, 6; Herbert L. Matthews, "The French Quota and Its Possible Results the Present Topic of Discussion," *New York Times,* 14 August 1932, X2.

17. Steven J. Boss, *Hollywood Left and Right: How Movie Stars Shaped American Politics* (New York: Oxford University Press, 2011), 1–2. Boss highlights the efforts of Louie B. Mayer, the legendary head of Metro-Goldwyn-Mayer (MGM), to establish links between the Republican Party and Hollywood and to create films that reflected conservative values (51–88, particularly 81–83).

18. Robert B. Ray, *A Certain Tendency of the Hollywood Cinema, 1930–1980* (Princeton, NJ: Princeton University Press, 1985), 57.

19. Interestingly, the film was remade as *The Magnificent Seven* (1960) in the United States with some plot changes.

20. Donald Richie, *The Films of Akira Kurosawa* (Berkeley: University of California Press, 1984), 99.

21. Robert Sklar, *Movie-Made America: A Social History of American Movies* (New York: Vintage, 1976), 267. Corkin, in his study of the political messages in westerns, makes a similar point, noting that the western film was designed to marry history and myth in order to appeal to the nationalism of American audiences. Corkin, *Cowboys as Cold Warriors,* 6.

22. Garth Jowett and Victoria O'Donnell, *Propaganda and Persuasion,* 2nd ed. (Newbury Park, CA: Sage, 1992), 4; Bruce L. Smith, "Propagandam" in *International Encyclopedia of the Social Sciences,* ed. David L. Sills (New York: Macmillan, 1968).

23. Sabine Hake, *German National Cinema* (New York: Routledge, 2002), 77.

24. Armand Schwerner, *Triumph of the Will* (Mt. Horeb, WI: Perishable, 1976). For more

information about the films and politics of Riefenstahl, see Rainer Rother, *Leni Riefenstahl: The Seduction of Genius* (New York: Continuum, 2002), 61–76; Jürgeb Trimborn, *Leni Riefenstahl: A Life* (New York: Faber & Faber, 2007), particularly 117–22; and the documentary film *Die Macht der Bilder: Leni Riefenstahl* (The Wonderful Horrible Life of Leni Riefenstahl, 1993).

25. David Denby, "Battle Lines," *New Yorker*, 23, 30 January 2006, 97.

26. Heather L. Lamarre, Kristen D. Landreville, and Michael A. Beam, "Irony of Satire: Political Ideology and the Motivation to See What You Want to See in *The Colbert Report*," *International Journal of Press/Politics* 14, no. 2 (2009): 212–31.

27. Jeffrey Hart, "Three Approaches to the Measurement of Power in International Relations," *International Organization* 30, no. 2 (1976): 284–305.

28. For a discussion of the problems of defining and measuring power, see John M. Rothgeb Jr., *Defining Power: Influence and Force in the Contemporary International System* (New York: St. Martin's, 1993).

29. Joseph S. Nye Jr., *Soft Power: The Means to Success in World Politics* (New York: Public Affairs, 2004), 7.

30. Harold Laswell and Abraham Kaplan, *Power and Society: A Framework for Political Inquiry* (New Haven, CT: Yale University Press, 1950), cited in Joseph S. Nye Jr., *The Future of Power* (New York: Public Affairs, 2011), 7.

31. Nye, *The Future of Power*, 21.

32. Nye refers to this as "invisible power," where the target does not even realize that the agenda is being shaped and that his or her preferences are molded by the preferences of others. Ibid., 14.

33. Meg Bortin, "Making Money in Senegal off Human Cargo," *International Herald Tribune*, 30 May 2006, 2.

34. Richard De Zoysa and O. Newman, "Globalization, Soft Power and the Challenge of Hollywood," *Contemporary Politics* 8, no. 3 (2002): 185–202; William Spencer Armour, "Learning Japanese by Reading 'Manga': The Rise of 'Soft Power Pedagogy,'" *RELC Journal* 42, no. 2 (2011): 125–40; Charles W. Hayford, "Crossing the Rivers of Time and Oceans of Culture: The Use of Films in American-East Asian Relations," *Journal of American–East Asian Relations* 18, no. 1 (2011): 1–9.

35. In rare cases, the film would be entirely remade in alternative languages. For example, Alfred Hitchcock's *Murder* (1930) was remade with German-language actors and released as *Mary* (1931). A number of Hollywood films had Spanish-language alternatives, such as the Spanish-language *Drácula* (1931), directed by George Melford, which were made simultaneously with Spanish-language actors for the Spanish-language markets of Central and South America.

36. Henry Kissinger, *Diplomacy* (New York: Simon & Schuster, 1994), 79.

2. A Primer on IR (International Relations) Perspectives

1. Karl Deutsch, "On Communication Models in the Social Sciences," *Public Opinion Quarterly* 16, no. 3 (1952): 356–80.

2. Gerard von Glahn, *Law among Nations: An Introduction to Public International Law*, 7th ed. (Boston: Allyn & Bacon, 1996), 52.

3. The modern international system was established under the moniker of the West-phalian System because the arrangements derived from the Peace of Westphalia in 1648. Under that arrangement, the rules and norms gave most prerogatives to states. Kalevi J. Hosti, *Peace and War: Armed Conflicts and International Order, 1648–1989* (New York: Cambridge University Press, 1991), 25, 39. For background on the importance of the Peace of Westphalia, see Leo Gross, "The Peace of Westphalia," *American Journal of International Law* 42, no. 1 (1948): 20–41.

4. For an account of why the work of Thucydides remains important in the current study of international politics, see Daniel Mendelsohn, "Theatres of War: Why Battles over Ancient Athens Still Rage," *New Yorker,* 12 January 2004, 79.

5. For further reading on the realist perspective, see Hans Joachim Morgenthau, *Politics among Nations: The Struggle for Power and Peace* (New York: Knopf, 1948); Kenneth Neal Waltz, *Man, the State, and War: A Theoretical Analysis* (New York: Columbia University Press, 1959); John J. Mearsheimer, *The Tragedy of Great Power Politics* (New York: Norton, 2001).

6. For further reading on the liberal perspective, see Michael W. Doyle, "Liberalism and World Politics," *American Political Science Review* 80, no. 4 (1986): 1151–69; Robert O. Keohane and Joseph S. Nye, *Power and Interdependence,* 2nd ed. (Glenview, IL: Scott, Fores-man, 1989); Bruce M. Russett, *Grasping the Democratic Peace: Principles for a Post–Cold War World* (Princeton, NJ: Princeton University Press, 1993).

7. For more readings from the social constructivist perspective, see Alexander Wendt, "Anarchy Is What States Make of It: The Social Construction of Power Politics," *International Organization* 46, no. 2 (1992): 391–425; Martha Finnemore, "Norms, Culture and World Politics: Insights from Sociology's Institutionalism," *International Organization* 50, no. 3 (1996): 347–60; John Gerard Ruggie, *Constructing the World Polity: Essays on International Institutions* (New York: Routledge, 1998).

8. For more readings from the structuralist perspectives, see Johan Galtung, "A Struc-tural Theory of Imperialism," *Journal of Peace Research* 8, no. 2 (1971): 81–98; Immanuel Wallerstein, *The Politics of the World-Economy* (New York: Cambridge University Press, 1984); J. Ann Tickner, *Gendering World Politics: Issues and Approaches in the Post–Cold War Era* (New York: Columbia University Press, 2001).

9. For additional readings on international relations theory, consult Stephen M. Walt, "International Relations: One World, Many Theories," *Foreign Policy* 110 (Spring 1998): 29–40; Paul R. Viotti and Mark V. Kauppi, *International Relations Theory,* 4th ed. (New York: Longman, 2010); Eric Leonard, ed., *International Relations Theory* (Lanham, MD: Rowman & Littlefield, 2014).

3. War Is Sometimes Unavoidable

1. John J. Mearsheimer, "Why We Will Soon Miss the Cold War," *Atlantic Monthly,* August 1990, 35–50; John J. Mearsheimer, "Back to the Future: Instability in Europe after the Cold War," *International Security* 15, no. 1 (1990): 5–56.

2. "We maintain . . . that war is nothing but a continuation of political intercourse with a mixture of other means." Carl von Clausewitz, *On War,* trans. Colonel J. J. Graham (London: Kegan Paul, Trench, Trübner, 1908), 121. Von Clausewitz goes on to argue, "Is not

War merely another kind of writing and language for political thoughts? It has certainly a grammar of its own, but its logic is not peculiar to itself" (122).

3. Kenneth N. Waltz, *Man, the State and War: A Theoretical Analysis* (New York: Columbia University Press, 1959).

4. See J. David Singer, "The Level-of-Analysis Problem in International Relations," *World Politics* 14, no. 1 (1961): 77–92.

5. Russett, *Grasping the Democratic Peace;* Michael W. Doyle, *Ways of War and Peace* (New York: Norton, 1997), 205–311.

6. Kenneth N. Waltz, "The Origins of War in Neorealist Theory," *Journal of Interdisciplinary History* 18, no. 4 (1988): 615–28.

7. Ibid., 71.

8. The security dilemma is demonstrated in the film *It's a Mad Mad Mad Mad World* (1963); for a further discussion, see Mark Sachleben and Kevan M. Yenerall, *Seeing the Bigger Picture: American and International Politics in Film and Popular Culture*, 2nd ed. (New York: Peter Lang, 2012), 217–18.

9. Because of references such as his adoption of the name Carpenter and the fact that he is a peacekeeper, Klaatu is generally regarded as representing Christ.

10. The story on which the film is based, "Farewell to the Master" by Harry Bates, was originally published in *Astounding Science Fiction,* October 1940.

11. For example, the American film *December 7th* (1943), the British film *London Can Take It!* (1940), and the Soviet film *Fascist Boots on Our Homeland* (1941).

12. This should not be confused with the documentary *Why We Fight* (2005), directed by Eugene Jarecki, which explores the warning contained in President Eisenhower's farewell speech that a military industrial complex made the use of military conflict nearly inevitable and the evidence that the United States had ignored this warning.

13. "America is Invaded Again in the Films," *New York Times,* 7 June 1916. This is a tactic that is used frequently to undermine opposition to military buildup; often those who are seen as pacifists or against military expenditures are cast as disloyal. In fact, in *Battle Cry of Peace,* the pacifists are portrayed as advocating peace during the day and building bombs at night for the invaders.

14. A remake of the film *Red Dawn,* released in 2012, features an invasion of the United States by North Korea.

15. Interestingly, Disney, the company that produced *Pearl Harbor,* had the film reedited for overseas markets and used advertising to focus attention away from politics and war. The film as shown in Japan, for example, attempted to focus more on the love story and downplay the aspects of war between the United States and Japan.

16. "Iran Condemns Hollywood War Epic," *BBC News,* 13 March 2007, http://news.bbc.co.uk/2/hi/entertainment/6446183.stm.

17. The full title of the film is *The Good Fight: The Abraham Lincoln Brigade in the Spanish Civil War;* the documentary visits several of the Americans who fought on behalf of the liberal government of Spain.

18. There are many films that take the approach of discussing the politics behind war without resorting to a military setting, such as *Abe Lincoln in Illinois* (1940).

19. Interestingly, at one point, future president Ronald Reagan was announced as the lead actor for the film.

20. Aljean Harmetz, *Round Up the Usual Suspects: The Making of "Casablanca"—Bogart, Bergman, and World War II* (New York: Hyperion, 1992), 280.

21. The film was fortunate to have incredible timing. It was released nationally on 23 January 1943. Unknown at the time, between 14 January and 24 January, an Allied conference between the American president Franklin Roosevelt and British prime minister Winston Churchill took place in Casablanca to map war strategy. Churchill and Roosevelt would demand the unconditional surrender of Axis forces. Because of a news blackout, the American public did not learn of the meeting until after Roosevelt had returned safely home. The film benefited from the additional publicity of the conference, which coincided with the opening of the film, adding to its legendary mystique. Harmetz, *Round Up the Usual Suspects*, 283.

22. There are a number of other interpretations that have been suggested as well. For instance, Donnelly has argued that the relationship between Rick and Renault is homosexual in nature. He argues that Renault's description of Rick to Ilsa ("He's the kind of man that, well, if I were a woman and I weren't around, I should be in love with Rick") and Rick's choice of male companionship over heterosexual romantic love is evidence of that relationship. William Donnelly, "Love and Death in Casablanca," in *Persistence of Vision: A Collection of Film Criticisms*, ed. Joseph McBride (Madison: Wisconsin Film Society Press, 1968), 103–7. For a summary of further interpretations, see Harmetz, *Round Up the Usual Suspects*, 347–54.

23. Julius Epstein (screenwriter), quoted in Harlan Lebo, *Casablanca: Behind the Scenes* (New York: Simon & Schuster, 1992), 13.

24. York went on to acknowledge that there had to be millions of Americans contemplating the same questions of morality as he did in 1917. Bosley Crowther, "Sergeant York," *New York Times,* 3 July 1941, 15.

25. Originally a poem published in *McClure's* magazine in 1899 that referenced the American role in the Philippines.

26. Here one can think about films such as *The Kaiser, the Beast of Berlin* (1918) as well as a slew of Cold War films.

27. *The Buffalo Boy* (2004) makes the point that regardless of the occupation forces (Japanese or French), life in rural Vietnam went on as normal.

28. The title of the film is literally translated as "We must help one another."

29. Stephen Hunter, "The Pentagon's Lessons from Reel Life," *Washington Post,* 4 September 2001, C1.

30. Studs Terkel, *The Good War: An Oral History of World War Two* (New York: Pantheon, 1984).

31. Harmetz, *Round Up the Usual Suspects*, 307–8.

4. The Case against War

1. Anthony Swofford, *Jarhead: A Marine's Chronicle of the Gulf War and Other Battles* (New York: Scribner, 2003), 7. Also quoted in Alex Cox, "Flashback: Alex Cox on *Fires on the Plain* (1959)," *Film Comment* 44, no. 3 (2008): 8. Swofford's book would be turned into a major motion picture, *Jarhead* (2005), starring Jake Gyllenhaal.

2. In the introduction to his account of the First World War, John Keegan encompasses the destruction and the effect on the psyche of European societies after the war: John Keegan,

The First World War (New York: Vintage Books, 2000), chapter 1, particularly 3–9. The most famous account of World War I is Barbara Tuchman, *The Guns of August* (New York: Macmillan, 1962), a good resource for learning more about the war. To help demonstrate the high casualty rates during the war, Tuchman recounts (174) an incident at Fort Barchon in which German soldiers continuously advanced toward Belgian lines, the dead and dying constituting a barricade that allowed their approach.

3. The Vietnam War helped to contribute to a number of antiwar art forms, including music. Popular songs such as Arlo Guthrie's "Alice's Restaurant Massacree," Bob Dylan's "Blowin' in the Wind," and Neil Young's "Ohio" became defining music of the period.

4. The film was heavily censored when it was screened in New York. This ultimately served to significantly disrupt the continuity. *New York Times* review, 19 June 1948, 19.

5. The project was filmed and released as *Operation Lysistrata* (2006). See Debra West, "No Sex as Anti War Protest? What Sex?" *New York Times,* 9 March 2003, WC14-1; Paula McCooey, "Actors Stage 2,400-Year-Old Comedy to Protest War in Iraq," *Ottawa Citizen,* 3 March 2003, D1. Because the Peloponnesian Wars were a conflict between Greeks, the play often resonates in communities that have been torn by civil strife, such as Northern Ireland; see "Hard-Hitting Message to Men," *Belfast Telegraph,* 3 March 2003. It also resonates during times in which there are unpopular wars. Note that there were several filmed versions during the Vietnam War and a revival of stage performances during the Iraq War (particularly 2003–2005), particularly the National Theater of Greece tour in 2004. See Charles Isherwood, "Antiwar Humor, Really Old School," *New York Times,* 8 October 2004, E-1.

6. Adam Roberts, "Lives and Statistics: Are 90% of War Victims Civilians?" *Survival* 52, no. 3 (2010): 115–36. Military doctrine usually dictates that civilians are not a legitimate target during times of war: Whitney Kaufmann, "What Is the Scope of Civilian Immunity in Wartime?" *Journal of Military Ethics* 2, no. 3 (2003): 186–94.

7. Wars were seen as sporting events by many. For example, during the first battle of Bull Run (Manassas), wealthy elites from Washington, assured of a Union victory, went to the battlefield to have a picnic while watching the fight: David J. Eicher, *The Longest Night: A Military History of the Civil War* (New York: Simon & Schuster, 2001), 98.

8. For example, *The Battle of the Somme* (1916), *The Kaiser, the Beast of Berlin* (1918), *Hearts of the World* (1918), and *Yankee Doodle in Berlin* (1919).

9. The ending segment of the film is shot in silence; soldiers, one by one, look over their shoulders and stare at the audience. The shot is superimposed over a hillside with dozens and dozens of white crosses, and is designed to implicate the viewer: we are the ones who allow these young men to be sent to the horrors and death of war.

10. This is a theme that is also explored in *The Razor's Edge* (1946), which tells the story of a World War I pilot who is so unsettled by his wartime experience that he departs on a spiritual quest to seek peace. For a thoughtful consideration of the effects of war on those who fight them, see Sebastian Junger's editorial, "Why Would Anyone Miss War?" *New York Times,* 17 July 2011, SR4.

11. Mourdant Hall wrote in his review that he thought the sounds of warfare were "a bit too loud and too prolonged": Mordaunt Hall, "A German War Film," *New York Times,* 20 February 1931, 18. Hall is missing an important element in the effectiveness of both *Westfront 1918* and *All Quiet on the Western Front.* The constant barrage of sound, along with the

constant fear, had a psychological impact on the soldiers in the trenches. The representation of the psychological pressures faced during warfare only begins to scratch the surface of confusion and dislocation that led to psychological problems.

12. Among the racially insensitive comments made, for example, a soldier refers to coffee as "negro sweat."

13. Michael Geisler, "The Battleground of Modernity: *Westfront 1918* (1930)," in *The Films of G. W. Pabst: An Extraterritorial Cinema,* ed. Eric Rentschler (New Brunswick, NJ: Rutgers University Press, 1990), 95–96.

14. Hall, "A German War Film."

15. Lee Atwell, *G. W. Pabst* (Boston: Twanye, 1977), 75–82; Geisler, "The Battleground of Modernity," 96. For more about G. W. Pabst and his films, see Eric Rentschler, "The Problematic Pabst: An Auteur Directed by History," in Rentschler, *The Films of G. W. Pabst.*

16. Kramer and Welsh, in their analysis of his career, wrote, "If Abel Gance never did another film, [*J'accuse*] alone would have earned him immortality": Steven Philip Kramer and James Michael Welsh, *Abel Gance* (Boston: Twayne, 1978), 62.

17. Kevin Brownlow, "The Waste of War: Abel Gance's *J'accuse*" (essay included with the DVD set), 4.

18. S. L. A. Marshall, *Men against Fire: The Problems of Battle Command in Future War* (Washington, DC: Infantry Journal, 1947); Sam Keen, *Faces of the Enemy: Reflections of the Hostile Imagination* (San Francisco: Harper & Row, 1986); Richard Holmes, *Acts of War: The Behavior of Men in Battle* (New York: Free Press, 1985).

19. One method of doing this is to dehumanize the enemy, as discussed above. See Michael Berenbaum, "I Can't Understand the Event, Therefore, I Will Try," in *Courage to Remember: Interviews on the Holocaust,* ed. Kinue Tokudome (St. Paul, MN: Paragon House, 1999); Ervin Staub, *The Roots of Evil: The Origin of Genocide and Other Group Violence* (New York: Cambridge University Press, 1989); Caroline Fournet, *The Crime of Destruction and the Law of Genocide: Their Impact on Collective Memory* (Burlington, VT: Ashgate, 2007). We see examples of this in Second World War–era films and cartoons, e.g., *Bugs Bunny Nips the Nips* (1944). This phenomenon is discussed further in chapter 13 on human rights.

20. Brownlow, "The Waste of War," 9.

21. Ibid.

22. Chris Hedges, *War Is a Force That Gives Us Meaning* (New York: Anchor, 2002). See also Kevin Ivison, *Red One: A Bomb Disposal Expert on the Front Line* (London: Weidenfeld & Nicholson, 2010).

23. The actor Harold Russell had lost his arms in a training accident in 1944 while in the army. Harold Russell and Dan Ferullo, *The Best Years of My Life* (Middlebury, VT: P. S. Eriksson, 1981).

24. Virginia Nicholson, *Singled Out: How Two Million Women Survived without Men after the First World War* (New York: Oxford University Press, 2007). The long-term implication was that a number of women of a certain age in Britain had no prospect of marriage. The number of available men substantially decreased across the European continent. Nicholson argues this has a dramatic impact on British society; for an example of this on screen, see the British television series *South Riding* (2011).

25. While not frequently written about until the 1990s, the victimization of women during

times of war regularly occurs; for a brief overview, consult Magnus Hirschfeld and Edward Podolsky, *The Sexual History of the World War* (New York: Panurge, 1934). More recently scholars have focused on the violence women face during war; for an overview, see Mark Ellis, "Breaking the Silence: Rape as an International Crime," *Case Western Reserve Journal of International Law* 38, no. 2 (2006/2007): 225–47; H. Patricia Hynes, "On the Battlefield of Women's Bodies: An Overview of the Harm of War to Women," *Women's Studies International Forum* 27 (2004): 431–45; Arpita Saha, "Rape as a War Crime: The Position of International Law since World War II," *Journal of East Asia and International Law* 2, no. 2 (2009): 497–516.

26. *A Woman in Berlin* (London: Virago, 2006).

27. For an overview of the humanitarian effects of war on women, consult the webpage of the International Committee of the Red Cross: http://www.icrc.org/eng/war-and-law/ protected-persons/women/overview-women-protected.htm.

28. Another intersection of children and warfare is the rise in the number of child soldiers, a topic that will be addressed in chapter 13.

29. John Costello, *Virtue under Fire: How World War II Changed Our Social and Sexual Attitudes* (Boston: Little, Brown, 1985), 7–8. The concerns that war brought a loosening of morals were not limited to the Second World War. For a discussion of how war provided the opportunity for more permissive discussions of sexual habits, see Angela Smith, "'Khaki Fever' and Its Control: Gender, Class, Age and Sexual Morality on the British Homefront," *Journal of Contemporary History* 29, no. 2 (1994): 325–47; Steven Humphries, *A Secret World of Sex: Forbidden Fruit; The British Experience, 1900–1950* (London: Sidgwick & Jackson, 1988), 16–26, 96–99, 104, 191; Penny Summerfield and Nicole Crockett, "'You Weren't Taught That with the Welding': Lessons in the Second World War," *Women's History Review* 1, no. 3 (1992): 435–54.

30. Beth L. Bailey, *Sex in the Heartland* (Cambridge, MA: Harvard University Press, 1999), 25.

31. The consequences were higher rates of venereal disease and pregnancies among the civilian population. Costello, *Virtue under Fire*, makes a point of discussing how the war changed what was considered morally acceptable during the war and argues that it lay the groundwork for the sexual revolution of the 1960s and 1970s. On the other hand, Bailey argues that sexual morality in the United States was already changing, but the war meant towns were less isolated and popular culture helped to bring these changes into the open (*Sex in the Heartland*, 29–39).

32. Jaroslav Hašek, *The Good Soldier Schweik* (New York: Penguin, 1965).

33. For background to the war, see Amos Harel and Avi Isacharoff, *34 Days: Israel, Hezbollah, and War in Lebanon* (New York: Palgrave Macmillan, 2008); Cathy Sultan, *Tragedy in South Lebanon: The Israeli-Hezbollah War of 2006* (Minneapolis: Scarletta, 2008). Many considered the war a setback for Lebanon; the country had experienced a civil war between 1975 and 1990, a war in which several outside forces intervened. For background to the civil war in Lebanon, see Farid El-Khazen, *The Breakdown of the State in Lebanon, 1967–1976* (Cambridge, MA: Harvard University Press, 2000); Elizabeth Picard, *Lebanon: A Shattered Country* (New York: Holmos & Meier, 1996). For journalistic and personal accounts, see Michael D. Dawahare, *No Country but War: A Reporter's Sketches of Lebanon* (Rockville, MD: Arc Manor, 2008); Thomas L. Friedman, *From Beirut to Jerusalem* (New York: Farrar, Straus,

Giroux, 1989). The film *Suspended Dreams* (1992) examines the devastating effects of the civil war in Lebanon and how the actions of the war made it difficult for the various sides to reconcile. For an interesting account of Lebanese cinema in the aftermath of the war, see Lina Khatib, *Lebanese Cinema: Imagining the Civil War and Beyond* (London: I. B. Tauris, 2008).

34. Stanley Weintraub, *Silent Night: The Story of the World War I Christmas Truce* (New York: Free Press, 2001).

35. Jack C. Ellis, *A History of Film,* 2nd ed. (Englewood Cliffs, NJ: Prentice-Hall, 1985), 352.

36. One of the characters in the original pilot movie was a pleasure girl (essentially a prostitute), but by the time of the series this fact was substantially toned down.

37. Similarly, *Popiól i diament* (Ashes and Diamonds, 1958) explores what soldiers are asked to do in time of warfare, even murdering a former schoolmate.

38. J. M. Winter, *Remembering War: The Great War between Memory and History in the Twentieth Century* (New York: Yale University Press, 2006), 186.

39. David A. Cook, *A History of Narrative Film* (New York: Norton, 1981), 338–39; Elizabeth Grottle Strebel, "Renoir and the Popular Front," *Sight and Sound* 49, no. 1 (1979): 36–41.

40. Kaes argues that this was a trend in post–First World War German films as well, especially expressed in Fritz Lang's *Metropolis* (1926): Anton Kaes, *Shell Shock Cinema: Weimar Culture and the Wounds of War* (Princeton, NJ: Princeton University Press, 2009), 186–93.

41. There are no known surviving prints of the film.

42. Animated shorts (cartoons) have been a source of many political and cultural messages. Certainly during the period that the United States was involved in the Second World War, cartoons were decidedly pro-war. As documented by Lehman, during the Vietnam War, animated films became increasingly antiwar in orientation: Christopher P. Lehman, *American Animated Cartoons of the Vietnam Era: A Study of Social Commentary in Film and Television Programs, 1961–1973* (Jefferson, NC: McFarland, 2006).

43. For background to these films and the war films of the Japanese cinema, see Liew Kai Khiun, "Self-Inflicted Pain: Japanese Cinema on the Pacific War," *New Cinemas: Journal of Contemporary Film* 8, no. 3 (2011): 189–201; Erik R. Lofgren, "Christianity Excised: Ichikawa Kon's Fires on the Plain," *Japanese Studies* 23, no. 3 (2003): 265–75; William B. Howser, "*Fires on the Plain:* The Human Cost of the Pacific War," in *Reframing Japanese Cinema: Authorship, Genre, History,* ed. Arthur Nolletti Jr. and David Desser (Bloomington: Indiana University Press, 1992); Keiko I. McDonald, *Cinema East: A Critical Study of Major Japanese Films* (Rutherford, NJ: Farleigh Dickinson University Press, 1983), 88–100.

44. The film *Pray the Devil Back to Hell* is discussed more in depth in chapter 8.

45. Mearsheimer, "Why We Will Soon Miss the Cold War," 38–40.

5. A Primer on Nuclear Weapons

1. For more in-depth information and background about the politics of nuclear weapons, see John Hersey, *Hiroshima* (New York: Knopf, 1946); Carol Cohn, "Sex and Death in the Rational World of Defense Intellectuals," *Signs* 12, no. 4 (1987): 687–718; Scott D. Sagan and Kenneth N. Waltz, *The Spread of Nuclear Weapons: A Debate* (New York: Norton, 1995); Ronald J. Bee, *Seven Minutes to Midnight: Nuclear Weapons after 9/11* (New York: Foreign

Policy Association, 2006); Colin Dueck and Ray Takeyh, "Iran's Nuclear Challenge," *Political Science Quarterly* 122, no. 2 (2007): 189–205. See also the website of the Federation of American Scientists: http://www.fas.org/nuke/index.html.

2. Avner Cohen, *The Worst-Kept Secret: Israel's Bargain with the Bomb* (New York: Columbia University Press, 2010).

3. The project to dismantle South Africa's nuclear arsenal took place between November 1989 and September 1991. After the arsenal was dismantled, South Africa signed a comprehensive safeguards agreement with the IAEA. Al J. Venter, *How South Africa Built Six Atomic Bombs: And Then Abandoned Its Nuclear Weapons Program* (Kyalami Estate: Ashanti, 2008).

4. Dietrich Fischer, *Preventing War in the Nuclear Age* (Totowa, NJ: Rowman & Allanheld, 1984), 11.

5. Federation of Atomic Scientists, *Nuclear Weapon Radiation Effects,* http://www.fas.org/nuke/intro/nuke/radiation.htm.

6. Indirectly related to humans is the effect known as an electromagnetic pulse (EMP). An EMP is the resulting magnetic field produced by a nuclear detonation, or potentially by geomagnetic storms produced by the sun. The effect of an EMP would be to burn out power lines and render most modern technologies, including automobiles, televisions, computers, and portable devices, useless. Dan Vergano, "Electromagnetic Pulse Impact Far and Wide," *USA Today,* 27 October 2012.

6. The War to End Humanity?

1. There is a rich literature on nuclear war and weapons in film and popular culture. See, among many others, Jack G. Shaheen, *Nuclear War Films* (Carbondale: Southern Illinois University Press, 1978); Paul Brians, *Nuclear Holocausts: Atomic War in Fiction, 1895–1984* (Kent, OH: Kent State University Press, 1987); Kim Newman, *Apocalypse Movies: End of the World Cinema* (New York: St. Martin's Griffin, 2000); Ronnie D. Lipschutz, "Nukes!" in *Cold War Fantasies: Film, Fiction, and Foreign Policy* (Lanham, MD: Rowman & Littlefield, 2001); Jerome F. Shapiro, *Atomic Bomb Cinema: The Apocalyptic Imagination on Film* (New York: Routledge, 2002); David Eldridge, "'There Is Hope for the Future': Retrospective Visions of the Bomb in 1950s Hollywood," *Historical Journal of Film, Radio and Television* 26, no. 3 (2006): 295–309.

2. Stanley Corkin notes that there was another genre that was very popular during the cold war, the western. He argues that films that focused on the mythical West (for example, *My Darling Clementine,* 1946, *High Noon,* 1952, *Gunfight at the OK Corral,* 1957, and *The Alamo,* 1960) helped to justify America's foreign policy and inform citizens, in particular about the need and desirability of military intervention in other countries (Korea, Vietnam). The "West" in the films of the genre was the wilderness, a metaphor, Corkin argues, for lesser-developed countries. Corkin, *Cowboys as Cold Warriors,* 10–12.

3. Consult Leif E. Peterson and Seymour Abrahamson, eds., *Effects of Ionizing Radiation: Atomic Bomb Survivors and Their Children, 1945–1995* (Washington, DC: Joseph Henry, 1998). In particular, see Dale L. Preston, "A Historical Review of Leukemia Risks in Atomic Bomb Survivors" and Kiyohiko Mabuchi, "Tumor Registries and Cancer Incidence Studies" in that volume.

4. John F. Kennedy, speech to the United Nations General Assembly, 25 September 1961.

5. One treaty, the Nuclear Non-proliferation Treaty (NPT), negotiated in 1968, sought to address the problems of proliferation. In recent years there are some interesting arguments about nuclear proliferation: John J. Mearsheimer, "The Case for a Ukrainian Nuclear Deterrent," *Foreign Affairs* 72, no. 3 (1993): 50–66; Scott D. Sagan and Kenneth N. Waltz, *The Spread of Nuclear Weapons: A Debate Renewed* (New York: Norton, 2002); James M. Lindsay and Ray Takeyh, "After Iran Gets the Bomb," *Foreign Affairs* 89, no. 2 (2010): 33–49.

6. For more on the logic and applicability of deterrence, see Frank C. Zagare, *The Dynamics of Deterrence* (Chicago: University of Chicago Press, 1987).

7. The concept of MAD was developed by the Rand Corporation in 1961.

8. Herman Kahn, *On Thermonuclear War*, 2nd ed. (Princeton, NJ: Princeton University Press, 1961), 145–47. It should be noted that Kahn allows that such a machine need not necessarily be nuclear. For more about Kahn, see Sharon Ghamari-Tabrizi, *The Worlds of Herman Kahn: The Intuitive Science of Thermonuclear War* (Cambridge, MA: Harvard University Press, 2005). Additionally, for an in-depth review of Ghamari-Tabrizi's biography, see Louis Menand, "Fat Man: Herman Kahn and the Nuclear Age," *New Yorker*, 27 June 2005.

9. In fact, in announcing that it had acquired nuclear weapons, the Democratic People's Republic of Korea (North Korea) used this logic and said that it had acquired a nuclear deterrent.

10. Bruce Reidel, "American Diplomacy and the 1999 Kargil Summit at Blair House" (working paper, Center for Advanced Study of India, University of Pennsylvania, 2002), http://media.sas.upenn.edu/casi/docs/research/papers/Riedel_2002.pdf. For some insight and details of the Kargil conflict, see S. Paul Kapur, *Dangerous Deterrent: Nuclear Weapons Proliferation and Conflict in South Asia* (Stanford, CA: Stanford University Press, 2007), 117–31.

11. *The Missiles of October* is largely based on Robert Kennedy's unfinished memoirs of the event, published as Robert F. Kennedy, *Thirteen Days: A Memoir of the Cuban Missile Crisis* (New York: Norton, 1971).

12. Don Munton and David A. Welch, *The Cuban Missile Crisis: A Concise History* (New York: Oxford University Press, 2007), 110–11. Monton and Welch's book is a resource for those interested in the missile crisis. Allison uses the Cuban missile crisis as a case study to explore how decisions were made in the classic text on decision-making processes: Graham T. Allison, *Essence of Decision: Explaining the Cuban Missile Crisis* (Boston: Little, Brown, 1971).

13. Joyce A. Evans, *Celluloid Mushroom Clouds: Hollywood and the Atomic Bomb* (Boulder, CO: Westview, 1998), 164. Evans argues that in the aftermath of the crisis, the public had tired of uncritical films about the military and hawkish strategy, instead embracing an interpretation that was both lighthearted and critical of the notion that nuclear wars could be won.

14. Ibid., 164. The parallels between Strangelove and Kahn are clear, and there is no doubt that the character is a satire of the scientist. Kenneth D. Rose, *One Nation Underground: The Fallout Shelter in American Culture* (New York: New York University Press, 2001), 73–76.

15. For an account of the parallels between *Fail Safe* and *Dr. Strangelove*, see Michael G. Wollscheidt, "Fail Safe," in Shaheen, *Nuclear War Films*, 68–70.

16. Bruce Blair, Harold Feiveson, and Frank N. von Hippel, "Who's Got the Button? Taking Nuclear Weapons off Hair-Trigger Alert," *Scientific American*, November 1997, 74–81; Richard Halloran, "Nuclear Missiles: Warning System and the Question of When to Fire," *New York Times*, 29 May 1983.

17. Robert Feleppa, "Black Rain: Reflections on Hiroshima and Nuclear War in Japanese Film," *Cross Currents* 54, no. 1 (2004): 112.

18. The film is reportedly all that remains of approximately three hours of footage shot. Robert W. Duncan, "Hiroshima-Nagasaki—August 1945," in Shaheen, *Nuclear War Films*. After limited availability, the film was released on videotape in 1982: John Dowling, "Hiroshima/Nagasaki August 1945: The Case of the A-Bomb Footage," *Bulletin of Atomic Scientists* 39, no. 1 (1983): 39. One of the best-known accounts of the immediate aftermath of the Hiroshima bombing is Hersey, *Hiroshima*. It tells the stories of six survivors of Hiroshima and was originally published in the *New Yorker* magazine.

19. Alternatively known as *Children of the Atomic Bomb.*

20. The story contained in the film is based on a collection of testimonials. Arata Osada, ed., *Children of Hiroshima* (Tokyo: Publishing Committee for "Children of Hiroshima," 1980). For a film review and a brief retrospective of the director, Kaneto Shindo, see A. O. Scott, "Japanese Survivors Shaded by Puzzlement and Sorrow," *New York Times*, 22 April 2011, C6.

21. Although the primary thrust of the film is the effects five years later, the flashback scenes of Hiroshima in the immediate aftermath of the detonation rely on accounts from various sources. They are realistic, graphic, and disturbing.

22. For background and the symbolic message contained in the film, listed under its alternative English title, *Record of a Living Being*, see Donald Richie with Joan Mellen, *The Films of Akira Kurosawa* (Berkeley: University of California Press, 1984), 109–14.

23. In the 1950s many radio programs, like *X Minus One, Arch Oboler's Plays*, and *Dimension X*, used the prospect of nuclear war in several stories. For an examination of how writers and popular culture understood the atomic bomb, see Paul S. Boyer, *By the Bomb's Early Light: American Thought and Culture at the Dawn of the Atomic Age* (New York: Pantheon, 1985).

24. For a critique of the plot holes and illogical events in *The World, the Flesh and the Devil*, see Frank W. Oglesbee, "*The World, the Flesh and the Devil*," in Shaheen, *Nuclear War Films*.

25. *Atomic Attack* was an episode in the anthology series *The Motorola Television Hour* and was originally aired on 18 May 1954. An interesting side note to the film is that one of the actors in the play is a young Walter Matthau, who would later play a prominent role in *Fail Safe.*

26. The documentary film *Atomic Café* (1982) collects propaganda, informational films, and news items to demonstrate the absurdities of the advice given during this period.

27. Nevil Shute, *On the Beach* (New York: Morrow, 1957); Shute was the pen name of Nevil Shute Norway, a British-Australian engineer.

28. The film has been criticized by Jack Shaheen and Stephen Weart for being a romantic film "masquerading as social consciousness." Shaheen, *Nuclear War Films*, 31. Weart notes that there are no depictions or images of the destruction caused by nuclear weapons: Stephen Weart, *Nuclear Fear: A History of Images* (Cambridge, MA: Harvard University Press, 1988), 219.

29. Rose, *One Nation Underground*, 43.

30. A more upbeat tempo accompanied Germany's "99 Luftballons" by Nena, a song about an accidental nuclear war that became a worldwide hit. While this chapter is concerned with nuclear weapons, the movement did extend to antinuclear energy as well. Many

protestors expressed fears about the potential environmental harm and danger to human health posed by nuclear power plants and the prospect of an accident. Films like *The China Syndrome* (1979), *The Quiet Earth* (1985) from New Zealand, and the German production *Die Wolke* (The Cloud, 2006) reflect these concerns. Incidents at nuclear power plants around the world—Three Mile Island near Harrisburg, Pennsylvania, in 1979, Chernobyl in Ukraine (then Soviet Union) in 1986, and the aftermath of the earthquake and tsunami at the Fukushima plant in Japan in 2011—have reinforced the fears among some.

31. Toni A. Perrine, *Film and the Nuclear Age: Representing Cultural Anxiety* (New York: Garland, 1998), 162–64.

32. Ronald Reagan, *An American Life* (New York: Simon & Schuster, 1990), 585–86. After this point, the president began to discuss an evolving belief that nuclear weapons should eventually be abolished. James Mann, *The Rebellion of Ronald Reagan: A History of the End of the Cold War* (New York: Penguin Books, 2009), 41–42.

33. Janet Maslin, "'Testament,' after a Nuclear Blast," *New York Times*, 4 November 1983.

34. David Crook, "CNN, WTBS Plan Nuclear Blitz This Month," *Los Angeles Times*, 1 January 1985; John J. O'Connor, "TV: Years after Nuclear Holocaust," *New York Times*, 12 January 1985.

35. The neutron bomb was designed to kill people but leave property intact. With the end of the cold war, the technology has been seen as largely obsolete. For background to the bomb, see the obituary of the inventor, Samuel Cohen: Robert D. McFadden, "Samuel T. Cohen, 89, Dies; Invented Neutron Bomb and Was Its Chief Advocate," *New York Times*, 2 December 2010, 35. Cohen also authored his own defense of the weapon: S. T. Cohen, *The Truth about the Neutron Bomb: The Inventor of the Bomb Speaks Out* (New York: Morrow, 1983).

36. The National Film Board of Canada (www.nfb.ca), which produced *23 Skidoo*, has made many films concerning nuclear war. Of particular note: *11 Steps to Survival* (1973), which was intended to help people build or stock a nuclear fallout shelter; *If You Love This Planet* (1982), an Oscar-winning short film, which uses a lecture by physician Dr. Helen Caldicott to highlight the medical implications of nuclear warfare; and *The Big Snit* (1985), about a couple so consumed with their Scrabble game and domestic dispute they miss the onset of a nuclear war.

37. *La jetée* was remade as *Twelve Monkeys* (1995), starring Bruce Willis and directed by Terry Gilliam (of Monty Python fame). Whereas in *La jetée* it is a nuclear war that destroys humanity, in *Twelve Monkeys* it is a virus that mutates and causes approximately 5 billion deaths.

38. Shapiro, *Atomic Bomb Cinema*, 13.

39. Likewise, *The Road* (2009), a film set in postapocalyptic America, fits into this group, but the cause of the devastation is never clearly defined. This might be a return to a normal pattern. Barkun has argued that nuclear war is simply a substitute for other types of natural disasters, rather than vice versa. In preindustrial times, natural disaster, plagues, floods, and earthquakes were seen to happen without human culpability. However, in modern times, disasters in popular imagination—atomic weapons, massacres, and so forth—happen with human involvement. Michael Barkun, *Disaster and the Millennium* (New Haven, CT: Yale University Press, 1974), 203–4.

7. Intrigue, Espionage, and Nuclear Secrets

1. For an overview and history of the German cinema, see Sabine Hake, *German National Cinema* (New York: Routledge, 2006).

2. Or, in German, the Deutsche Demokratische Republik (DDR).

3. Anderson provides an analysis of the psychological difficulty in reuniting Germany: Jeffrey J. Anderson, "The Federal Republic at Twenty: Of Blind Spots and Peripheral Visions," *German Politics and Society* 28, no. 2 (2010): 17–53.

4. Hensel provides a justification and explanation for the remembrances of the GDR in her memoirs: Jana Hensel, *After the Wall: Confessions from an East German Childhood and the Life That Came Next* (New York: Public Affairs, 2004). For a critical analysis of *Goodbye Lenin!* and *The Lives of Others* in terms of representing the integration of Easterners (Ossies) into the West juxtaposed with the integration of Turks into German society, see Gareth Dale, "Heimat, 'Ostalgie' and the Stasi: The GDR in German Cinema, 1999–2006," *Review of Contemporary German Affairs* 15, no. 2 (2007): 155–75. See also Jennifer M. Kapczynski, "Negotiating Nostalgia: The GDR Past in *Berlin Is in Germany* and *Good Bye Lenin!*" *Germanic Review* 82, no. 1 (2007): 78–100.

5. The film even helped to revive the product after reunification. Richard Bernstein, "Eisenhüttstadt Journal; Warm, Fuzzy Feelings for East Germany's Gray Old Days," *New York Times*, 13 January 2004.

8. Is International Cooperation Possible?

1. Richard Sennett, *Together: The Rituals, Pleasures, and Politics of Cooperation* (New Haven, CT: Yale University Press, 2012), 5–6.

2. I. William Zartman and Saadia Touval, "Introduction: Return to the Theories of Cooperation," in *International Cooperation: The Extents and Limits of Multilateralism*, ed. I. William Zartman and Saadia Touval (New York: Cambridge University Press, 2010), 1.

3. This was the argument made by Thomas Hobbes in *Leviathan* (1651).

4. For a detailed examination of the Stag Hunt, see Brian Skyrms, *The Stag Hunt and Evolution of Social Structure* (Cambridge: Cambridge University Press, 2004).

5. Ibid., 4–9.

6. William Poundstone, *Prisoner's Dilemma* (New York: Doubleday, 1992); Anatol Rapport and Albert M. Chammah, *Prisoner's Dilemma: A Study in Conflict and Cooperation* (Ann Arbor: University of Michigan Press, 1965); Richard Campbell and Lanning Sowden, *Paradoxes of Rationality and Cooperation: Prisoner's Dilemma and Newcomb's Problem* (Vancouver: University of British Columbia Press, 1985).

7. Robert K. Axelrod, *The Evolution of Cooperation* (New York: Basic Books, 1984).

8. Ibid., 73–87. Axelrod relies primarily on the work of Tony Ashworth, who used interviews, letters, and memoirs to demonstrate these informal alliances between soldiers on both sides. Of course, officers, who were not involved in the day-to-day trench life, would urge the soldiers to fire on their enemies at will. See Tony Ashworth, *Trench Warfare, 1914–1918: The Live and Let Live System* (New York: Holmes & Meier, 1980).

9. Ashworth, *Trench Warfare,* 19–20, 25–26.

10. David R. Woodward, "Christmas Truce of 1914: Empathy under Fire," *Phi Kappa*

Phi Forum 91, no. 1 (2011): 18–19; Michael Brown and Shirley Seaton, *The Christmas Truce* (New York: Hippocrene Books, 1984); Weintraub, *Silent Night*.

11. The events of Christmas 1914 are also depicted in the music video of Paul McCartney's "Pipes of Peace."

12. Several episodes of the original series of *Star Trek* (1966–1969), particularly the interchange between the Federation and the Klingons, were often seen as a metaphor for the relationship between the Soviet Union and the United States. Richards makes an interesting case for the numerous allusions to the Roman Empire in *Star Trek* as well. Thomas Richards, *The Meaning of Star Trek* (New York: Doubleday, 1997), 24. For a critical interpretation of the *Star Trek* franchise, including the series as a justification of American foreign policy, see Jutta Weldes, "Going Cultural: *Star Trek*, State Action, and Popular Culture," *Millennium—Journal of International Studies* 28, no. 1 (1999): 117–34.

13. Stanger confirms that in cooperation the past can be an inhibitor to future cooperation. Allison Stanger, "The Shadow of the Past over Conflict and Cooperation," in Zartman and Touval, *International Cooperation*, 134.

14. King James version, Psalm 133:1.

15. Hannah Arendt, *The Human Condition* (Chicago: University of Chicago Press, 1998), 200.

16. François Truffaut and Helen G. Scott, *Hitchcock* (New York: Simon & Schuster, 1967), 113–14.

17. In the original novel, *The Life and Adventures of Robinson Crusoe,* written by Daniel Defoe in 1718, Crusoe is initially self-sufficient but comes to rely on a native he encounters whom he names Friday. For an example of someone stranded on an island, see the case of Alexander Selkirk: Bruce Selcraig, "The Real Robinson Crusoe," *Smithsonian* 36, no. 4 (2005): 82–90.

18. Determining who is a member of a community (especially in an age of high immigration) can be difficult. *Little Mosque on the Prairie* and the issue of belonging to a community will be explored further in chapter 11.

19. William Deresiewicz, "A Man. A Woman. Just Friends?" *New York Times,* 8 April 2012, SR4.

20. David Letwin, Joe Stockdale, and Robin Stockdale, *The Architecture of Drama: Plot, Character, Theme, Genre, and Style* (Lanham, MD: Scarecrow, 2008), 1–2.

21. Moses L. Malevinsky, *The Science of Playwriting* (New York: Brentano's, 1925), 182–86.

22. Letwin, Stockdale, and Stockdale, *The Architecture of Drama*, xii–xiii.

23. Geisler, "The Battleground of Modernity," 92, 96.

24. It should be noted that the incident upon which the film was based occurred in 1911. Berman criticizes the message of *Kameradschaft* because it is ambiguous and unrealistic, arguing that this would not have happened in 1931. Russell A. Berman, "A Solidarity of Repression: *Kameradschaft* (1931)," in Rentschler, *The Films of G. W. Pabst*.

25. Zartman and Touval, "Introduction: Return to the Theories of Cooperation," 3.

26. Many scholars point to the Rush-Bagot Treaty of 1817 as the starting point of this cooperative relationship. Negotiated in the immediate aftermath of the War of 1812, the treaty provided for the demilitarization of the Great Lakes and Lake Champlain. It laid the basic framework for the demilitarization of the entire border between the two countries.

Subsequently there were a number of treaties to facilitate cooperation between the two countries, most notably the Boundary Waters Treaty (1909), Migratory Birds Treaty (1916), Canada–United States Free Trade Agreement (1988), and the North American Free Trade Agreement (NAFTA), along with Mexico in 1994.

27. The online archives of the Canadian Broadcasting Corporation (CBC), *The CBC Digital Archives Website,* contain several helpful clips about Canadian-American cooperation, including "NORAD and September 11" (http://archives.cbc.ca/war_conflict/defence/topics/1552-10476/) and "Deter, Detect, Defend" (http://archives.cbc.ca/war_conflict/defence/topics/1552-10469/).

28. The film is a part of the Canadian television series *On the Spot* (1953–1954) and is available online through the National Film Board of Canada: http://www.nfb.ca/film/two_countries_one_street.

29. See, for example, Malcolm McKinnor, *Independence and Foreign Policy: New Zealand in the World since 1935* (Auckland: Auckland University Press, 1993). The Entente cordiale, a series of agreements between France and the United Kingdom in 1904, set the stage for increased cooperation and consultation between the two countries.

30. For example, Emily J. Pudden and David L. VanderZwaag, "Canada-USA Bilateral Fisheries Management: Under the Radar Screen," *Review of European Community and International Environmental Law* 16, no. 1 (2007): 36–44; Geoffrey Hale, "Politics, People and Passports: Contesting Security, Travel and Trade on the US-Canadian Border," *Geopolitics* 16, no. 1 (2011): 27–69.

31. Inis L. Claude Jr., *Swords into Plowshares: The Problems and Progress of International Organizations,* 3rd ed. (New York: Random House, 1964) 14, 111.

32. Ibid., 112, 117. For a history and analysis of the implications of the move toward majoritarianism in international institutions, see 113–19.

33. In terms of forms of government, this is why benevolent dictators are seen with suspicion. Goldstone explores one such variation, the sultanate: Jack A. Goldstone, "Understanding the Revolutions of 2011: Weakness and Resilience in Middle Eastern Autocracies," *Foreign Affairs* 90, no. 3 (2011): 9–10.

34. Alexis de Tocqueville, *Democracy in America* (1835).

35. For background on when, how, and why QMV is used in the European Union, see Stephen C. Sieberson, "Inching toward EU Supernationalism? Qualified Majority Voting and Unanimity under the Treaty of Lisbon," *Virginia Journal of International Law* 50, no. 4 (2010): 936–67.

36. David Mitrany, *A Working Peace System* (Chicago: Quadrangle Books, 1966); David Mitrany, *The Functional Theory of Politics* (New York: St. Martin's, 1976).

37. John Oneal and Bruce Russett, "The Kantian Peace: The Pacific Benefits of Democracy, Interdependence and International Organizations, 1885–1992," *World Politics* 52, no. 1 (1999): 1–37; Charles Boehmer, Erik Gartzke, and Timothy Nordstrom, "Do Intergovernmental Organizations Promote Peace?" *World Politics* 57, no. 1 (2004): 1–38.

38. For further background on the concepts of functionalism and complex interdependence, see Ernst B. Haas, *Beyond the Nation-State: Functionalism and International Organization* (Stanford, CA: Stanford University Press, 1964); Keohane and Nye, *Power and Interdependence;* Robert O. Keohane and Joseph S. Nye, "Power and Interdependence

Revisited," *International Organization* 41, no. 4 (1987): 725–53; George T. Crane and Abla Amawi, *The Theoretical Evolution of International Political Economy: A Reader* (New York: Oxford University Press, 1991).

39. Zartman and Touval, "Introduction: Return to the Theories of Cooperation," 2.

40. Richard Norton-Taylor, "Spy Swaps of the Cold War," *Guardian.co.uk*, 8 July 2010, http://www.guardian.co.uk/world/2010/jul/08/spy-swaps-history-russia.

41. Melanie M. Ziegler, *U.S.-Cuban Cooperation, Past, Present and Future* (Gainesville: University Press of Florida, 2007).

9. Iranian Cinema

1. See, for example, the biography of the Iranian prime minister from 1951 to 1953, Muhammed Mussadegh: Christopher de Bellaique, *Patriot of Persia: Muhammed Mossadegh and a Tragic Anglo-American Coup* (New York: Harper, 2012).

2. One might also notice that many films feature children in an attempt to avoid censorship.

3. Robin Wright, *The Last Great Revolution: Turmoil and Transformation in Iran* (New York: Vintage Books, 2001), 122. For an overview of Iranian cinema in the postrevolutionary period (since 1979), consult ibid., 117–32; Richard Tapper, *The New Iranian Cinema: Politics, Representation and Identity* (New York: I. B. Tauris, 2008); Negar Mottahedeh, *Displaced Allegories: Post Revolutionary Iranian Cinema* (Durham, NC: Duke University Press, 2008).

4. Azadeh Faramand, "Perspectives on Recent (International Acclaim for) Iranian Cinema," in Tapper, *The New Iranian Cinema*, 88.

5. Richard Tapper, introduction to Tapper, *The New Iranian Cinema*, 4.

6. Wright, *The Last Great Revolution*, 126–30.

7. Agnès Devictor, "Classic Tools, Original Goals: Cinema and Public Policy in the Islamic Republic of Iran (1979–97)" in Tapper, *The New Iranian Cinema*, 73. Robin Wright interviewed Akbar Abdi, the star of *The Snowman*, and provides background to the film and the controversy; see Wright, *The Last Great Revolution*, 117–21. The film found a receptive audience outside Iran as well, and it took home many awards from film festivals around the world.

8. Significant portions of the film were shot during the actual match under the guise of filming a completely different story.

9. A. O. Scott, "In Tehran Stadium, Women out of Bounds," *New York Times*, 23 March 2007.

10. The film's director, Jafar Panahi, has made several films that have criticized the Iranian government, including *The White Balloon* (1995), which won the Palme d'Or at the Cannes Film Festival, and *The Circle* (2000), which criticized the treatment of women in Iran. In 2010, Panahi was arrested and jailed for a few months for publicly supporting the opposition after disputed presidential elections the previous year. Ian Black, "Jafar Panahi Freed from Jail in Iran," *Guardian*, 26 May 2010, 17.

11. The film is also known by its international title, *Songs of My Motherland*.

12. There are a number of Iranian films available internationally that one might want to consider, including *Badkonahe sefid* (The White Balloon, 1995), *Bacheha-Ye aseman* (Chil-

dren of Heaven, 1997), *Ta'm e guilass* (Taste of Cherry, 1997), *Sib* (The Apple, 1998), *Rang-e khoda* (The Color of Paradise, 1999), and *Dayereh* (The Circle, 2000).

10. Patterns of Consumption and Poverty

1. In his classic text, *The Stages of Economic Growth: A Non-Communist Manifesto* (Cambridge: Cambridge University Press, 1960), W. W. Rostow equated development with an economy that was termed "high mass consumption," where consumer demands drive the economy.

2. This is not dissimilar from *Fahrenheit 451* (1966), in which the burning of books is to achieve an economic goal rather than a political end.

3. Barber, *Jihad vs. McWorld.*

4. For a discussion of the parallels between *Roger Rabbit* and the demise of the Pacific Electric Railway, see Sy Adley, "The Transformation of the Pacific Electric Railway: Bradford Snell, Roger Rabbit, and the Politics of Transportation in Los Angeles," *Urban Affairs Quarterly* 27, no. 1 (1991): 51–86. The novel on which the film is based focuses on the duality of individuals rather than commercialization.

5. To the corporate interests, land is a commodity, easily bought and sold. Additionally, note that the names of the female leads in the film, Marina and Stella, refer to the sea and the sky.

6. On the other hand, Wayne argues that the film is ultimately unsatisfactory because it does not adequately deal with the sense of dislocation and people will give in to the allure of rampant commercialization. Mike Wayne, "Utopianism and Film," *Historical Materialism* 10, no. 4 (2002): 148–53.

7. This is a calculation also made, for example, by unmarried American women in the 1920s working in large cities. Because of the disparity in pay it was almost a necessity to have a male partner to help pay the bills, in what was often an unspoken exchange for sexual favors. Joanne J. Meyerowitz, *Women Adrift: Independent Wage Earners in Chicago, 1880–1930* (Chicago: University of Chicago Press, 1988), 39–42; Joshua Zeitz, *Flapper: A Madcap Story of Sex, Style, Celebrity and the Women Who Made America Modern* (New York: Three Rivers, 2006), 36, 253.

8. Dan Bilefsky, "Dark Film on Teenagers Echoes from Mall to Church," *International Herald Tribune,* 16 March 2010, A8.

9. Kariithi and Kareithi argue that mass media and popular culture not only promote neoliberal economics but ensure mass consumer spending as well. Nixon Kariithi and Peter Kareithi, "It's Off to Work You Go! A Critical Discourse Analysis of Media Coverage of the Anti-privatization Strike in South Africa in October 2002," *Journalism Studies* 8, no. 3 (2007): 465–80.

10. Dan Mitchell, "What's Online: Shying Away from Degeneracy," *New York Times,* 9 September 2008.

11. Shaw argues that *Wall-E i*s useful in highlighting the philosophy of Alain Badiou. Ian Graham Ronald Shaw, "Wall-E's World: Animating Badiou's Philosophy," *Cultural Geographies* 17, no. 3 (2010): 391–405.

12. In an odd coincidence, television advertisements in 2010 for Hoveround, a chair

to aid the mobility of patients who have trouble walking, used intricately choreographed sequences to tout the benefits of the product. The advertisements were reminiscent of the chairs used by humans in *Wall-E.*

13. The release of new consumer products, such as the iPad and iPhone, often engenders a great deal of excitement and news. So frenzied was the rush for iPad2 in China that a near riot broke out in Beijing's Apple Store in May 2011. Nichola Saminather, "IPad2's International Release Met with Long Lines," *San Francisco Chronicle,* 26 March 2011, D2; "Beijing Consumers 'Riot' over New iPad," NTDTV, 9 May 2011, http://english.ntdtv.com/ntdtv_en/news_business/2011-05-09/beijing-consumers-riot-over-new-ipad.html.

14. Robert D. Putnam, "Bowling Alone: America's Declining Social Capital," *Journal of Democracy* 6, no. 10 (1995): 65–78.

15. The exact relationship between connectivity and happiness has been difficult to define. Are less happy people inclined to become more connected, or do people become unhappy as their use of the Internet or social media increases? For an overview, see Janet Morahan-Martin and Phyllis Schumacher, "Loneliness and Social Uses of the Internet," *Computers in Human Behavior* 19, no. 6 (2003): 659–71; Mustafa Koc and Seval Gulyagci, "Facebook Addiction among Turkish College Students: The Role of Psychological Health, Demographic, and Usage Characteristics," *Cyberpsychology, Behavior, and Social Networking* 16, no. 4 (2013): 279–84.

16. Frank Rich, "Wall-E for President," *New York Times,* 6 July 2008.

17. Patrick J. Ford, "WALL-E's Conservative Critics," *American Conservative,* 30 June 2008, http://www.amconmag.com/blog/2008/06/30/wall-es-conservative-critics/.

18. Reed Johnson, "Sci-fi Films: TheApes Weren't Cuddly," *Los Angeles Times,* 13 July 2008.

19. A. O. Scott, "Portrait of a Marriage: Eco-Greens Unplugged," *New York Times,* 11 September 2009.

20. Thomas L. Friedman and Ignacio Ramonet, "Dueling Globalizations," *Foreign Policy* 116 (Autumn 1999): 110–27.

21. Despite the quest for materialistic goods, researchers have often questioned the assumption that wealth and materialism lead to happiness. Most research indicates that the opposite is true. See, for example, James A. Roberts and Aimee Clement, "Materialism and Satisfaction with Over-all Quality of Life and Eight Life Domains," *Social Indicators Research* 82, no. 1 (2007): 79–92.

22. Films such as *East Side, West Side* (1927), *It* (1927), and *Little Annie Rooney* (1925) are all examples of this concern about poverty. Because of the gap between rich and poor and the desperate living conditions of some urban residents, American films were more conscious of the issues of poverty during the silent era. For a discussion of this topic, see Kevin Brownlow, *Behind the Mask of Innocence: Sex, Violence, Crime: Films of Social Conscience in the Silent Era* (Berkeley: University of California Press, 1992), 264–99.

23. Occasionally there are romanticized versions of what it is like to be poor, such as *Hallelujah, I'm a Bum* (1933). There are notable exceptions to this trend, however, including the Italian film *Lardi de biciclette* (Bicycle Thieves, 1948) and the Chinese film *Yi ge dou du neng shao* (Not One Less, 1999).

24. Naím, "Dangerously Unique."

25. See Millennium Development Goals, http://www.un.org/millenniumgoals/.

26. Stephen C. Smith, *Ending Global Poverty: A Guide to What Works* (New York: Palgrave Macmillan, 2005).

27. Ibid., 11. Smith goes on to discuss the difficulties of a poverty trap and escaping chronic poverty in general (12–17).

28. Actually the word *slumdog* was an invention of the filmmakers and there was some controversy over its use concerning whether it conveyed an insult. Rick Westhead, "Child Star of *Slumdog Millionaire* Kicked Out of Slums: From Oscar to Homelessness," *Toronto Sun,* 15 May 2009, A1.

29. Erika Kinetz, "No Happily Ever After for *Slumdog* Kid Stars: 9-Year-Old Actress Shares Sewage-Filled One-Room Shack with Rats, Scorpions," *Seattle Times,* 23 May 2009. Eventually the actors moved to apartments purchased for them through the trust set up to be custodians of the money earned from the film.

30. This is the argument made by Robert Kaplan in an influential article, "The Coming Anarchy," *Atlantic Monthly,* February 1994. The article was so persuasive that then President Clinton ordered copies to be faxed to all U.S. embassies around the world.

11. Human Migration

1. For statistical and background information, consult http://iom.int/jahia/Jahia/about-migration/facts-and-figures/lang/en.

2. For an overview of the issue of immigration in film and political culture, see Rachel Rubin and Jeffrey Melnick, *Immigration and American Popular Culture: An Introduction* (New York: New York University Press, 2007).

3. Groucho Marx was actually concerned about the impact of immigration and foreign cultures in the United States. Michael A. Krysko, "'Gibberish' On the Air: Foreign Language Radio and American Broadcasting, 1920–1940," *Historical Journal of Film, Radio and Television* 27, no. 3 (2007): 333–34.

4. For an overview of the theories about what prompts immigration, see Alejandro Portes and József Böröcz, "Contemporary Immigration: Theoretical Perspectives on Its Determinants and Modes of Incorporation," *International Migration Review* 23, no. 3 (1989): 606–30.

5. Alejandro Portes, "Determinants of the Brain Drain," *International Migration Review* 10, no. 4 (1976): 489–508; B. Schmitter-Heisler, "Sending Countries and the Politics of Emigration and Destination," *International Migration Review* 19, no. 3 (1985): 469–84.

6. See Carol Nohmer and Amy Shuman, *Rejecting Refugees: Political Asylum in the 21st Century* (New York: Routledge, 2008); Jennifer Hyndman, *Managing Displacement: Refugees and the Politics of Humanitarianism* (Minneapolis: University of Minnesota Press, 2000), 12–13; David J. Whitaker, *Asylum Seekers and Refugees in the Contemporary World* (New York: Routledge, 2006), 3–11. Globalization has meant, Marfleet argues, that the distinction between voluntary and involuntary migration is increasingly blurred. Philip Marfleet, *Refugees in a Global Era* (Basingstoke, UK: Palgrave Macmillan, 2006), 12–14.

7. Nosheen Iqbal, Anna Leach, and Henry Barnes, "David Baddiel and Omid Djalili on *The Infidel:* 'It's Not a Message Movie,'" *Guardian.co.uk,* 8 April 2010, http://www.guardian.co.uk/film/video/2010/apr/08/david-baddiel-omid-djalili-the-infidel?intcmp=239. Ander-

son, in his classic work on the subject, explores how political identities are shaped by shared narratives: Anderson, *Imagined Communities*.

8. Samuel P. Huntington, "The Hispanic Challenge," *Foreign Policy* 141 (March/April 2004): 30–45. Auster, an advocate of curtailing immigration to the United States, argues that a substantial influx to the United States will have a devastating effect on the ability of the country to keep social peace and that the negative traits of (donor) countries will be transferred to the United States. Lawrence Auster, *The Path to National Suicide: An Essay on Immigration and Multiculturalism* (Monterey, VA: American Immigration Control Foundation, 1990), 2. Earlier waves of immigration prompted political reactions within the United States as well. For example, the "Know-Nothing Party" of the 1840s and 1850s opposed Irish and German Catholic immigration for fear the immigrants were under the control of the pope and would greatly change American politics. See Tyler Anbinder, *Nativism and Slavery: The Northern Know Nothings and the Politics of the 1850s* (New York: Oxford University Press, 1992).

9. Stephan-Götz Richter, "The Immigration Safety Valve: Keeping a Lid on Inflation," *Foreign Affairs* 79, no. 2 (2000): 13–16; Joseph E. Altonji and David Card, "The Effects of Immigration on Labor Market Outcomes of Less-Skilled Natives," in *Immigration, Trade and Labor Markets,* ed. John M. Abowd and Richard B. Freeman (Chicago: University of Chicago Press, 1991); Aviva Chomsky, *"They Take Our Jobs!" And 20 Other Myths about Immigration* (Boston: Beacon, 2007); Noah Smith, "The Secret to U.S. Growth in the 21st Century, More Asians," *Atlantic.com,* http://www.theatlantic.com/business/archive/2012/10/the-secret-to-us-growth-in-the-21st-century-more-asians/263161/.

10. The treatment of illegal migrants has created tensions within the European Union; Charlemagne, "The Unstoppable Flow," *Economist,* 19 February 2011, 60.

11. In the United States, the payroll tax of illegal immigrants helps to fund Social Security and Medicare—programs that noncitizens will never benefit from. Edward Schumacher-Matos, "How Illegal Immigrants Are Helping Social Security," *Washington Post,* 3 September 2010. Corporate interests also might push to maintain the current system because it helps to keep payrolls low, thus maximizing corporate earnings. Schlosser reports on how meatpacking plants have used undocumented workers to perform undesirable jobs: Eric Schlosser, *Fast Food Nation: The Dark Side of the All-American Meal* (Boston: Houghton-Mifflin, 2001), 160–63.

12. The documentary series *Moguls and Movie Stars: A History of Hollywood* (2010) explored the issue of immigrant movie executives. See specifically episode 2, "The Birth of Hollywood, 1907–1920." See also Neil Gabler, *An Empire of Their Own: How the Jews Invented Hollywood* (New York: Anchor Books, 1989).

13. For a discussion of the modern sex-trade industry, see chapter 10 on consumption and poverty, specifically the film *Lilya 4-ever* (2002).

14. David Robinson, *Chaplin: His Life and Art* (New York: Da Capo, 1994), 199.

15. Famed immigrant director Frank Capra also made a series of films that celebrated both the immigrant and the American experience. Jonathan J. Cavallero, "Frank Capra's 1920s Immigrant Trilogy: Immigration, Assimilation, and the American Dream," *MELUS* 29, no. 2 (2004): 27–53.

16. For a discussion of the film's message and portrayal of Irish immigrants (as well as the portrayal of Jewish Irving Berlin), see Meaghan Dwyer-Ryan, "'Yankee-Doodle Paddy':

Themes of Ethnic Acculturation in *Yankee Doodle Dandy,*" *Journal of American Ethnic History* 30, no. 4 (2011): 57–62.

17. Interestingly, the sacrifice of the son in the First World War is used to demonstrate the family's acceptance of American values and the price of freedom in the United States. Military service as a path to citizenship is a recurrent issue in American politics. Julia Preston, "U.S. Military Will Offer Path to Citizenship," *New York Times,* 15 February 2009, A1.

18. For an analysis of *Border Incident,* see Jonathan Auerbach, "Noir Citizenship: Anthony Mann's Border Incident," *Cinema Journal* 47, no. 4 (2008): 102–20.

19. Huntington, "The Hispanic Challenge," 36–39. Huntington cites the film *Falling Down* (1993) as an example of how "White Nativism" might be a reaction to the multicultural society immigration might bring (41).

20. Historically, bad things happen to Homer when he works on the roof, and he occasionally wakes up in the hospital.

21. George J. Borjas, *Mexican Immigration to the United States* (Chicago: University of Chicago Press, 2007).

22. In the episode, the residents of Springfield create a local militia known as the Goofballs, clearly inspired by the Minuteman Project, established and self-appointed to guard the border between the United States and Mexico. The group has routinely been labeled extremist and racist. The Star-Spangled Goofballs, unorganized and amateur, fail to prevent border crossings, so the town decides to build a wall to prevent migration. Again, the writers are drawing on the border fence that was built along the U.S.-Mexican border, but note that other walls, such as the wall between Israel and Palestinian lands, also exist. The residents of Springfield, completely inept at building a wall, have to rely on Ogdenville to do it for them. Heidi Beirich, "The Anti-immigrant Movement," Southern Poverty Law Center, http://www.splcenter.org/get-informed/intelligence-files/ideology/anti-immigrant/the-anti-immigrant-movement.

23. Everett S. Lee, "A Theory of Migration," *Demography* 3, no. 1 (1966): 47–57; Peter Doerschler, "Push-Pull Factors and Immigrant Political Integration in Germany," *Social Science Quarterly* 87, no. 5 (2006): 1100–16.

24. James A. Clapp, "Streets of Gold: Immigrants in the City and the Cinema," *Visual Anthropology* 22, no. 1 (2009): 15.

25. Loshitzky refers to Europe as a "promised land" for many immigrants, where they can pursue dreams of wealth and success (15). The concept of the promised land is explored in depth (specifically 14–76), but as in the United States, the prospect of increased migration is a cause for alarm and vigilance for some in Europe. Yosefa Loshitzky, *Screening Strangers: Migration and Diaspora in Contemporary European Cinema* (Bloomington: Indiana University Press, 2010).

26. For an actual story of illegal immigration based on a series that was originally published in the *Los Angeles Times,* see Sonia Nazario, *Enrique's Journey* (New York: Random House, 2006).

27. There is an extensive literature about immigration (documented and undocumented) upon which to draw. As a starting point, consider the following: Daniels provides a history of American immigration policy, while Ngai examines the history of undocumented immigration to the United States. Roger Daniels, *Guarding the Golden Door: American Immigration Policy and Immigrants since 1882* (New York: Hill & Wang, 2004); Mae M. Ngai, *Impossible*

Subjects: Illegal Aliens and the Making of Modern America (Princeton, NJ: Princeton University Press, 2004). Swain offers a good overview of debates surrounding modern immigration, and Chomsky provides a vigorous defense of immigration and immigrants. Carol M. Swain, ed., *Debating Immigration* (New York: Cambridge University Press, 2007); Chomsky, *"They Take Our Jobs!"* LeMay provides a historical perspective focusing on the security risks and factors associated with immigration: Michael C. LeMay, *Guarding the Gates: Immigration and National Security* (Westport, CT: Praeger Security Information, 2006).

28. In particular, films such as *The Birth of a Nation* (1915) and *Gone with the Wind* (1939). For more information, consult Ed Guerrero, *Framing Blackness: The African American Image in Film* (Philadelphia: Temple University Press, 1993); Vincent F. Rocchio, *Reel Racism: Confronting Hollywood's Construction of Afro-American Culture* (Boulder, CO: Westview, 2000); Henry T. Sampson, *Blacks in Black and White: A Source Book on Black Films* (Metuchen, NJ: Scarecrow, 1977). See chapter 13 for more on racial and cultural stereotypes.

29. The film *The Italian* (1915), while indulging in some stereotypes, does provide a positive image of the immigrant known as Beppo. The scenes with his sick son are particularly humanizing.

30. Lehman, *American Animated Cartoons of the Vietnam Era*, 5–6.

31. Shaheen, *Reel Bad Arabs*, 4–10, 14–33. The book has been turned into a documentary film by the same name (2006), directed by Sut Jhally. See also other titles by Jack Shaheen, including *Arab and Muslim Stereotyping in American Popular Culture* (Washington, DC: Center for Muslim-Christian Understanding, 1997), and *The TV Arab* (Bowling Green, OH: Bowling Green State University Press, 1984).

32. In September 2012, a little-known Internet film, *The Innocence of Muslims,* sparked riots and protests around the world because of its mocking of the prophet Muhammad. Matt Bradley and Dion Nissenbaum, "U.S. Missions Stormed in Libya, Egypt," *Wall Street Journal,* 12 September 2012, A8.

33. As pointed out by Lehman, the subsequent animated version of the series *My Favorite Martians* (1973–1975) was more direct in its reference to immigration in the United States; Lehman, *American Animated Cartoons of the Vietnam Era*, 198.

34. Rubin and Melnick, *Immigration and American Popular Culture*, 1–3.

35. The film is most often associated with a commentary on the apartheid era of South African politics, but can also be seen as a wider message on the treatment of others. Matthew Jones, "*District 9* (2009)," *Film and History* 40, no. 1 (2010): 120–22. See also Bernard Beck, "The People Next Door: Getting Along with the Neighbors in *Yoo-Hoo Mrs. Goldberg* and *District 9,*" *Multicultural Perspectives* 12, no. 2 (2010): 87–90.

36. There is an ongoing debate about the efficacy and effect of emigration on the sending community as well. Often these debates center around two key issues: the perceived "brain drain" versus the remittances that can be sent home.

37. See "Interview with John Sharry," *The John Murray Show,* RTÉ Radio One, 15 February 2011.

38. Mirca Madianou and Daniel Miller, "Mobile Phone Parenting: Reconfiguring Relationships between Filipina Migrant Mothers and Their Left-Behind Children," *New Media and Society* 13, no. 3 (2011): 457–70.

39. Ed Pilkington, "Joaquin Luna: Undocumented Migrant Whose Lack of Hope Drove

Him to Suicide," *Guardian.co.uk,* 29 November 2011, http://www.guardian.co.uk/world/2011/nov/29/joaquin-luna-immigration-texas-suicide.

40. The film was inspired in part by another film in this genre, Elia Kazan's *America, America* (1963); press kit for the film: http://www.filmmovement.com/downloads/press/InchPressKit.pdf.

41. One of the interesting implications of recent technological developments is that immigrants increasingly use new technologies to keep in contact with relatives and friends from home. This helps to alleviate the alienation that émigrés feel when arriving in a new country. Monika Metykova, "Only a Mouse Click Away from Home: Transnational Practices of Eastern European Migrants in the United Kingdom," *Social Identities* 16, no. 3 (2010): 325–38. Recent innovations have also substantially reduced the cost of international communication: Steven Vertovec, "Cheap Calls: The Social Glue of Migrant Transnationalism," *Global Networks* 4, no. 2 (2004): 219–24.

42. Kalvero Oberg, *Culture Shock* (Indianapolis: Bobbs-Merrill Reprint Series in the Social Sciences, A-329, 1959), reprinted in *Practical Anthropology* 7 (1960): 177–82.

43. Ibid., 180–81.

44. Clapp, "Streets of Gold," 16.

45. Guido Rings, "Questions of Identity: Cultural Encounters in Gurinder Chadha's *Bend It Like Beckham,*" *Journal of Popular Film and Television* 39, no. 3 (2011): 114–23. See also Mary Ann Chacko, "*Bend It Like Beckham:* Dribbling the Self through a Cross-cultural Space," *Multicultural Perspectives* 12, no. 2 (2010): 81–86.

46. For more about the Turkish cinema in Germany, see Ayca Tunc Cox, "Three Generations of Turkish Filmmakers in Germany: Three Different Narratives," *Turkish Studies* 12, no. 1 (2011): 115–27; Noah Isenberg, "Faith Akin's Cinema of Intersection," *Film Quarterly* 64, no. 4 (2011): 53–61.

47. Alan Riding, "On Screen, Tackling Europe's New Reality," *New York Times,* 18 January 2005.

48. This figure does not include Internally Displaced People (IDP), individuals who must leave their homes but who do not cross an international border. Altogether, there were roughly 25 million people protected (refugees and IDPs) by the UNHCR: UNHCR, *Global Trends 2010: 60 Years and Still Counting* (Geneva, 2011), http://www.unhcr.org/4dfa11499.html. Article 1 of the Convention on the Status of Refugees (1951) defines a refugee as a person who, due to a "well-founded fear of being persecuted for reasons of race, religion, nationality, membership of a particular social group or political opinion, is outside the country of his nationality, and is unable, or owing to such fear, is unwilling to avail himself of the protection of that country." For analysis of the convention, see James C. Hathaway, *The Law of Refugee Status* (Toronto: Butterworths, 1991). For a briefer description of the convention and its politics, see Mark Sachleben, *Human Rights Treaties: Considering Patterns of Participation, 1948–2000* (New York: Routledge, 2006), 57–59.

49. D. Silove, I. Sinnerbrink, A. Field, V. Manicavasagar, and Z. Steel, "Anxiety, Depression and PTSD in Asylum-Seekers: Associations with Pre-migration Trauma and Post-migration Stressors," *British Journal of Psychiatry* 170, no. 4 (1997): 351–57. Porter and Haslam found that older, more educated, female, and more economically displaced refugees and IDPs were more likely to have issues of diminished mental health. Matthew Porter and Nick Haslam,

"Predisplacement and Postdisplacement Factors Associated with Mental Health of Refugees and Internally Displaced Persons: A Meta-analysis," *Journal of the American Medical Association* 294, no. 5 (2005): 602–12.

50. For background and information, see Refugees International, http://www.refintl.org/.

51. Will H. Moore and Stephen M. Shellman, "Whither Will They Go? A Global Study of Refugees' Destinations, 1965–1995," *International Studies Quarterly* 51, no. 4 (2007), 812, 831.

52. Sheila Murphy, "Environmental Migrants and Canada's Refugee Policy," *Refuge* 27, no. 1 (2011): 89–102.

53. Holly Yeager, "'Star-Spangled Banner' in Spanish Brings Discord," *Financial Times,* 28 April 2006; Martin Miller, "'Nuestro Himno' Foes Say U.S. Song Should Be in English," *Los Angeles Times,* 29 April 2006.

54. One of the findings of scholars has been that immigrants often seek news and information from alternative sources, especially if the information is related to their home or ethnicity. See Anne-Katrin Arnold and Beate Schneider, "Communicating Separation? Ethnic Media and Ethnic Journalism as Institutions of Integration in Germany," *Journalism* 8, no. 2 (2007): 115–36; Connie Carøe Christiansen, "News Media Consumption among Immigrants in Europe: The Relevance of Diaspora," *Ethnicities* 4, no. 2 (2004): 185–207; Marie Gillespie, "Transnational Television Audiences after September 11," *Journal of Ethnic and Migration Studies* 32, no. 6 (2006): 903–21.

55. Canada, Multiculturalism Directorate, *Multiculturalism and the Government of Canada* (Ottawa: Multiculturalism Canada, 1984). Canada has continuingly sought to increase immigration with little or no public opposition. Jason DeParle, "Defying Trends, Canada Lures More Migrants," *New York Times,* 13 November 2010, A1.

56. Matthew Clark, "Germany's Angela Merkel: Multiculturalism Has 'Utterly Failed,'" *Christian Science Monitor,* 17 October 2010; John F. Burns, "Cameron Criticizes 'Multiculturalism' in Britain," *New York Times,* 6 February 2011, A6. Jacoby briefly summarizes the challenges that immigration poses for German elites; see Tamar Jacoby, "Germany's Immigration Dilemma: How Can Germany Attract the Workers It Needs?" *Foreign Affairs* 90, no. 2 (2011): 8–14.

57. Croucher reports that many Americans living in Mexico continue to interact with the government of the United States, seeking the extension of benefits (e.g., Social Security) and advantageous tax laws. Sheila L. Croucher, *The Other Side of the Fence: American Migrants in Mexico* (Austin: University of Texas Press, 2009), 108–35, 142–43.

12. A Primer on Human Rights

1. David P. Forsythe, *Human Rights in International Relations* (New York: Cambridge University Press, 2000), 3.

2. For additional information and background to human rights, see William F. Schulz, *In Our Own Best Interest: How Defending Human Rights Benefits Us All* (Boston: Beacon, 2001); Mary Ann Glendon, *A World Made New: Eleanor Roosevelt and the Universal Declaration of Human Rights* (New York: Random House, 2001); Samantha Power, *A Problem from Hell: America and the Age of Genocide* (New York: Perennial, 2003); Samuel Totten and Rafiki Ubaldo, eds., *We Cannot Forget: Interviews with Survivors of the 1994 Genocide in Rwanda*

(New Brunswick, NJ: Rutgers University Press, 2011). See also the following organizations and documents: Amnesty International (www.amnesty.org); Human Rights Watch (www.hrw.org); the Universal Declaration of Human Rights (http://www.un.org/en/documents/udhr); the European Convention for the Protection of Human Rights and Fundamental Freedoms (http://conventions.coe.int/treaty/en/treaties/html/005.htm); and the American Convention on Human Rights (http://www.hrcr.org/docs/American_Convention/oashr.html).

3. See Glendon, *A World Made New.*

4. Ibid., 73–76.

5. For the text of the Universal Declaration of Human Rights, see http://www.un.org/en/documents/udhr/. For a commentary on the role and impact of the declaration, see David Matas, "The Universal Declaration of Human Rights: Fifty Years Later," *McGill Law Journal* 46 (2000): 203–15.

6. Schulz, *In Our Own Best Interest,* 4–5.

7. The reason why countries adopt and ratify international human rights treaties is a point of debate among scholars. For a review of motivations, see Sachleben, *Human Rights Treaties,* 7–31.

8. Josef L. Kunz, "The United Nations Convention on Genocide," *American Journal of International Law* 43, no. 4 (1949): 738.

9. Frank Chalk, "Redefining Genocide," in *Genocide: Conceptual and Historical Dimensions,* ed. George J. Andreopoulos (Philadelphia: University of Pennsylvania Press, 1997), 52. See also Irving Louis Horowitz, *Taking Lives: Genocide and State Power,* 5th ed. (New Brunswick: Transnational, 2002), 13–26.

10. For background, see Adam Jones, *Genocide: A Comprehensive Introduction* (New York: Routledge, 2010). Lamarchand reviews some of the lesser-known genocidal events and provides some excellent background and analysis: René Lamarchand, *Forgotten Genocides: Oblivion, Denial and Memory* (Philadelphia: University of Pennsylvania Press, 2011). One of the most controversial events in terms of whether it should be classified as a genocide is the case of Armenia during the First World War; see Michael M. Gunter, *Armenian History and the Question of Genocide* (New York: Palgrave Macmillan, 2011).

13. Human Rights and Modern World Politics

1. For a review of the depiction and history of African Americans in film prior to the Second World War, see Thomas Cripps, *Slow Fade to Black: The Negro in American Film, 1900–1942* (New York: Oxford University Press, 1977). While images of African Americans improved in the 1960s and 1970s, films about blacks were often violent and/or highly sexualized, which confirmed many of the stereotypes of the day. Daniel L. Leab, *From Sambo to Superspade: The Black Experience in Motion Pictures* (Boston: Houghton Mifflin, 1975), 233–60; Dan Leab, "Blacks in American Cinema," in *The Political Companion to American Film,* ed. Gary Crowdus (Chicago: Lake View, 1994); Donald Bogle, *Toms, Coons, Mulattoes, Mammies and Bucks: An Interpretive History of Blacks in American Film* (New York: Continuum, 2001), 231–44.

2. For sources of African American cinema, see Sampson, *Blacks in Black and White.*

3. Wayne King, "Fact vs. Fiction in Mississippi," *New York Times,* 4 December 1988.

King was the reporter who covered the civil rights movement for the *New York Times* during the 1960s.

4. For a more in-depth discussion of films about the politics of race in the United States, see Sachleben and Yenerall, *Seeing the Bigger Picture*, 154–170.

5. One of the more bizarre practices associated with lynching is that often photographs were taken by professional photographers and copies would be sold in local communities. James Allen, Hilton Als, John Lewis, and Leon F. Litwack, *Without Sanctuary: Lynching Photography in America* (Santa Fe, NM: Twin Palms, 2000). In an essay in that collection entitled "Hellhounds," Litwack describes in graphic detail the torture that several victims of lynching faced prior to their death. Apel argues that these photographs were part of a phenomenon known as spectacle lynching, which amounted to perpetuating a situation of intimidation. Dora Apel and Shawn Michelle Smith, *Lynching Photographs* (Berkeley: University of California Press, 2007), 43–44. For a discussion of spectacle lynching in motion pictures, see Amy Louise Wood, *Lynching and Spectacle: Witnessing Racial Violence in America, 1890–1940* (Chapel Hill: University of North Carolina Press, 2009). For a history of lynching, see Philip Dray, *At the Hands of Persons Unknown; The Lynching of Black America* (New York: Random House, 2002); Robert W. Thurston, *Lynching: American Mob Murder in Global Perspective* (Burlington, VT: Ashgate, 2011).

6. Abel Meeropol had other connections with history; he adopted the children of Ethel and Julius Rosenberg, convicted of spying for the Soviet Union, after their parents were executed by the United States. Meeropol was a progressive Jewish schoolteacher from New York who had a passion for fighting intolerance. He would later write the song "The House I Live In," performed by Frank Sinatra, which was a plea for religious tolerance. The film short associated with the song won the Academy Award in 1946.

7. The film was criticized for underplaying the difficulties of interracial marriage and for Poitier's character being too good to be true. Bogle, *Toms, Coons, Mulattoes, Mammies and Bucks*, 217.

8. *Loving v. Virginia*, 388 U.S. 1 (1967), argued 10 April 1967, decided 12 June 1967. For background on the case, see Peter Wallenstein, *Tell the Court I Love My Wife: Race, Marriage and Law—An American History* (New York: Palgrave Macmillan, 2004), 173–230. Wallenstein also provides background to the entire history of antimiscegenation laws in the United States.

9. For an overview of the treatment of Native Americans in films, see the edited volume by Peter C. Rollins and John O'Connor, *Hollywood's Indian: The Portrayal of the Native American in Film* (Lexington: University Press of Kentucky, 1998). Two chapters serve as an excellent introduction to the topic: Peter C. Rollins and John O'Connor, "Introduction: The Study of Hollywood's Indian; Still on the Scholarly Frontier?" and Ted Jojola, "Absurd Reality II: Hollywood Goes to the Indians." For a historical overview, see Ralph E. Friar and Natasha A. Friar, *The Only Good Indian . . . The Hollywood Gospel* (New York: Drama Book Specialists, 1972). Boscombe offers a more up-to-date overview of the genre, as well as the treatment of Native Americans in European cinema and popular culture (181–220): Edward Boscombe, *"Injuns!" Native Americans in the Movies* (Bodmin, UK: Reaktion Books, 2006). For the characterization of women, including Native American women as highly sexualized, see M. Elise Marubbio, *Killing the Indian Maiden: Images of Native American Women in Film* (Lexington: University Press of Kentucky, 2006).

10. Griffith's *Intolerance* was a bold new way of conceiving story on film. The story jumped among the four stories, not following a chronological order. This is thought to have confused contemporary audiences. The film was a box office disaster; however, today many film historians consider it one of the best of Griffith's films, if not the best. Cook, *A History of Narrative Film*, 96–99.

11. David Desser and Lester D. Friedman, *American Jewish Filmmakers*, 2nd ed. (Urbana: University of Illinois Press, 2004), 1–9.

12. Henry Gonshak, "Pre-Holocaust Christianity in *The Passion of the Christ*," *Peace Review; A Journal of Social Justice* 20, no. 2 (2008): 218–25. For a series of essays on the impact and consequences of the film, see Zev Garber, ed., *Mel Gibson's "Passion": The Film, the Controversy and Its Implications* (West Lafayette, IN: Purdue University Press, 2006).

13. Shaheen, *Reel Bad Arabs*, 1–37. For a further discussion of the portrayal of Muslims in film, see chapter 11 on immigration.

14. Randy Astle and Gideon O. Burton, "A History of Mormon Cinema," *BYU Studies* 46, no. 2 (2007): 12–163.

15. In December 2011, however, the series *All-American Muslim* generated controversy when a Florida-based group began pressuring advertisers to withdraw advertisements from the programs. The group claimed that the series hid an Islamic agenda and was a "clear and present danger to American liberties and traditional values." As a result some advertisers, most notably the home improvement chain Lowe's, pulled advertisements. Shan Li, "Lowe's Faces Backlash after It Pulls Ads; Politicians, Activists Slam the Chain after It Disengages from a Show about Muslims," *Los Angeles Times*, 13 December 2011, B1.

16. For an overview of films about women's suffrage in silent films, see Brownlow, *Behind the Mask of Innocence*, 226–37.

17. Claudio Grossman, "The Inter-American System of Human Rights: Challenges for the Future," *Indiana Law Journal* 83, no. 4 (2008): 1267–82; Neil A. Englehart, "State Capacity, State Failure, and Human Rights," *Journal of Peace Research* 46, no. 2 (2009): 163–80.

18. John J. Michalczyk, *Costa-Garvas: The Political Fiction Film* (Philadelphia: Art Alliance, 1984), 234–45. Patrick Buchanan, an aide to President Richard Nixon during the incident, has said that if people want to know what happened in Chile, seeing *Missing* would not help. Flora Lewis, "New Film by Costa-Garvas Examines the Chilean Coup," *New York Times*, 7 February 1982, cited in Robert Brent Toplin, *History by Hollywood: The Use and Abuse of the American Past* (Chicago: University of Illinois Press, 1996), 113.

19. Toplin, *History by Hollywood*, 115. In November 2011, a Chilean judge indicted a former American naval officer for accessory to the murder of Charles Holman and his friend Frank Teruggi. Pascale Bonnefoy, "Chile Indicts Ex-U.S. Officer in 1973 Killings," *New York Times*, 30 November 2011, A12.

20. For examples of how disappearance works in practice, consider the Dirty War in Argentina (1976–1983). The report known as Nunca Más contains detailed accounts of the practice. Argentina, Comisión Nacional sobre la Desaparición de Personas, *Nunca Más: The Report of the Argentine National Commission on the Disappeared* (New York: Farrar, Straus, Giroux, 1986).

21. Iain Guest, *Behind the Disappearances: Argentina's Dirty War against Human Rights and the United Nations* (Philadelphia: University of Pennsylvania Press, 1990). The war is also the subject of *No habrá más penas ni olvido* (Funny Dirty Little War, 1983).

22. The film is not dissimilar from actual historical events. Alexei Barrionuevo, "A Child of War Discovers 'Dad' Is Parents' Killer," *New York Times,* 9 October 2011, A1.

23. John Simpson and Jana Bennett, *The Disappeared and the Mothers of the Plaza: The Story of 11,000 Argentineans Who Vanished* (New York: St. Martin's, 1985). The story of the Mothers of the Disappeared is also the subject of a song by Sting entitled, "They Dance Alone."

24. Michael G. Wessells, *Child Soldiers: From Violence to Protection* (Cambridge, MA: Harvard University Press, 2006), 5–7.

25. For the impact of brutality, deprivation, and violence on child soldiers, see Rachel Brett and Margaret McCallin, *Children: The Invisible Soldiers* (Vaxjö, Sweden: Radda Barnen, 1996). For an overview of child soldiering, see Garça Machel, *The Impact of War on Children* (New York: Palgrave, 2001); Aleinda Manuel Hawana, *Child Soldiers in Africa* (Philadelphia: University of Pennsylvania Press, 2006). Additionally, the violence and sexual violence directed at female child soldiers, often resulting in pregnancies and HIV/AIDS, is notable. There is also a stigma attached to the female survivors of child soldiering: Wessels, *Child Soldiers,* 1–2, 92–97. There are numerous memoirs and stories about child soldiers that help contextualize the practice. See, for example, Janine di Giovanni, "Girl's Seven Years as Slave of Rebel Forces," *The Times* (London), 13 May 2000; Ishmael Beah, *A Long Way Gone: Memoirs of a Boy Soldier* (New York: Farrar, Straus and Giroux, 2007); Robert Marquand, "Lubanga Trial: Is an Army of Child Soldiers a War Crime?" *Christian Science Monitor,* 8 October 2009; Peter H. Eichstaedt, *First Kill Your Family: Child Soldiers of Uganda and the Lord's Resistance Army* (Chicago: Lawrence Hill Books, 2009).

26. For background to the LRA, see Kevin Dunn, "Killing for Christ? The Lord's Resistance Army of Uganda," *Current History* 103 (2004): 206–10. For an accounting of the human rights violations committed by the LRA, see Phuong N. Pham, Patrick Vinck, and Eric Stover, "The Lord's Resistance Army and Forced Conscription in Northern Uganda," *Human Rights Quarterly* 30 (2008): 404–11.

27. The Optional Protocol to the Convention on the Rights of the Child on Involvement of Children in Armed Conflicts opened for signature in May 2000 and entered into force on 12 February 2002. For background to the treaty, see Michael J. Dennis, "Newly Adopted Protocols to the Convention on the Rights of the Child," *American Journal of International Law* 94, no. 4 (2000): 789–96.

28. The film's website is http://childrenofwarfilm.com/.

29. The campaign's website is http://zerounder18.0rg/.

30. The website for the film is http://www.invisiblechildren.com/.

31. See, for example, the Amnesty International advertisement for banning the use of child soldiers: http://www.youtube.com/watch?v=ibW01ICn03k.

32. Gregory Stanton, "The 8 Stages of Genocide," State Department Briefing Paper (1996), http://www.genocidewatch.org/images/8StagesBriefingpaper.pdf.

33. Howard Ball, *Prosecuting War Crimes and Genocide: The Twentieth Century Experience* (Lawrence: University Press of Kansas, 1999), 220–22. Goldhagen explores how the roots of anti-Semitism, including stereotypes and classifications, evolved into dehumanizing policies under the Nazis: Daniel J. Goldhagen, *Hitler's Willing Executioners: Ordinary Germans and the Holocaust* (New York: Knopf, 1996), 39–45, 80–81. See also Christopher R. Browning, *Ordinary Men: Reserve Police Battalion 101 and the Final Solution in Poland* (New York: Harper, 1992).

34. TNA PRO FO 1060/1233, *Anklageschrift gegen Veit Harlan,* 15 July 1948, cited and quoted in Jo Fox, *Propaganda in Britain and Nazi Germany: World War II Cinema* (New York: Berg, 2007), 273.

35. Ibid., 273–75.

36. Vande Winkel, "Nazi Germany's Fritz Hippler, 1909–2002," *Historical Journal of Film, Radio and Television* 23, no. 2 (2003): 92. Winkel's essay, published shortly after Hippler's death, details his denial about his own work and about Germany's responsibility for the Second World War (94–95). For more on the cinema of Nazi Germany, see Erwin Leiser, *Nazi Cinema* (New York: Macmillan, 1974); Richard Taylor, *Film Propaganda: Soviet Russia and Nazi Germany,* 2nd ed. (New York: I. B. Tauris, 1998).

37. For a review of the cinematic importance of *The Birth of a Nation,* see Cook, *A History of Narrative Film,* 4th ed., 64–72; Kevin Brownlow, *The Parade's Gone By* (Berkeley: University of California Press, 1968), 26. Bogle specifically details the incorrect and offensive characterization of blacks in *The Birth of a Nation:* Bogle, *Toms, Coons, Mulattoes, Mammies and Bucks,* 10–13.

38. When the film was released and rereleased during the 1910s and 1920s, this was a common view among many Americans. Upon a screening of the film at the White House (the first film to be screened at the executive mansion), Woodrow Wilson stated that it was "like writing history in lightning." Terry Christensen, *Reel Politics: American Political Movies from "Birth of a Nation" to "Platoon"* (New York: Basil Blackwell, 1987), 16–21.

Although the film was a sensational commercial success, there was a backlash against it. The *New York Times* acknowledged the success of the film, but also stated that the inflammatory material from which the story was drawn was likely to reopen old wounds: *New York Times,* 4 March 1915, 9. Protests and confrontations broke out in many cities over the original release and subsequent rereleases of the film over the years. Melvyn Stokes, *D. W. Griffith's "The Birth of a Nation": A History of "The Most Controversial Film of All Time"* (New York: Oxford University Press, 2007), in particular, 146–47, 154–55, 158, 161–62, 277–78.

There was even a film response to Griffith called *The Birth of a Race* (1918), directed by John W. Noble. Originally conceived as a vehicle to chronicle the achievements of Africans throughout history, the film went on to argue that the United States, in its adherence to democracy, created a race unto itself. *The American Film Institute Catalog of Motion Pictures Produced in the United States—Feature Films, 1911–1920: Film Entries* (Berkeley: University of California Press, 1988), 71. Unfortunately, only a few minutes of the film still survive.

After receiving so much criticism, Griffith would answer his critics by making *Intolerance* (1916) a chronicle of "man's inhumanity to man" throughout the ages (discussed above). A few years later Griffith would make *Broken Blossoms* (1919), alternatively titled *The Yellowman and the Girl,* as a plea for racial tolerance directed toward Asians.

39. Linda Kirschke, *Broadcasting Genocide: Censorship, Propaganda and State-Sponsored Violence in Rwanda, 1990–1994* (London: Article 19, 1996), 85–86. See also Darryl Li, "Echoes of Violence: Considerations on Radio and Genocide in Rwanda," *Journal of Genocide Research* 6, no. 1 (2004): 19–27. The RTLM propaganda was considered by French historian Gérard Prunier as more effective than the standard government propaganda. The government would regularly make references to the Tutsi monarchy that existed prior to 1959. For most youths, born after the 1959 revolution, such references had little or no meaning (Prunier's interview with Article 19, reported in Kirschke, *Broadcasting Genocide,* 86–87).

40. In the 1947 film *Monsieur Verdoux,* Charles Chaplin, the writer-director and star, plays a character who has murdered, or attempted to murder, several of his wives. Standing trial, the title character draws the distinction between himself and those who perpetuate wars: "That's the history of many a big business: wars, conflicts, it's all business. One murder makes a villain, millions a hero. Numbers sanctify my good fellow."

41. Oftentimes, particularly in Israel, the word *Shoah* is used instead of Holocaust as the name of the genocide.

42. The website for the film is http://www.pbs.org/wgbh/pages/frontline/camp/. For background on the history of the film, see Sussex, "The Fate of *F3080.*"

43. Leila Levinson, "The Loss of Faith among the Jewish GI Liberators," *Cross Currents* 61, no. 1 (2011): 27–38.

44. The film was remade as a television series in Britain in 2009 and broadcast on the BBC.

45. Doneson, *The Holocaust in American Film,* 143. Doneson is critical of other Holocaust films, such as *Distant Journey, The Last Stop,* and *Schindler's List* because Jews are often not the main protagonists. Instead it is gentiles who are often rescuing Jews (200).

46. Ibid., 191–93.

47. John Ardagh, *Germany and the Germans,* 3rd ed. (New York: Penguins Books, 1985), 501.

48. Most versions of the DVD contain bonus material featuring details of Schindler's life and the people he saved. Oskar Schindler survived the war and died an unsuccessful businessman but nonetheless was revered and respected for his work during the Second World War saving so many Jews. United Press International, "Oskar Schindler, Saved 1,200 Jews," *New York Times,* 13 October 1974.

49. In news reports and other media outlets, Oskar Schindler's name is used in association with others who performed similar acts. A lesser-known individual who has been called the female Oskar Schindler, Irena Sendler, is featured in the American television film *The Courageous Heart of Irena Sendler* (2009). Sendler saved at least two thousand Jewish children by smuggling them out of the Warsaw ghetto so that they would be adopted and raised by Polish Catholic families until they could be reunited with their families after the war. Ginia Bellafante, "A Female Oskar Schindler of the Warsaw Ghetto," *New York Times,* 18 April 2009. Alternatively, Giorgio Perlasca, who is credited with saving thousands of Jewish lives, is the subject of the Italian made-for-TV movie *Perlasca: Un eroe italiano* (Perlasca: The Courage of a Just Man, 2002). Anita Gates, "An Oskar Schindler in Italy," *New York Times,* 15 April 2005.

50. Polanski, a Polish Jew who survived the Holocaust and was married to Sharon Tate (victim of a horrific murder by the Manson gang), fled the United States in 1974 after being convicted of statutory rape. Consequently, *The Pianist* is not an American film, but Polanski continues to have a major influence on American cinema, including working with a number of American actors. For background, see Vanessa Thorpe, "Waiting to Come In from the Cold," *Observer,* 6 December 2008, 53; Michael Cieph, "Polanski Appeal Alleges More Secret Dealings by Judge in '77 Case," *New York Times,* 19 March 2010, A13.

51. Richard von Weizsäcker, speech to the Bundestag, 8 May 1985, http://mediaculture-online.de/fileadmin/bibliothek/weizsaecker_speech_may85/weizsaecker_speech_may85.pdf. For a discussion of the importance of the speech and the legacy of the Nazi period on German politics, see Ardagh, *Germany and the Germans,* 497–512.

52. The film was banned in Czechoslovakia (during the Communist period) because it was considered a Zionist film. Antonín J. Liehm, *Closely Watched Films: The Czechoslovak Experience* (White Plains, NY: International Arts and Sciences, 1974), 69.

53. For an overview and analysis of films made in Czechoslovakia, and subsequently in the Czech Republic, concerning the Holocaust, see Peter Hames, *Czech and Slovak Cinema: Theme and Tradition* (Edinburgh: Edinburgh University Press, 2009), 95–111.

54. Van der Knaap argues that *Night and Fog* served to start the process of memorializing the Second World War and the victims of the Holocaust. Ewout van der Knaap, "Transmitting the Memory of the Holocaust," in *Uncovering the Holocaust: The International Reception of "Night and Fog,"* ed. Ewout van der Knaap (New York: Wallflower, 2006), 1. Subsequent chapters in the book also consider the importance of the film to the cultural understandings of the events.

55. André Pierre Colombat, *The Holocaust in French Film* (Metuchen, NJ: Scarecrow Press, 1993).

56. Philip Martin, "A Troubling Appraisal of Holocaust Movie: Does It Trivialize Evil?" *Arkansas Democrat-Gazette,* 4 April 1999, J2.

57. The original title of the novel and film uses the British spelling of "pajamas": *The Boy in the Striped Pyjamas.*

58. Roger Ebert, "Loyalty Shrouds Evil for Child, but What of Adults? *Striped Pajamas* Poses Moral Questions," *Chicago Sun-Times,* 7 November 2008, A7.

59. Manohla Pargis, "Horror through a Child's Eyes," *New York Times,* 6 November 2008, C15.

60. Kenneth B. Noble, "Cambodian Physician Who Won an Oscar for *Killing Fields* is Slain, *New York Times,* 27 February 1996.

61. Seth Mydans, "Survivors Seek Answers at Khmer Rouge Trial," *New York Times,* 21 November 2011, A12; Sebastian Strangio, "Khmer Rouge No. 2 Gives Insights to His Role in Cambodia's *Killing Fields,*" *Christian Science Monitor,* 22 November 2011.

62. Christian P. Scherrer, *Genocide and Crisis in Central Africa: Conflict Roots, Mass Violence, and Regional War* (Westport, CT: Praeger, 2002), xi. For U.S. State Department documents relating to the genocide in Rwanda, see http://www.state.gov/m/a/ips/c44620. htm. For background to the Rwandan genocide, see Gérard Prunier, *The Rwandan Crisis: History of a Genocide* (London: Hurst, 1995); Linda Melvern, *A People Betrayed: The Role of the West in Rwanda's Genocide* (New York: Zed Books, 2000); Philip Gourevitch, *We Wish to Inform You That Tomorrow We Will Be Killed with Our Families: Stories from Rwanda* (New York: Farrar, Straus, Giroux, 1998); Christina Fisanick, ed., *The Rwanda Genocide* (San Diego, CA: Greenhaven, 2004).

63. Norbert Ehrenfreund, *The Nuremberg Legacy: How the Nazi War Crimes Trial Changed the Course of History* (New York: Palgrave Macmillan, 2007); Hans Kelsen, "Will Judgment in the Nuremberg Trial Constitute a Precedent in International Law?" *International Law Quarterly* 1, no. 2 (1947): 153–71. Some of the more prominent ad hoc courts have been in Rwanda, the former Yugoslavia, Cambodia, and Bangladesh. Anjana Pasricha, "Bangladesh Begins 1971 War Crimes Trial," *Voice of America News,* 21 November 2011, http://www.voanews. com/english/news/asia/south/—Bangladesh-Begins-1971-War-Crimes-Trial-134235283. html. See also Elizabeth Neuffer, *The Key to My Neighbor's House: Seeking Justice in Bosnia and Rwanda* (New York: Picador, 2001).

64. This section of the film is recounted in Claude Lanzmann, *Shoah: An Oral History of the Holocaust, the Complete Text of the Film* (New York: Pantheon Books, 1985), 83–92. There is a discussion of this phenomenon found in the preface of the book by Simone de Beauvoir, vii–ix.

65. Daniel Goleman, *Vital Lies, Simple Truths: The Psychology of Self-Deception* (New York: Simon & Schuster, 1985), 114–17.

66. Nicholas Kristof, "Save the Darfur Puppy," *New York Times,* 10 May 2007, A33.

Conclusion

1. See, for example, the case of Abdol-Hussein Sardari, an Iranian diplomat who used his position and personal fortune to save thousands of Jews in Europe from the Nazis. A celebrated book about his life and exploits (and subsequent reviews) reference Schindler as a person against whom he should be compared. Fariborz L. Mokhtari, *In the Lion's Shadow: Sardari, the Iranian Schindler* (Stroud, UK: History, 2011); Brian Wheeler, "The 'Iranian Schindler' Who Saved Jews from the Nazis," *BBC News,* 20 December 2011, http://www.bbc.co.uk/news/magazine-16190541.

2. Robert Sklar, "Oh! A Husser! Historiography and the Rise of Cinema Studies," in *Resisting Images: Essays on Cinema and History,* ed. Robert Sklar and Charles Musser (Philadelphia: Temple University Press, 1990), 20–21.

3. For example, African Americans led protests and boycotts against the exhibition of *The Birth of a Nation* (1915); disability groups advocated a boycott of the film *Tropic Thunder* (2008) because of its portrayal of the intellectually disabled; and some Indians protested the portrayal of poor slum dwellers as "dogs" in the film *Slumdog Millionaire* (2008). Brownlow, *The Parade's Gone By,* 26; Michael Cieply, "Nationwide *Thunder* Boycott in the Works," *New York Times,* 11 August 2008, E1; Matthew Weaver, "Protests at Indian Cinemas over *Slumdog Millionaire,*" *Guardian.co.uk,* 27 January 2009, http://www.guardian.co.uk/world/2009/jan/27/riots-india-slumdog-millionaire. The depiction of other countries by Hollywood films has also been a point of contention. The film *Cuban Love Song* (1931), which depicted Cubans as half-clothed, barefooted natives, was highly offensive and the target of a boycott in Cuba in 1931. "*Cuban Love Song* Protested in Havana," *New York Times,* 2 December 1931, 16.

4. "Producers Resent Boycott of Films," *New York Times,* 8 December 1934; "Asks Film Boycott by All Catholics," *New York Times,* 9 December 1934; "Spellman Urges *Miracle* Boycott," *New York Times,* 8 January 1951, 1, 14; "Plan Film Boycott; Los Angeles Catholics Decide on Protests during February," *New York Times,* 4 February 1947, 34; "Boycott Threat Ends Film's Run," *New York Times,* 5 January 1956; Ian Fisher, "Vatican Official Urges Boycott of *Da Vinci* Film," *New York Times,* 29 April 2006.

5. "Baptists to Fight 'Improper' Films," *New York Times,* 11 May 1947, 53.

6. Aljean Harmetz, "Ministers Vow Boycott over Scorsese Film on Jesus," *New York Times,* 13 July 1988.

7. "Film Termed Anti-labor," *New York Times,* 15 August 1939.

8. Tepper examines the protests over art and culture in the United States and concludes that those cities that have experienced the most immigration in the previous decade are likely to be the cities most prone to protest over art. He surmises that there are concerns about

the changing values of the communities that produce fears among people. Steven J. Tepper, *Not Here, Not Now, Not That! Protest over Art and Culture in America* (Chicago: University of Chicago Press, 2011).

9. Although the messages can be unintentional, they can be, nonetheless, considered harmful or undesirable. A recent study suggests that European adolescents who watch Hollywood films in which actors engage in alcohol drinking were more likely to binge drink. Reiner Hanewinkel et al., "Alcohol Consumption in Movies and Adolescent Binge Drinking in 6 European Countries," *Pediatrics,* 5 March 2012, http://pediatrics.aappublications.org/content/early/2012/02/29/peds.2011-2809.full.pdf+html.

10. Kariithi and Kareithi, "It's Off to Work You Go!"

11. Putnam, "Bowling Alone."

12. Jovan Byford, *Conspiracy Theories: A Critical Introduction* (New York: Palgrave Macmillan, 2011); David Aaronovitch, *Voodoo Histories: How Conspiracy Theory Has Shaped Modern History* (New York: Riverhead Books, 2010).

13. Bob Sonneclar, "The VNR Top Ten: How Much Video PR Gets on the Evening News?" *Columbia Journalism Review* 29, no. 6 (1991): 14; K. Tim Wulfemeyer and Lowell Frazier, "The Ethics of Video News Releases: A Qualitative Analysis," *Journal of Mass Media Ethics* 7, no. 3 (1992): 151–68.

14. David Tewksbury, Jakob Jensen, and Kevin Coe, "Video News Releases and the Public: The Impact of Source Labeling on the Perceived Credibility of Television News," *Journal of Communications* 61, no. 2 (2011): 328–48.

15. Paul Lewis, "Churnalism or News? How PRs Have Taken Over the Media," *Guardian,* 24 February 2011, 14.

16. Doneson, *The Holocaust in American Film,* 229–30.

INDEX

CPSIA information can be obtained at www.ICGtesting.com
Printed in the USA
BVOW07*0928270114

342628BV00002B/2/P